PARKER PILLSBURY

PARKER
Pillsbury

Radical Abolitionist, Male Feminist

Stacey M. Robertson

Cornell University Press

Ithaca and London

Copyright © 2000 by Cornell University

All rights reserved. Except for brief quotations in a review, this book, or parts thereof, must not be reproduced in any form without permission in writing from the publisher. For information, address Cornell University Press, Sage House, 512 East State Street, Ithaca, New York 14850.

First published 2000 by Cornell University Press.

Printed in the United States of America.

Library of Congress Cataloging-in-Publication Data

Robertson, Stacey M.
  Parker Pillsbury : radical abolitionist, male feminist / Stacey M. Robertson.
    p. cm.
  Includes bibliographical references (p.) and index.
  ISBN 0-8014-3634-6 (cloth)
  1. Pillsbury, Parker, 1809–1898.   2. Abolitionists—United States—Biography.   3. Antislavery movements—United States—History—19th century.   4. Radicals—United States—Biography.   5. Social reformers—United States—Biography.   6. Feminists—United States—Biography.   7. Antislavery movements—New Hampshire—History—19th century.
  I. Title

E449.P643 R63 2000
973.7'114'092—dc21   99-046230
[B]

Cornell University Press strives to use environmentally responsible suppliers and materials to the fullest extent possible in the publishing of its books. Such materials include vegetable-based, low-VOC inks and acid-free papers that are either recycled, totally chlorine-free, or partly composed of nonwood fibers. Books that bear the logo of the FSC (Forest Stewardship Council) use paper taken from forests that have been inspected and certified as meeting the highest standards for environmental and social responsibility. For further information, visit our website at www.cornellpress.cornell.edu.

Cloth printing   10   9   8   7   6   5   4   3   2   1

To my family

Contents

Illustrations

Acknowledgments

I began this book more than ten years ago, when Richard Archer introduced me to the collection of Pillsbury's letters in the Wardman Library at Whittier College. I will always be grateful for this introduction, as well as for the persistent encouragement and friendship Archer has generously offered me over the years. Faculty members at the University of California, Santa Barbara, including Patricia Cline Cohen, Sarah Fenstermaker, Nancy Gallagher, and Carl Harris, taught me to be a critical and creative historian. In particular, Pat Cohen encouraged me to develop a project that proved untraditional for a women's historian. She introduced me to the study of masculinity and thereby added a critical new dimension to the manuscript. Moreover, her ability to maintain an unimaginably hectic schedule, balancing scholarship, administration, teaching, and family, continues to inspire me.

Many colleagues at Santa Barbara and elsewhere have read parts of this manuscript. I am grateful to Robert Abzug, Erik Ching, Jane DeHart, Heather Fowler-Salamini, Gerald Horne, Karen Mead, Brett Schmoll, and Ula Taylor. I thank those who commented on early chapters presented at various conferences, including Clyde Griffen, Jack Maddex, Jenni Parish, Rita Roberts, and Will Roscoe. I am especially indebted to Hal Morris, who generously read the entire manuscript at the last minute.

Part of this book appeared previously in two journals: " 'Aunt Nancy Men': Parker Pillsbury, Masculinity, and Women's Rights Activism in the Nineteenth-Century United States," *American Studies* 37 (Fall 1996): 33–60; and " 'A Hard, Cold, Stern Life': Parker Pillsbury and Grassroots Abolitionism, 1840–1865," *New England Quarterly* 70 (June 1997): 179–210. I am grateful to the editors at *American Studies*, David M. Katzman and Norman R. Yetman, and the editors at the *New England Quarterly*, William M. Fowler, Jr., and Linda Smith Rhoads.

I am indebted to the staff at the libraries and archives I visited and corresponded with over the last decade. Special thanks to Ronald Baumann at Oberlin College; Elizabeth Hamlin-Morin and Sherry Wilding-White at the New Hampshire Historical Society; Phillip O'Brien at Wardman Library, Whittier College; and R. Eugene Zepp at the Boston Public Library. I gratefully acknowledge the following for permission to quote from documents in their possession: the American Antiquarian Society; Franklin Trask Library, Andover-Newton Theological Seminary; The Trustees of the Boston Public Library; Cleveland Colby Colgate Archives, Colby-Sawyer College; Rare Book and Manuscripts Library, Columbia University; Cornell University Library; Dartmouth College Library; Haverford College Library; Houghton Library, Harvard University; The Huntington Library; Concord Public Library Materials Collection, part of the New Hampshire Historical Society manuscript collections; New-York Historical Society; Oberlin College Archives; Ohio Historical Society; Phillips Library, Peabody Essex Museum; Schlesinger Library, Radcliffe College; The Sophia Smith Collection, Smith College; Department of Special Collections, Syracuse University Library; Wardman Library, Whittier College; and Yale University Library. Thanks also to the Bentley Historical Library and the Clements Library at the University of Michigan; Illinois State Historical Society; Kent State University Library; Library of Congress; Moorland-Spingarn Research Center, Howard University; Vassar College Library; and the Western Reserve Historical Society, for responding to inquiries and copying letters.

I gratefully acknowledge generous funding from the University of California, Santa Barbara, and Bradley University, which helped support the research and writing for this project. Arnold Shober, my terrific research assistant, devoted endless hours to this project, and I am very appreciative. I also thank my colleagues in the History Department and Women's Studies Program at Bradley.

For their friendship and collegiality I express my gratitude to my fellow historians of antislavery, including Carol Lasser, John Quist, Beth Salerno, and Deborah Van Broekhoven. I am especially grateful to Michael Pierson for his good humor, intellectual incisiveness, and encouragement. I also acknowledge John Mack Faragher for generously offering his friendship and support to a young scholar he barely knew.

My friends and family deserve much more than the thanks I can offer on these pages. Chris Belden, Cindi Carrell, Mary Galvin, John Gonsalves, Paul and Kit Kassel, Seth and Barb Katz, Susan Levine, Randy Lindquist, Clare Lyons, Jill Orr, Roman Padilla, Mia Picerno, Jeff Ramsey, Micheal Schwartz, Frank Venegas, Devaughn Williams, John Williams, and Henry Wilson, your affection and goodwill are priceless. Christine Erickson, Karen Mead, and Demetrice Worley, have provided love, laughter, and constant support over the years. I deeply appreciate the gracious encouragement of Clif and Victoria Brown, Creighton Brown, Seth Maiman, and especially Marissa Brown. My parents, Scotty and Shirley Robertson, gave me the self-confidence and imagination to write this book and they continue to offer their love and encouragement. My sister, Sharon Robertson, is an extraordinary source of inspiration. She nurtured my passion for writing and knowledge. My brother and sister-in-law, Scott and Michelle Robertson, have been generous and gracious in their support.

I am deeply grateful to Cornell University Press and especially my editor, Peter Agree, who responded with kindness and thoughtfulness to all my impatient E-mails. He guided me through the publishing process with gentleness and good humor. I am indebted to the reviewers at Cornell, Robert Abzug and Nancy Hewitt, whose careful and insightful reading of this manuscript proved remarkably beneficial.

To my husband and dearest friend, Brad Brown, I owe the largest debt of gratitude. A more generous, thoughtful, and loving partner could not be found. He read and reread every word of this manuscript with extraordinary patience and devotion. His keen intelligence and graceful style have significantly improved this book. And finally, to my son Evan, thank you for bringing a new joy to my life as I concluded Parker Pillsbury's story.

STACEY M. ROBERTSON

Abbreviations

AAS — American Antiquarian Society, Worcester, Mass.

ALutz — Alma Lutz Collection, Schlesinger Library, Radcliffe College, Cambridge, Mass.

BPL — Boston Public Library, Boston, Mass.

CSC — Cleveland-Colby-Colgate Archives, Susan Colgate Cleveland Library, Colby-Sawyer College, New London, N.H.

FTL — Franklin Trask Library, Andover Newton Theological School, Newton Centre, Mass.

HAV — Nathaniel Peabody Rogers Papers, Haverford College Library, Haverford, Mass.

HouL — Houghton Library, Harvard University, Cambridge, Mass.

JGW — John Greenleaf Whittier Collection, Wardman Library, Whittier College, Whittier, Calif.

LOC — Library of Congress, Washington D.C.

NHHS — Concord Public Library Historical Materials Collection, New Hampshire Historical Society, Concord, N.H.

PEM — Peabody Essex Museum, Salem, Mass.

SSC — Sophia Smith Collection, Smith College, Northampton, Mass.

SYR — Gerrit Smith Papers, Syracuse University Library, Syracuse, N.Y.

Yale — Yale University Library, New Haven, Conn.

PARKER PILLSBURY

Introduction

When Peleg Clark asked Parker Pillsbury if he would be willing to have his "head examined" by a famous phrenologist, the young New Hampshire abolitionist cheerfully complied. Pillsbury was intrigued by the new science of phrenology, which held that a careful physical examination of the bumps and protrusions on the skull could reveal specific personality traits. Orson Fowler, the leading American expert on phrenology, was blindfolded as he probed Pillsbury's head. The results of the exam astonished and delighted Pillsbury's friends, who felt that Fowler had brilliantly captured the young man's dynamic and complicated identity. His report extolled Pillsbury's mental and physical strength, describing him as someone who could "endure more wear and tear than almost any other person." It also recognized Pillsbury's prickly side, noting that "combativeness" and "resistance" were the strongest elements of his character. The report praised his "moral principle" and his deep love for his family and friends, and concluded by observing that Pillsbury was "too humble" and lacked "self esteem," but nonetheless did his own thinking and "let others do theirs."[1]

Scientists have long since debunked Fowler's misguided phrenological theories, but his profile of Parker Pillsbury remains more convincing than scholarly depictions. Mentioned in almost every study of the abolition movement, Pillsbury is usually classed among the small squadron of anticlerical field lecturers considered to be zealous at best, fanatical at worst. In one characterization of "cranks" and "oddities" among the abolitionists, Carlos Martyn, a nineteenth-century scholar, portrayed Pillsbury as "individualism run mad."[2] A twentieth-century historian, Merton L. Dillon, placed Pillsbury among a group of "New Englanders . . . especially prone to . . . eccentricities." He characterized their antislavery tactics as "irritating" and "disruptive" and their message "heavily laced with sexual allusions that some understandably found offensive."[3] In general, scholars have emphasized Pillsbury's confrontational tactics, his "hostility to authority," and his contentious position among his abolitionist colleagues.[4]

The story of Pillsbury's life does not fit a simple descriptive formula. Sometimes he was a disruptive eccentric who lashed out at authority and irritated his own colleagues, as when, during the Civil War, he deemed Lincoln the worst president in the nation's history and concluded that Confederate leader Jefferson Davis would be preferable. Pillsbury was also, however, a sensitive visionary whose commitment to social justice drove him to lecture across New Hampshire for little or no pay, enduring cold winters and meager accommodations. It was, in fact, the combination of these two distinct aspects of his identity which made Pillsbury such an extraordinary figure in the abolitionist movement. His "notorious" positions caught the attention of the public, and his unswerving dedication to the cause guaranteed the respect of his peers.

Up to now there has been no full-length biographical study of Pillsbury.[5] This may, in part, be due to the fact that his correspondence is widely scattered in over thirty archives across the country.[6] Yet Pillsbury's rich and captivating life story is worth the telling, not least because it challenges our understanding of the antislavery movement. Despite the proliferation of scholarly studies on abolition, there has been little attention paid to the inner workings of antislavery organizations. How did these small groups manage to attract the attention of the nation? How did they develop tactics, create consensus, coordinate actions, and implement policies? Pillsbury's life offers a window into the elaborate orchestration of the abolition movement. He devoted twenty-five years to antislavery field lecturing and held elected posts with almost every major abolitionist organization. As a field worker he became intimately familiar with the impact of the movement at the local level. He lived and worked with community abolitionists in every state across the North and he understood the tactics and strategies of their opponents. He spent several months every year traveling and speaking in the West, familiarizing himself with the perspective of frontier abolitionists. Although Pillsbury worked primarily with the radical Garrisonian wing of the movement, his position required regular interaction with abolitionists of all stripes. He was more than a foot soldier in the movement, however. He was also a policymaker and influential tactician. He forged strong bonds with the elites of the American Anti-Slavery Society, including William Lloyd Garrison and Wendell Phillips, and he eventually entered the inner circle of leaders. As both a field lecturer and a strategist, Pillsbury developed a uniquely comprehensive understanding of the movement, which he persistently employed to affect the direction of antislavery.

Pillsbury's significance for scholars of antislavery is also connected with his uncompromising radicalism. Though he was deemed a "fanatic" by historians and even some of his contemporaries, Pillsbury's confrontational tactics, perfectionist philosophy, and anticlerical tendencies challenged and stimulated the abolition movement. Working with a small group of grassroots radicals, Pillsbury pushed William Lloyd Garrison and the antislavery leadership toward uncompromising positions throughout the 1840s and early 1850s. "Chasing the illusion of purity," as one historian deemed their radical strategy, these itinerant agitators constantly demanded complete separation from the corrupt influences of church and state.[7] Because Pillsbury and other field lecturers remained far from the central abolitionist leadership in Boston, their importance has been underestimated by historians. Yet it was this field experience that catalyzed their radicalism and provided them with their influence. Constantly battling opponents for the hearts of their audiences, lecturing agents developed a confrontational understanding of the movement.

Another aspect of Pillsbury's life that is worth exploring involves the youthful experiences and personal relationships that made possible his exceptional public life. These offer singular insights into the diverse and overlapping motivations that propelled an earnest young minister to abandon a promising career with the church for an uncertain future as a radical abolitionist. This side of Pillsbury's life also reveals the difficulties faced by professional agitators in balancing family life and radical politics. Struggling to maintain their egalitarian ideals in their public roles, many abolitionists like Pillsbury failed to hold to these standards in their personal relationships. By focusing on Pillsbury's family life we are led to acknowledge women's critical contribution to the antislavery movement, above all in the area of the unheralded role of abolitionist spouses.[8]

While scholarship on women abolitionists has recently flourished, much work is still needed on the important influence of gender on the movement. A few recent studies have begun to reveal the pervasiveness of traditional gender ideals in antislavery literature and rhetoric.[9] Gender as a category of analysis is especially illuminating in the case of Pillsbury's complicated life history, as he subverted traditional notions of manly strength and self-control to construct a vision of manhood that rejected male dominance. This central element of his identity strongly influenced his political philosophy and personal relationships. It led him to support women's rights even at the expense of his abolitionist friendships, and it also allowed him to establish affectionate attachments to innumerable progressive women.

While research on gender and antislavery is slowly evolving, historians have long since produced scholarship on the complicated connection between religion and abolition.[10] Pillsbury's career furthers our understanding of this relationship by highlighting the motivations and experiences of one of the most anticlerical abolitionists in the movement. Although Pillsbury is known for his deeply antagonistic relationship with the church, it was his early religious experiences that motivated his initial connection with antislavery. Even as his relationship with the church grew even thornier over the years due to his constant run-ins with clergy during his field meetings, Pillsbury continued to be religiously motivated. A committed perfectionist, he devoted his life to preparing the nation for the millennium through provocation and agitation. Although he was more stubborn in his critique of the clergy than most abolitionists, his hostile relationship with the church reveals a great deal about the connections between antislavery and religion.

Pillsbury's frustrations with the church did not end with Northern victory in the Civil War and the abolition of slavery. Because he remained a determined agitator and public lecturer through the 1890s, Pillsbury allows us an unusual perspective—lacking in most antislavery scholarship which tends to focus exclusively on the period up to 1865—on the connections between antebellum and postwar reform activism. While continuing to denounce the church for its corruption and backwardness, Pillsbury joined a new generation of reformers in integrating the exciting discoveries of science into their social agitation. Lecturing in support of numerous progressive causes, Pillsbury merged his perfectionist philosophy with the hopefulness of science. Although his postwar reform work never rivaled the abolition movement, whether in terms of challenging the status quo or of his own personal fulfillment, Pillsbury never abandoned his goal of welcoming the millennium.

This biography is at heart the tale of a man who devoted his life to social justice and human equality. It attempts to understand his motivations and experiences in the context of nineteenth-century social reform, but it never strays far from Pillsbury himself. His voice—irascible, fiery, whimsical, and compassionate—reminds us that history is the story of individual lives.

1

The Roots of Radicalism

This time, he went too far. Though certainly the antislavery gatherings of Parker Pillsbury, a licensed Congregational minister, had always irritated the august cadre of men who made up the Suffolk North Association of Congregational Ministers, his latest speech, in January 1841, proved intolerable. A broad-shouldered man with piercing brown eyes, a dark complexion, and a deep booming voice, Pillsbury called the meeting to order.[1] "Resolved," he began slowly, attracting the attention of the large crowd, "that the great body of northern clergy . . . by their continued silence on the wrongs of two and a half millions of slaves . . . have proved themselves . . . a *great brotherhood of thieves*; and instead of being supported as the ministers of righteousness, they should be held (on their own principles) in execration and abhorrence by the whole human race."[2]

The Suffolk North Association responded with vigor, threatening to revoke Pillsbury's license to preach if he did not appear before them to defend himself against charges of "unchristian" behavior.[3] Pillsbury, in turn, reacted with his usual determined irreverence, especially when it came to powerful men and their institutions. Refusing to be summoned, he responded in a letter, reminding these "grave and venerable ministers" of their own culpability in the sin of slaveholding. He meticulously documented their persistent refusal to separate themselves from Southern slaveholding ministers and churches, and suggested that their accusations represented a thinly veiled attack on his antislavery successes. After excommunicating the entire Suffolk North Association "for the sin of conniving at American slavery" and solemnly warning them to repent, Pillsbury concluded: "When . . . you, and

I, stand at the tribunal of God . . . it shall be known who has served God and who has not. And justice shall be meted out."⁴ Earthly justice, however, did not favor Pillsbury; the association revoked his license.⁵

This episode—recounted by Pillsbury in his autobiographical history of the antislavery movement—marks the point at which the fledgling radical self-consciously and with abandon rejected traditional values and institutional authority. Although he had already forsaken the ministry by the time he offered his sanctimonious reply to the Suffolk Association, his refusal to defend himself guaranteed that he would never return to the Congregational fold. The thirty-one-year-old, however, made this decision with confidence. He had already accepted a sense of his own identity as an "outsider"—a radical who stood apart from the social order, speaking the dictates of his conscience.

This chapter chronicles the development of Pillsbury's radicalism throughout several stages of his early history, including his family life and youthful experiences, his religious education and early ministry, and his decision to join the antislavery movement. Growing up in the backwoods of New Hampshire, the uneducated son of a farmer, Parker Pillsbury learned the lessons of manhood which would mold him into a "rugged and indomitable John the Baptist" and deeply affect his political thought.⁶ He would also experience the exhilaration and disappointment of Christian revivalism as he struggled to find meaning in his life. The frustrations of his family background and religious experiences, however, eventually evoked in Pillsbury a sense of alienation and influenced him to embrace the radical abolitionists.

In October 1842, Parker Pillsbury traveled with Nathaniel P. Rogers, editor of the radical antislavery newspaper *Herald of Freedom*, across New Hampshire's rocky countryside to attend a convention in Hancock. Rogers took the opportunity to mention Pillsbury's background: "We passed . . . the rugged, mountain homestead where he was bred from earliest childhood— bred to toil. Where he worked through all his young life, hard and faithfully, as his manhood is laboring for the slave."⁷ Rogers also sketched Pillsbury's sparse academic education, and concluded by eulogizing his young colleague's unrefined upbringing: "He was educating all the better for humanity's service on that rugged farm. He there taught himself to be a MAN, a great lesson he had effectually learned before he came in contact with Seminaries and with a Priesthood. These proved unequal, on that account, to overmatch and cower down his homespun nobility of soul." This vision of youthful Parker's early life—harsh but invigorating, poor but honest, uneducated but courageous—well reflected Pillsbury's paradoxical understanding of his rural upbringing.

Parker Pillsbury was a seventh-generation descendant of William Pillsbury, who emigrated to Boston in 1641. William, who had fled from legal trouble in England, had an inauspicious beginning in Massachusetts. Soon after he arrived he found himself called before local authorities, accused of violating the proprieties of courtship. William quickly made reparation and married the young woman, Dorothy Crosbey, in the summer of 1641. Over the next four decades the Pillsburys bought land in Newbury, Massachusetts, built a home, and raised ten children. More than a century later, Oliver Pillsbury, Parker's father, was born in the same house William built.[8] Oliver spent his youth in Newbury and eventually continued the tradition of large families established by his seventeenth-century forefather. He and his wife, Anna Smith, married in 1808 and had eleven children—the eldest, Parker, arriving in November 1809. The first three children, all boys, were born in Hamilton, Massachusetts, where their father worked as a blacksmith. Economic difficulties caused by the Embargo Act and the War of 1812, however, forced the family to move to a farm in the rural village of Henniker, New Hampshire, in 1814.[9]

Throughout the antebellum period most New Hampshire families lived and worked on small farms.[10] Rocky, thin soil, however, made farming a physically demanding occupation. The Pillsbury family would have devoted endless hours to back-breaking labor in the fields, probably growing corn, peas, beans, wheat, and potatoes.[11] A family garden would have provided a variety of fruits and vegetables as well. The growing season was bounded on either side by the bitter cold of winter and the exhausting heat of summer. Parker and his siblings would have had little opportunity for schooling, even during the off season, and the quality of their education was probably very poor.[12] Travel across rocky and hilly New Hampshire proved difficult through the 1840s, when railroad development finally began to spread across the Granite State.[13] Confined, therefore, to Henniker and the surrounding area, Parker grew up in a rustic environment.

In hindsight, Parker Pillsbury both bemoaned and celebrated his upbringing in Henniker. When lamenting his youth, he focused on the community's lack of education and culture. "From the time I was four years old," wrote Pillsbury to his own daughter in 1853, "I never was washed all over till I was twelve—and then only by going into the pond, perhaps twice in a summer. Nobody considered it necessary. And my mind was as foul and neglected as my skin."[14] Although perhaps exaggerating to remind his daughter of her privileges, he nonetheless clearly believed his had been a deprived

Fig. 1. Anna and Oliver Pillsbury. Courtesy of the New Hampshire Historical Society, S1998.519.02.

childhood. His youthful education, he told one reporter late in life, consisted of "attending the Dirtiest school (generally a very poor one even for those times) ten or twelve weeks in the winter, until about twenty years old."[15] Moreover, he considered New Hampshire both unsophisticated and uncultured: "The Granite state . . . is good ground for wolves and bears and the bearish."[16] This perceived lack of education and culture created an insecurity in Parker and he would often apologize to his better-educated and wealthy comrades in the antislavery movement for his lack of refinement. "I presume my incapacities and blunders have troubled you often," Pillsbury once suggested to his friend Wendell Phillips, a wealthy Bostonian, "but if you knew the early history of my life and experience, my associates, means and mode of culture, my school, books and amusements, you would pardon me all, before I had half time to cry 'be merciful to me.' "[17]

Yet disdain and regret were often mixed with pride in Pillsbury's memories of his provincial background. Emphasizing the hardy farming heritage of the Pillsbury clan, he described himself as one of the common people and promoted this image among abolitionists. Known as a "Theseus in stout cow-hide boots," he became legendary for his feats of courage and endurance, his bouts with mobs, and his demanding lecturing schedule.[18] Pillsbury attributed this physical hardihood to his rustic New Hampshire background. "New Hampshire granite is hard to work, and tries the temper of the most sublimated steel. . . . But once beaten into form, it is good for all time. . . . A good proportion of their native hills and mountains is wrought into the character of the people."[19] Those stony hills not only toughened Pillsbury, they sparked in him a sense of adventure. Once, at the age of nine, he walked alone through a memorable thunderstorm to a neighboring town some fifteen miles away. "It did not rain very hard," he later recalled, "but the thunder and lightning were quite severe—at least they seemed so, to such a young traveler."[20] Instead of returning directly home he detoured to witness a house-raising, which "took me a little out of my way, and it troubled me some to get back to my road. But at last I found it, and reached home all safe—and after felt that I had done a brave deed." Childhood taught Pillsbury to take the more interesting path, despite the dangers. His later career as a radical abolitionist, a job that required both fearlessness and endurance, would reflect these earlier experiences.

Pillsbury's childhood history included the influence of a "public spirited and religious" father.[21] Oliver Pillsbury, a figure noticeably absent in Parker's private and public writings, actively promoted "the general welfare of the town," according to a New Hampshire biographer.[22] Despite his own large financial debt, incurred during the War of 1812, Oliver advocated and willingly helped finance extensive community improvement, including the building and repair of churches, schoolhouses, roads, and bridges.[23] Like many of his neighbors, he felt that such improvements would lead to increased economic opportunities as well as a strong moral foundation for the community.[24] He taught Sunday school regularly and he expanded his home to provide space for a singing school. Moreover, according to a community historian, "He was among the first to espouse the cause of temperance and anti-slavery, and took a deep interest in all the benevolent and philanthropic objects of the day."[25] Oliver's reform tendencies influenced all of his children, who participated in a variety of benevolent organizations throughout their lives.[26]

Oliver Pillsbury's commitment to his community probably derived from his religion. An orthodox Congregationalist and longtime deacon of his church, Oliver enthusiastically embraced the benevolent awakening of the 1820s. For many New Englanders of the time, the church was a bastion of stability and order in a time of great economic and political dislocation.[27] Despite his financial failures, Oliver found both success and purpose in the reform activities of his church, becoming a philanthropic leader in his community. Unlike his son Parker and many of the reformers of a younger generation, however, Oliver continued to adhere to religious orthodoxy. He remained committed to his Calvinist training, focusing on "daily prayer and reading of God's holy word."[28] Parker eventually came to resent his parent's narrow Calvinism, believing it unnecessarily dreary and joyless. "My own pupilage in the Sunday School . . . involved committing [to memory] chapters of Scripture, hymns, psalms and calvinistic catechisms," he recalled in 1869. "Everything about it was shrouded in a drapery of gloom. Death was the climax of all terrors, and life, even young life, must be made as terrible as possible, as if to acclimate the spirit to it, as the one only aim for which life was given."[29] Moreover, Pillsbury blamed his parents and this "drapery of gloom" for his poor self-confidence. "My folks were so afraid I should think myself of some consequence, that they stood hammer in hand, over my organ of self esteem, until they made it as *concave* as it ought to have been *convex*," he explained to a friend who inquired regarding the source of his modesty. "Ever since, I have been creeping through the world, *on all fours*, begging pardon of all creation, for having been born, and thrusting my sorry self into its august presence."[30]

While less than grateful for this indoctrination, Parker nonetheless adopted his father's public-spirited commitment. Oliver, however, never approved of the uncompromising zeal with which Parker pursued moral reform, and all of Parker's extant references to his father and mother reflect a tension over his religious radicalism. For example, when Nathaniel Rogers and Parker traveled through Henniker on their way to an antislavery convention in 1844, they spent the night at the home of Parker's parents. This rare visit with his family probably discouraged the young radical from further such calls. Rogers commented, "Our first tarry was at Henniker, at the paternal home of my fellow traveler, Parker Pillsbury, where we were kindly received *notwithstanding our heresies*."[31] Parker's parents did not disguise their disapproval, even vilifying him in the presence of his spouse, Sarah, who recalled the unpleasant interaction for Parker: "I told Father and Mother [Pillsbury] yesterday that they ought to feel proud of you. They replied 'the time had been when they had reason to be proud of your course, but now they saw reason only for mourning at your willful determination to deny Jesus, and his cause on earth.' "[32] The deep divide between Pillsbury and his parents remained evident throughout his antislavery career, only softening after the Civil War and the public acceptance of abolitionists.[33] This opportunity for reconciliation came too late, though, for Parker and his father, who had died in 1857. Anna apparently eventually mended relations with her prodigal son. "When I joined the abolitionists in 1840, and renounced the congregational church," explained Pillsbury, his mother mourned him as "one lost forever." However, "she has lived, I trust, to see her son, who to her, was dead, alive again, and her lost one, found."[34]

Even before Pillsbury's radicalism forced him to sever his ties with church and family, he developed a reputation for uncompromising moral independence. In 1829, at the age of twenty, he moved away from his family and spent three years in Lynn, Massachusetts, working as an express wagon driver and soap boiler.[35] Although little is known about this important period in his life, it is clear that during these years of difficult manual labor Pillsbury learned the costs of defying social norms. As a wagon driver Pillsbury joined a poorly paid and lonely contingent of "rootless" men who often turned to whiskey or rum to help them endure the boredom of their occupation.[36] Alcohol became a means not only of forgetting their drudge jobs and lack of independence but also of resisting their middle-class employers, who often demanded abstinence of their workers.[37] Pillsbury, however, probably influenced by his teetotaling father, refused to join his co-workers in their drinking binges. "While in Lynn he endured the jeers and sneers of his fellow-teamsters, because, on principle, he would never taste liquor of any kind, which was the general custom of that day," wrote longtime family friend Charles Buffum.[38] Perhaps perceived as disloyal and snobbish for adopting the customs of employers, not employees, Pillsbury found himself estranged from his fellow drivers.[39] He was unwilling to abandon his reform convictions in order to gain social acceptance, however, and so he stubbornly established himself as an outsider even among the working class of Lynn.

Pillsbury's experience as a wage worker nonetheless produced in him strong sympathies with the laboring population of New England. Although he rarely reminisced about his life as an express driver in Lynn, he became an outspoken supporter of the labor movement, referring to working men and women as the "bone and sinew of the nation."[40] His years in Lynn also contributed to his future reputation as a man of the people and a hardened toiler: "Mr. Pillsbury is a self-made man," explained one admirer. "He has literally hewn out his own place among men, and that place is a pre-eminent one. He was a truck-man . . . who drove his own horses and with his own stalwart arms loaded and unloaded his own trucks."[41]

Pillsbury returned home to work on the family farm in 1832, after three unsatisfying years earning his own living. By his own account, he returned in order to lift the burden of labor from two of his younger brothers, so that they might attend school to train for the ministry.[42] Probably eager to escape the tiresome life of an unskilled laborer, Pillsbury expressed little resentment toward his brothers as they left for school. He did not, however, pleasantly recall his agricultural duties during those years on the family farm. "[I] was brought up, or rather, *drove* up, a farmer," he bitterly recollected.[43] Twenty-three years old, still dependent on his parents, and unable to find a fulfilling career, Pillsbury toiled with his father and wondered about his destiny.

Over the next few years, however, he experienced a religious conversion that would dramatically affect his future. As he struggled to find meaning and purpose in his life, the countryside of New England was ignited by evangelical revivals. Vibrant ministers Lyman Beecher and Charles Finney had initiated a powerful religious awakening in the 1830s which led to the decline of Calvinism and its cold, formal theology. Enthusiastic new converts began to question the old ways and celebrate personal experience instead of complex theological texts.[44] Searching for opportunities to fulfill their new religious convictions, many took the advice of Beecher and Finney and turned to benevolent activism. Religious conversion now required constant regeneration in the form of a lifelong commitment to good works. This emphasis on benevolence led directly to the rise of many reform movements of the period, including temperance and abolition.[45] Like thousands of other New Englanders, Pillsbury wholeheartedly embraced the Congregational religion of Finney and Beecher in the mid-1830s. He became an active leader in the church, traveling to other towns to aid in revival meetings.[46] He also began participating in moral reform organizations, including the temperance movement. He even accepted a captain's commission in the militia solely in order to take a stand against the widespread drunkenness that occurred at military occasions. Although his efforts to eliminate alcohol from the military met with some resistance among his company and the local "rumsellers and their drunken dupes," he passionately pursued his convictions.[47]

Perhaps more important, it was during this religious awakening that Pillsbury first became interested in abolition. He was probably influenced by his younger brothers, who were converted to antislavery during their stay at Phillips Academy in Andover, Massachusetts.[48] Although it is unclear exactly when he joined the movement, he recalled working with local antislavery Quakers and Methodists during the mid-1830s, probably circulating pamphlets and petitions.[49] Pillsbury's interest in abolition was also influenced by his friendship with Stephen Symonds Foster, a young teacher whom he met in 1834.[50] Foster and Pillsbury would later become infamous for their anticlerical lectures and activities; at the time they befriended each other, however, they were still forming their radical sensibilities. Foster, who was already some way down this road, influenced Pillsbury significantly, exposing him to what one contemporary called the "lessons in ethics which made of him an abolitionist."[51] Pillsbury, however, described his meeting with Foster as significant less for its antislavery influence than its religious impact.[52] Not long after his friendship with Foster, began he took the advice of both friends and family and, at the age of twenty-six, entered Gilmanton Theological Seminary to train for the ministry.[53]

Many of the personal characteristics and beliefs that dominated Pillsbury's later reform career were already in place before he entered the seminary. His Calvinist upbringing, though repudiated, left its mark in the form of a gloomy personality. As one friend wrote following his death, "Pillsbury possessed some humor of a grim sort, but he was too terribly in earnest to make much use of it. . . . He saw the dark side and rarely the bright side of a reform."[54] More important, Pillsbury's contradictory feelings toward his upbringing and his strongly independent self-identity would lead him to turn for comfort and satisfaction to radical reform. His simple education and rustic physique, qualities that would make him feel like an outsider among the well-educated teachers and students in the seminary, proved useful in the radical antislavery movement. Indeed, he would develop a reputation as both a "wit and a bully,"—not mutually exclusive characteristics among abolitionists, who had to be quick-thinking and quick-footed. "A great burly fellow from the White Mountains of New Hampshire" who forged "abolition thunder," Pillsbury would cow his audiences, but he also earned a reputation as "a thinker, a seer, and a scholar."[55] Radicalism would allow him to fulfill the physically oriented standards of manhood he learned among the farmers of Henniker, but also permit him to transform his bothersome lack of education into an admirable virtue that allowed him to outwit "seminaries and the Priesthood" and maintain a "homespun nobility of soul."[56]

Before he discovered his natural place among the radicals, however, Pillsbury remained keenly aware of his shortcomings. While seeking to fill in the gaps of his education, he came to see himself as an outsider in the wider world of reform, beyond the borders of Henniker and New Hampshire.

When Pillsbury began his religious education in the mid-1830s, the clergy-led colonization movement, which called for the gradual emancipation of slaves followed by their emigration, was effectively overwhelmed by the movement for immediate emancipation. Although free Northern blacks had long since rejected colonization and demanded unconditional abolition, it was young William Lloyd Garrison who converted thousands to the immediate antislavery movement. Influenced by the evangelical trends of perfectionism and millennialism, Garrison became convinced that slavery was a sin that required immediate repentance. He believed, as perfectionism preached, in the possibility of a pure Christian society, and therefore refused to tolerate any form of evil, especially slavery. Millennialism convinced Garrison and other Christians that "no social problem, including slavery, was intractable, because their work was in fulfillment of a divinely ordained plan."[57] Many young revivalists, white and black, joined Garrison in the movement for immediate emancipation.

Established churches, however, continued to consider slavery more in relation to political and economic issues than moral issues. Hoping to avoid alienating their Southern counterparts, Northern church leaders discouraged their congregations from even discussing slavery. They reluctantly acknowledged antislavery sentiment among their parishioners by endorsing only voluntary manumission and gradualist programs.[58] Although churches adopted a variety of positions on slavery, ranging from the notion that the Bible sanctioned slavery to the argument that slavery was sinful but that individual slaveholders were not sinners, no major denomination endorsed immediate emancipation prior to the Civil War.[59]

The Northern public was even less sympathetic toward the antislavery movement. Between 1835 and 1838—while Pillsbury studied the latest theological debates—New England abolitionists experienced dozens of acts of violence, resulting in shocking personal injury and property destruction. After violently invading a meeting of the Boston Female Anti-Slavery Society in October 1835, a Massachusetts mob paraded William Lloyd Garrison around the streets of Boston with a rope around his neck. In 1837, a determined group shot and killed abolitionist editor Elijah Lovejoy in the town of Alton, Illinois, as he attempted to defend his antislavery press. And in May 1838, an anti-abolition crowd razed Pennsylvania Hall in Philadelphia and terrorized the local black population.[60] More close to home, mob turbulence in Concord, New Hampshire, prevented a lecture by famed English abolitionist George Thompson in 1835, and the stalwart antislavery advocate George Storrs experienced explosive resistance across the state in the mid-1830s.[61] Pillsbury did not remain oblivious to this violence. In fact, he was so disturbed by the anti-abolition attacks that he felt compelled to respond to the Boston mob that assaulted Garrison. A subscriber to the *Boston Recorder*, he was appalled by the paper's unsympathetic coverage of the incident: "I at once wrote to the Editor that his course towards that outrage had destroyed my confidence in him, and I would rather have my postage money for the rest of the year than his paper, and begged him to discontinue it."[62]

Although he remained concerned about the abolition movement, Pillsbury devoted himself to study while at Gilmanton Theological Seminary. With only a few years' education in New Hampshire's public school system, he entered the seminary with minimal academic skills. This weakness inspired him to work diligently, day and night. "I applied myself to study with a zeal that well nigh ruined my health," he later wrote a friend.[63] When he entered the school in the autumn of 1835, he was the only student, at least for the first few weeks. Attached to the Gilmanton Academy, the seminary opened its doors for the first time in September 1835, and Pillsbury was the first student to arrive. Although he was joined by six other eager students that year, the seminary remained small, averaging between three and ten graduates each year.[64] Gilmanton was located some sixty miles northeast of Henniker and his family, and Pillsbury must have felt lonely there. Nonetheless, he learned the tenets of Calvinism, as well as the intricacies of the latest theological debates, during his three years there. Afterwards, he would reveal little nostalgia for Gilmanton, a second-rate orthodox institution with a short and obscure existence.

Whether to improve his employment opportunities or to enrich his education, Pillsbury moved to the more reputable and conservative Andover Theological Seminary in 1838, after graduating from Gilmanton. It was at Andover that he experienced firsthand the tension between the abolition movement and the church. For several years prior to his attendance Andover had enraged immediatist abolitionists because of its refusal to allow antislavery activity among its students. A "rigorously orthodox" seminary founded in 1808, Andover produced many influential church leaders, whom antislavery activists wanted to mold into abolitionists.[65] The immediatists realized the power and potential influence of these young ministers as they graduated from Andover and spread out among the communities of New England.[66] But Andover had advocated colonization as an answer to slavery since 1823, and its faculty wanted to continue this tradition despite the emergence of the immediatist movement. After George Thompson spoke on campus in 1835, converting a large portion of Andover students to immediatism, the Andover faculty "requested" that students refrain from antislavery activity in the future. The teachers argued that abolitionism created antagonism among students, sidetracked them from their studies, and alienated potential benefactors.[67] Many students accepted this advice and no organized antislavery association formed on campus, but Thompson and Garrison continued to lecture in Andover and convert more students.

Despite personal sympathies for the immediatist position, Pillsbury was reluctant at first to speak openly at Andover. "I dreaded to be denounced as the enemy of the church, and therefore did not dare to speak out what I knew," he later admitted in an antislavery editorial.[68] Pillsbury was not yet prepared to challenge his religious mentors and risk losing his hard-earned educational credentials. He did, however, defy Andover regulations and deliver an antislavery lecture in a nearby community.[69] But even as he wrote to a friend in November 1838, casually mentioning his first abolition address, he extolled the "beautiful and effecting [*sic*]" sermon of Moses Stuart, an Andover professor who argued that the Bible sanctioned slavery.[70]

Pillsbury was clearly still unsure about how far he was willing to take his reform convictions, but a few well-timed incidents served to further embolden his abolitionism. He was shocked when a professor urged the graduating class to go into Missouri, a slave state, and even offered to pay their traveling expenses.[71] Pillsbury probably believed that any clerical appointment in the South would involve an acceptance of slavery because religious abolitionism had been effectively eradicated there. This seemingly proslavery manipulation of his fellow students enraged him. Later, Pillsbury requested a leave of absence at the end of his second term in order to accept a temporary antislavery lecturing position with the Massachusetts Anti-Slavery Society. Not only did Andover officials refuse his request, they warned him of the negative consequences antislavery activity would have for his chances of gaining a parish position. "The Institution . . . tried to tempt and flatter me with promises and prophecies of Great usefulness and success in the ministry, which even a three months service in your behalf as a society, would greatly impair," Pillsbury later recalled to Garrison.[72] By this time, however, full-time reform activism had become a career option, so Pillsbury was not intimidated by the threats of his Andover teachers.[73] Confident in his ability to make a living, he requested to be discharged. Despite the recent dismissal of fellow student John A. Collins for his abolitionism, Andover refused to release Pillsbury. This proved to be the last straw: "I escaped a fugitive," Pillsbury wrote, "and am free."[74]

In many ways, Pillsbury's religious experiences reflected the effects of the Second Great Awakening and the changing nature of the New England ministry. Hundreds of young working-class men experienced a call for religious regeneration during the height of revivalism in the 1820s and 1830s, and decided to train for the ministry. They, like Pillsbury, hoped to fulfill "God's ultimate millennial purpose" through their ministry, which they closely associated with moral reform such as temperance and antislavery.[75] These young men crowded into the newly opened seminaries across New England and significantly transformed the character of the clergy. Ministers no longer came primarily from elite families and they no longer maintained a stable and long-term commitment to a single parish. They hailed from rural farming families and they were more interested in advancing the millennium through moral reform than in maintaining social order through a stable town ministry.[76] The conservative old guard attempted to control this new cadre of recruits by regulating and restricting their reform tendencies. Not surprisingly, many young ministers felt betrayed.

Holding only "vague reformist and humanitarian convictions," even the leaders of evangelical revivalism did not live up to the standards of "purity and intensity of faith" they preached.[77] Many young moral reformers, including Pillsbury, considered the ambivalent attitude of their mentors toward slavery utterly unacceptable and in contradiction to everything they understood Christian revivalism to represent. Inspired by this feeling of frustration, they enthusiastically turned to the abolition movement. Antislavery "injected a sense of purpose and direction into lives thwarted by inadequate religions," and "satisfied religious yearnings and reforming impulses traditional institutions could not fulfill."[78] Pillsbury, for example, dated the beginning of his "life mission and labor" from his introduction to William Lloyd Garrison and his first experience as an antislavery agent in the spring of 1839.[79] He considered his work as an abolitionist to be the labor of any faithful Christian "apostle." Several of Pillsbury's closest Garrisonian associates experienced similar conversions to the "religion" of antislavery. Henry C. Wright, one of the most vehemently anticlerical Garrisonians, abandoned his Calvinist upbringing and Andover education for the life of an itinerant "infidel." Stephen Foster, also a New Hampshire native, rejected his Congregational ministry to become a Garrisonian apostle.[80]

Pillsbury left Andover a committed abolitionist, yet for the time being he remained an orthodox minister: for a brief and unhappy period, following his antislavery agency, he held a parish position in Loudon, New Hampshire.[81] In fact, his religious education and experiences proved to be critical in the development of his radical philosophy. Gilmanton and Andover provided Pillsbury with critical thinking skills and a thorough grounding in religious history, theory, and dogma, which served him well in his assault upon the Christian ministry. More important, his experiences at these institutions nourished his feelings of outsiderness. He considered his education at Gilmanton barely adequate and consistently referred to his years at this short-lived seminary with bitterness. "At 27 I was induced to enter an Institution of Theology grafted, probably illegally, on to the charter of Gilmanton N. H. Academy," he caustically explained. "One professor, Rev. Herman Hood, and myself, composed 'Gilmanton Theological Seminary,' when as such, it was first introduced by the newspapers to a wondering world."[82] His attempt to improve his status at Andover failed miserably. He felt disconnected from his fellow students because he was older and yet less learned than most of them (for seminary recruits usually had some type of college education).[83] His final break with the faculty ensured that he would remain outside the elite inner circle of Andover graduates.

Pillsbury did not immediately embark on his abolition career upon leaving Andover. His interactions with radical antislavery leaders and his first ministry, however, would push him toward a full-time career in reform.

In November 1839, Pillsbury took great pleasure in repeating for an anti-slavery colleague the comments of a Boston clergyman's wife on the divisions among abolitionists in the state of Massachusetts. " 'Do you not know,' said she, 'that the *New* Organization has all the *pious* abolitionists in the state belonging to it?' Really, I told her I was not aware of it. How long has it been? 'Well,' said she, 'it is so, and the ministers of this state who are abolitionists are with them.' "[84] Pillsbury, a member of the "Old Organization," agreed that "the ministers of this state . . . who *profess* to be abolitionists were with them." However, Pillsbury assured his hostess that his recent experience traveling through the towns of Massachusetts had convinced him that the only abolitionists who could be relied on were those of the "Old Organization," who "had been fed on *Liberators* and could eat and digest them, as well as an old Kentucky hunter could eat raw bear and buffalo."[85]

This anecdote highlights the three issues that propelled Pillsbury closer toward radicalism during his short-lived first ministry and his early antislavery experiences. First, the momentous division in the antislavery movement, which occurred between 1837 and 1840, forced all abolitionists, including Pillsbury, to take sides. Second, antislavery radicals like Garrison, with his *Liberator*, actively courted young, talented, and committed abolitionists like Pillsbury. And finally, the perceived personal and political betrayal by the church sealed his decision.

In the spring of 1839, Pillsbury undertook a position as a temporary lecturing agent with the Massachusetts Anti-Slavery Society, and traveled across the state attending antislavery conventions and meetings.[86] During this lecturing tour Pillsbury learned of the various sources of division among abolitionists, the most contentious of which was the debate over the role of women in antislavery organizations.[87] When the Grimké sisters began lecturing before audiences of both men and women in 1837, some abolitionists expressed their disapproval.[88] Many of the more conservative ministers in the movement considered the Grimkés' public lecturing an activity outside the boundaries of women's "sphere" and, most important, an intrusion into their own domain: public oratory on moral issues.[89] Even as they clashed over women's public lecturing, abolitionists also differed over the appropriateness of political activity within the movement. The Garrisonians argued that politics required compromise and expediency, thus effectively eliminating the possibility of a moral movement. Others disagreed, contending that the political arena offered the only practical avenue for real change.[90] Finally, abolitionists also divided over the increasing predominance of "nonresistance" within the movement. Garrison, influenced by John Humphrey Noyes, asserted that abolitionists should not participate at all in government (especially not voting) as long as the Constitution sanctioned and defended slavery. Believing that civil government usurped the power of God, some Garrisonians went even further in their nonresistance philosophy, asserting that any government that relied on arms or violence in any form should not be supported.[91] These various internal conflicts proved devastating for the unity of the antislavery movement. By the late 1830s, individual abolitionists found themselves called upon to take sides as the major antislavery societies, including the American Anti-Slavery Society, divided into separate, competing organizations.[92] Little middle ground remained.

In 1839, Pillsbury did not easily or automatically adopt a radical position. His orthodox religious training was still a powerful influence and, furthermore, he intended to pursue a career as a Congregationalist minister. In reminiscing about his first meeting with Pillsbury, the Boston Brahmin abolitionist Wendell Phillips recalled that his young friend struggled with his decision to deliver an antislavery oration on the Garrisonian platform. "I well remember the deliberation and the reluctance with which you came to a decision and then the manly, eloquent, upright, and downright speech, near the close of the day, with which you regaled the meeting."[93] Not long after that speech, Pillsbury wrote that while "I have no doubt brother Garrison and myself might differ in our views of the Christian ministry and some other subjects," he still loved "to vindicate [Garrison's] general course whenever it is assailed."[94] Conservative abolitionists also worked diligently to gain the support of the impressive young Pillsbury, hoping to lure him away from the Garrisonians. "He is a young man of strong mind, determined energy and fearlessness, and thorough-going in his principles and opposition to Slavery," explained one anti-Garrisonian to a colleague, "but I am sorry to say rather inclined to fall in with the views of Garrison on other subjects."[95]

While Pillsbury was strongly drawn to the Garrisonians, practical issues may have initially influenced him to choose a parish ministry over the more precarious career of radical agitation. Sometime during 1839, Pillsbury met and courted fellow New Hampshire abolitionist Sarah Sargent. Probably drawn to one another because of their common interest in the antislavery movement, the young couple quickly fell in love and married on New Year's Day, 1840. Although his new wife strongly supported abolition, the responsibilities of married life required that Pillsbury provide a safe and comfortable home for Sarah. A parish ministry certainly offered a more reliable source of income than antislavery lecturing. Later, after he had chosen abolition over the ministry, he would admit to a friend, "My poor wife supposed she was marrying a Congregational minister. So never was little woman more disappointed."[96] Probably suspecting Sarah's preference for his stable employment in the church, Parker at first chose to remain a member of the clergy. His relationship with a few leading male abolitionists, however, and his frustration as a minister, would cause him to reconsider this decision.

Many young evangelical ministers were "converted" to abolition through the influence of an older male mentor.[97] Just before Pillsbury began his lecturing tour in the spring of 1839 he attended a meeting of the Executive Committee of the Massachusetts Anti-Slavery Society in order to clarify the arrangements for his meetings. Here he met William Lloyd Garrison, who, at the close of the meeting, invited the young man to pass the night at his home.[98] Inspired by this act of generosity and impressed with Garrison's limitless enthusiasm, Pillsbury conducted a successful tour of Worcester County, converting many to immediate abolition. He later wrote to a friend, "I trust I am no flatterer, but I must say I esteem Bro[ther] Garrison more highly than ever. . . . I stand away up here on the granite hills of New Hampshire and watch his course with admiration."[99] By this time Garrison had become a powerful central figure in antislavery, attracting either earnestly devoted followers or unforgiving critics. His supporters developed into a tightly knit radical "clique," as one historian described the Garrisonians.[100] Beguiled by Garrison's charm, warmth, and intensity, Pillsbury quickly found himself drawn into this intimate family of "infidels." He confided to a friend that he considered the Boston abolitionists to be "the most important moral engine that now moves and ever has moved on the Earth. I regard them as *my friends* though they belong to the Universe."[101]

Other abolitionists besides Garrison inspired Pillsbury to work full-time in the antislavery movement and abandon the church. Just after he finished his abolition lecture tour and settled into his first ministerial position in the autumn of 1839, Pillsbury received a letter from John Collins, his friend who had also abandoned Andover Seminary on account of his antislavery inclinations.[102] Collins had quickly become a close associate of Garrison and general agent of the Massachusetts Anti-Slavery Society. Searching for earnest young recruits, Collins pleaded with Pillsbury to return to Massachusetts and "assist in the struggle for freedom." Pillsbury assured Collins that he greatly desired to leave his parish in Loudon, New Hampshire. "I do not like the place at all," he admitted, "and nothing but a sense of duty would retain me in it a single day. It is however a good place to plant an Anti Slavery battery upon and unless I am driven out . . . I intend here to plant one."[103] Pillsbury remained convinced that his role as a minister would allow him to most effectively advance the antislavery movement and fulfill his commitment to moral reform. More practically, Pillsbury probably felt hesitant to sacrifice his hard-earned career and many personal ties for the cause of abolition. As he later explained, joining the radical Garrisonians came with many costs: "With a large circle of relatives, almost every one in the orthodox church, including Father and Mother, I learned by a painful experience, what it was to 'forsake all' for the truth."[104]

Abolitionist editor Nathaniel Rogers assailed Pillsbury with even greater pressure to leave the ministry and join the movement—more particularly, the New Hampshire movement. Rogers, the undisputed leader of New Hampshire antislavery, had forged a prominent position in the movement since the mid-1830s, often influencing Garrison and his Boston contingent toward more progressive positions on nonviolence, women's rights, and religion.[105] Because the New Hampshire antislavery radicals had already lost their best lecturer, Stephen Foster, to the Boston movement, they proved unwilling to allow another native son to work in Massachusetts. Moreover, as the New Hampshire antislavery movement began to divide in 1839—conservatives battling radicals for supporters and finances—Rogers desperately needed the assistance of every radical abolitionist he could find.

Rogers cleverly employed familiar images of manhood to entice Pillsbury out of his religious career. In an article written for the *Herald of Freedom*, he publicly appealed to Pillsbury to "forego . . . the contracted and hampered position of a parish minister."[106] After describing the antislavery movement as a revolutionary campaign, employing military jargon and metaphors, Rogers raised the issue of Pillsbury's courage and willingness to meet challenges. "Bro[ther] P[illsbury] is not a man who will avoid the fatigues and sacrifices of the abolition service, for the sake of settlement and a parish. . . . No, duty, and not ease or interest is the question with him," explained Rogers, portraying the ministry as a spineless and selfish career choice. An antislavery lectureship, on the other hand, represented a "manly, generous, philanthropic" vocation.[107]

Rogers also tried to sway Pillsbury with the abundant confidence he consistently expressed in his friend's abilities and talents. In May 1840, when Rogers temporarily left his editor's desk to attend the World Anti-Slavery Convention in London, he asked Pillsbury to take charge of the *Herald*. "I have the satisfaction of leaving the paper . . . in the able and faithful charge of our beloved brother, Parker Pillsbury," gushed Rogers in his last editorial.[108] During Pillsbury's tenure as editor of the radical *Herald of Freedom* he attempted to maintain Rogers's progressive standards. For example, when the American Anti-Slavery Society confronted the debate about women's appropriate position in the movement by electing Abby Kelley, an experienced young female lecturer, to the all-important Business Committee, Pillsbury expressed enthusiastic support. He scolded the conservative and religious members of the organization who walked out in protest.[109]

Rogers's influence on Pillsbury proved to be deep and long lasting.[110] He became both a father figure and a role model for Pillsbury, whose real father

had by this time shunned his eldest son. Indeed, Rogers often protected and
advised his young friend, treating him like one of the family. When Pillsbury
fell ill in 1844, Rogers wrote with fatherly suggestions for recovery. "Don't
take too much second advent medicine," he warned. "Would not the simple
waters invigorate you more? . . . Don't be discouraged or *too brave*."[111] Rogers
used his editorial position to promote Pillsbury among abolitionists when he
felt his friend was neglected.[112] He also wrote several articles in 1844 appealing to abolitionists for contributions in order to help Pillsbury purchase a
home.[113] Even following Rogers's bitter falling-out with the Garrisonians in
1845, a conflict that tortured Pillsbury, the young radical had only kind
words for his mentor, who would die a year later. "My regard for friend
Rogers has been greater than for any other man alive," he wrote.[114]

While the call of antislavery radicals like Rogers profoundly moved Pillsbury, his dreadful experiences as a minister in Loudon made him particularly
susceptible to their appeal. After leaving Andover and completing his anti-
slavery lecturing agency, Pillsbury received five invitations from various
parishes in New Hampshire and Massachusetts to preach as a candidate for
settlement.[115] He accepted a position in Loudon and he and his new wife
moved to this small community. According to Pillsbury, he immediately met
with resistance among his flock. His sermons on temperance, antislavery,
and the imperative of moral reform angered his congregation, who found
this focus on "works" instead of salvation unpalatable.[116] "I pleaded guilty as
to the charge of dwelling more on *works*," explained Pillsbury, "and gave as
reason that I thought we failed less in faith than in works."[117] He quickly
sensed that his congregation preferred a minister who did not challenge or
even question the moral status quo. Pillsbury, however, did not capitulate: "I
did not harken to certain influential *christians*, and take an inventory of all the
sins done in the parish, and then preach on anything else but them."[118]

Pillsbury's congregation did not act alone in undermining his position;
some of his peers in the Congregational clergy and his opponents among the
conservative moral reform movement worked diligently to weaken his influence. For example, he found "neighboring ministers prowling about among
the church and people of my congregation whispering surmises that my anti-
slavery zeal and my intimacy with the 'Infidel Garrison' and the already suspected Rogers were shaking my own orthodoxy too."[119] Most clergymen
from all denominations opposed Garrison's abolitionism and barred anti-
slavery lecturers from their pulpits. Even the Congregationalists enacted ecclesiastical "gag laws" forbidding any discussion of the controversial topic.[120]
Pillsbury's antislavery sermons as well as his association with Garrison,
therefore, would have made him a target for his more conservative colleagues. Even worse, Pillsbury learned that a powerful and conservative

benevolent organization, the American Home Missionary Society, had "officially assured two parishes at least, where there was some prospect that I might be called to labor, that they must avoid me, or forfeit the aid and the favor of that Society."[121] An interdenominational association that eschewed immediate emancipation because of its potential effect on all-important Southern donations, the society unquestionably found radical abolitionists like Pillsbury to be intolerable.[122]

These personal attacks frustrated Pillsbury as he attempted to defend himself against his diverse antagonists. It was in this frame of mind that he came across James G. Birney's anticlerical monograph, *American Churches, the Bulwarks of American Slavery*.[123] Birney, a former slaveholder from Alabama, had been converted to abolition by Theodore Weld in 1831. He abandoned a lucrative legal career to become an agent for the American Colonization Society and then the American Anti-Slavery Society, all the while writing his anticlerical interpretation of American slavery.[124] Birney documented the varying ways in which all denominations of the Christian church in the North helped to support and maintain the Southern slave system. Reading Birney, Pillsbury realized that his own experience typified the hypocrisy of the Christian ministry.[125] His religious education and his employment in Loudon seemed to verify Birney's accusations, and he decided to leave the Congregational ministry for a career in antislavery reform. In the transition from respected minister to despised abolitionist, Pillsbury became convinced that the Christian church represented the most dangerous and powerful enemy of the organized antislavery movement and he dedicated himself to exposing this fact. "Our religious institutions have made themselves the body-guard of slavery," he wrote grimly to Stephen Foster. "We cannot come at the monster but through them. Let us not then mistake. A pro-slavery religion must be hunted out of the land. . . . It has fattened on human misery. . . . But her hour has come."[126] Pillsbury thus began a lifelong campaign to overthrow one of the most powerful institutions in the nation.

Pillsbury's disappointment with revivalism and the Christian ministry and his "conversion" to antislavery were similar to the experiences of many young men. He was atypical, however, in his ultimate rejection of institutionalized Christianity and his radical position on women's rights, racism, and various other issues. Many moral reformers chose to remain within the church and work toward converting both individuals and the institution itself. For example, Samuel Joseph May, a leading Garrisonian abolitionist, remained a Unitarian minister throughout his antislavery career.[127] Other abolitionists, including Lewis Tappan and Joshua Leavitt, embraced evangelicalism and attempted to push their colleagues toward a stronger antislavery position.[128] Most of these evangelical abolitionists adopted moderate positions on the issues of women's rights and racism.[129]

Pillsbury, on the other hand, helped to formulate and promulgate what the majority of his colleagues considered an extreme position in regard to the Christian church.[130] During his first years as an antislavery lecturer Pillsbury discovered the church to be his strongest and most persistent opponent. In response, he and his antislavery coadjutor Stephen Foster argued that true Christians should "come out" of their respective churches, thereby freeing themselves from the corrupt influence of these tainted institutions which accepted the sin of slavery.[131] Pillsbury and Foster actively promoted this "come-outer" philosophy through tactics that ultimately fostered their reputation as extremists—and once so labeled, they labored to live up to that reputation. In 1841, Pillsbury wrote excitedly to Foster: "We must show ourselves what we are already called, 'dangerous men.' Devise some plan, if you can, by which we may improve on the operations of the past. If we scourged a pro-slavery church and ministry last year with whips, let us this year with scorpions!"[132] Foster responded with a plan that involved entering churches during Sunday sermons, rising during a quiet moment, and delivering an antislavery lecture.[133] These aggressive tactics brought both men widespread opprobrium, many bumps and bruises, and even jail time for Foster. During a lecturing tour in the fall of 1841, for example, Pillsbury and Foster experienced a series of escalating attacks as they were verbally abused at one meeting, found their carriage covered with cow manure after the next gathering, and then were physically assaulted at the following lecture. Foster described his efforts at this last meeting to protect frightened women while Pillsbury was left with their assailants. When the mob quieted, Foster found that Pillsbury, "with an unresisting demeanor, had protected himself from personal injury, although for a time entirely in the power of infuriated drunkards."[134] These types of violent encounters proved fairly common for the two radicals and probably increased their antipathy toward the church, which they inevitably blamed for the mobs. Although Pillsbury was less interested in disrupting church services than Foster, his religious radicalism remained indomitable. He supported antisabbatarianism, flirted with spiritualism, and eventually spent some twenty years denouncing "spiritual slavery" as a traveling lecturer in the Free Religion movement following the Civil War.[135]

Pillsbury's religious radicalism was closely connected to his feeling of being an outsider. Although this important aspect of his self-identity was well developed by the time he left Andover, his relationship with antislavery leaders further catalyzed his sense of alienation. Even among abolitionists, he considered himself second-tier because the leaders of the movement hailed from Massachusetts and most boasted wealthy and cultured backgrounds. Although certainly non-Bostonians like Henry C. Wright, Rogers, and Foster earned an esteemed place among the leading Garrisonians, the wealthy Boston "patricians," including Edmund Quincy, Francis Jackson, Wendell Phillips, and Maria Weston Chapman, controlled the day-to-day operations of the group and strongly influenced their leader, Garrison.[136] Rogers lived and worked away from the central gathering spot of the Garrisonians—Chapman's comfortable home in Boston—while Foster, Wright, and Pillsbury spent most of their time traveling and lecturing, especially in the West. Moreover, the wealth, education, and culture of the Garrisonian patricians produced in Pillsbury feelings of insecurity and inferiority. Writing to his wife in 1850 about the possibility of boarding with one of their privileged Boston colleagues, for example, Pillsbury sullenly concluded, "We have been to some of their houses a great deal, and we can make them no return. And besides, they can look upon us, at best, only as 'country cousins,' and indeed not even that; while they are among the best of the city and have company in abundance of people of their own quality."[137] As Pillsbury leaned more and more toward radicalism, however, as his tactics and philosophy evolved and his reputation as a fanatic increased, his status within the antislavery movement improved and he began to feel less like a "country cousin." Although some of his colleagues continued to regret his unforgiving anticlericalism, Pillsbury slowly emerged as a leading thinker among radical abolitionists. No longer an outsider, but rather a role model and an influential tactician, Pillsbury found his calling.

Perhaps more important, Pillsbury's sense of being an outsider merged comfortably with the predominant theological self-image among the Garrisonians of being a "minority among sinners." Envisioning themselves as "distressed outsiders," radicals looked in on the world and saw a population of unrepentant sinners. Convinced that their duty as apostles of the Christian millennium was to convert the world, they sought to persuade both individuals and institutions to adhere to the "ethic of love" and repent of their sins, but they always remained outside the sinful world.[138] Pillsbury abandoned his career, his upbringing, his religion, his relatives, and his friends, and became a professional outsider. The Garrisonians, with their celebration of outsiderness, offered Pillsbury new friends and family, a new religion, and a new career.

2

Marriage, Family, and the Business of Reform

Wed on New Year's Day in 1840, Parker Pillsbury and Sarah Sargent remained married until their deaths in 1898, within four months of each other. Their fifty-eight-year marriage is a testimony to their ability to balance reform activism and family commitment, despite many overwhelming obstacles. Long separations, financial problems, illnesses, and distrust threatened the Pillsburys over the years, but they stubbornly continued to negotiate a workable family life. For Parker, his roles as husband and father offered a mixed blessing. He gloried in the intimacy and boundless love that his family eagerly offered him, but he also struggled to harmonize domestic responsibilities and the business of reform. Sarah wrestled with her own challenges, attempting to find the strength to run a household with an absent husband.

As they tried to build a satisfying family life, Sarah and Parker also experienced the difficulties of integrating the values of the age with their unconventional household. Many radical abolitionists tried to weave their egalitarian politics into their home life, rejecting traditional gender and familial relations. Political ideals, however, were not so easily converted into personal relationships. Sarah and Parker attempted to develop a relationship guided by respect and equality, but over the years they found it increasingly difficult to escape society's traditions and norms.

Born in 1818, Sarah Sargent grew up in the small town of Loudon, New Hampshire. Her father, John L. Sargent, joined the growing class of young men who chose a profession over farming. A successful physician and surgeon, he boasted an extensive practice and probably provided his family with a comfortable home.[1] Sarah's mother, Sally Wilkins, was known as a woman "of rare excellence of character, of refined taste and culture."[2] She had at least four children, including a daughter who died during childhood.[3] Her three surviving offspring, Charles, Sarah, and Frances, remained close throughout their lives, often staying in each other's homes and caring for one another's children. Sally Sargent also maintained intimate ties with her three children. She lived with Charles (presumably after the death of her husband) only a few blocks from Sarah, in Concord. Frances also lived in Concord sporadically. Sarah's father, who is never mentioned in her letters, probably died prior to her marriage to Parker Pillsbury.

Sarah Sargent came of age during a period when New England abounded with new ideas about womanhood. As the economy changed and men increasingly began working outside the home, women became leaders in the domestic arena. Expected to provide a comfortable home for their work-weary husbands and raise strong, intelligent children, women were charged with important and respected work. In fulfilling these responsibilities women built their own "female world of love and ritual," centered around the domestic sphere.[4] For some women, this female world offered a source of confidence and emboldened them to challenge the conventional norms of womanhood. They employed the ideology of domesticity, which deemed women morally superior to men, to justify their involvement in moral reform organizations, and in some cases, women's rights groups. While the domestic sphere continued to limit women's political, economic, and social opportunities, some women cleverly used it to establish untraditional roles and activities.[5]

One of the most important elements of women's expanded roles was access to education. In the antebellum period new perceptions of femininity led to the opening of many private academies for girls. Although early educational reformers like Emma Willard and Catharine Beecher focused on the importance of domestic training for young girls, these female schools often inspired women to pursue careers and challenge constricting traditions.[6] Sarah Sargent may have attended a female academy, or at least a local school. Her "Remembrance Book," a collection of school essays written from age fourteen to eighteen, suggests that she received an excellent education. These essays reveal an independent and thoughtful young woman, who did not hesitate to express her own opinion. Perhaps more important, the "Remembrance Book" illuminates Sarah's obsession with her relationship to God and her responsibilities as a virtuous Christian.

Sarah, like many young New Englanders in the 1830s, experienced a religious awakening that left her deeply concerned with the spiritual aspect of all her activities. From choosing friends to listening to her parents, Sarah judged her behavior through the lens of evangelical Christianity. She also judged those around her, often criticizing her youthful peers for their lack of spiritual concern. A great lover of music as a form of worship, for example, she was deeply disturbed by those who "when singing the most sacred music," show "the utmost indifference and inattention."[7] She considered music a spiritual activity—not a form of entertainment or a pleasurable pastime— and thus pointedly disapproved of her peers' indifference toward this sacred vocation. A serious and studious young woman, Sarah disdained the amusements and recreation that seemed to occupy the youth of Loudon. Writing about the "trifling" conversation at parties, Sarah concluded that such social gatherings, instead of improving the minds and health of their participants, resulted in gossip, overeating, and overdrinking. The women dressed in useless costumes and decorated themselves with "artificial ornaments that give them the appearance of *distracted* beings."[8] Unlike the growing contingent of young urban working women who enjoyed social events, fancy dress, and late nights whenever they found time and money, Sarah disapproved of such behavior as frivolous and unchristian.[9]

Sarah's passionate sense of appropriate Christian duty and behavior probably found an outlet in benevolent activism. Unlike Parker Pillsbury, who could translate his evangelical convictions into a career in the ministry, Sarah Sargent had few opportunities to act publicly on her religious beliefs. Many New England women responded to this dilemma by creating female moral reform organizations which were dedicated to eradicating society's ills and beckoning the millennium. Armed with a passionate evangelicalism and the popular presumption of female moral superiority, these groups moved beyond the limited benevolent societies of the 1820s which had focused on charities and orphans.[10]

Some women also joined the growing number of female antislavery societies which emerged in the 1830s. These reformers earnestly concurred with Elizabeth Chandler's declaration that women's sensitive moral nature and sisterly connection to female slaves created in them a special obligation to help free those in bondage.[11] Sarah Sargent joined this small but vocal contingent of women abolitionists in the mid-1830s, while still a teenager. Blending her love of music with her religious faith, in 1838 she wrote an antislavery song entitled "Freedom's Alarm, or Lovejoy's Voice from the Grave," which bemoaned the murder of Elijah Lovejoy, who had been shot by a mob in Alton, Illinois, in 1837.[12] Following Chandler's lead, she employed traditional gender roles to encourage opposition to slavery, pleading with her listeners to hear "the voice of woman's wail" and not "coldly turn your ear."

Sarah Sargent had probably already developed her interest in the abolition movement by the time she met Parker Pillsbury. Though little is known about their courtship, they likely encountered one another in southern New Hampshire, where they grew up within twenty miles of one another. Perhaps they became acquainted while Parker studied for the ministry in the neighboring village of Gilmanton, falling in love through their mutual interest in orthodox religion. Abolition may have drawn them together, as well. As a member of the small New Hampshire abolition community, Parker certainly heard Sarah's antislavery song performed. Or perhaps Sarah learned of Parker's successful antislavery tour of Massachusetts in 1839 and looked for him when he returned to New Hampshire. In any case, they married on 1 January 1840, and settled in Sarah's hometown when Parker began his short-lived ministry there. By the summer of 1840, they had moved a few miles west, to Concord, and Parker had begun his antislavery lecturing agency.

Parker's decision to leave his clerical position was undoubtedly difficult for Sarah. Although an eager advocate of antislavery, she was also a devoted Christian. By 1841, however, Sarah had wholeheartedly adopted Parker's critical position toward the church. At the same time Parker excommunicated his former Congregational brethren in the Suffolk North Association, Sarah also initiated a movement among a small group of women to renounce their membership of the church in protest against its acceptance of slavery.[13] Repudiating the orthodox religion of her youth, Sarah even defied the church representatives who came to question her rebellion. "I expressed as strong an assurance that I should never come back to that body, to be a part of it, till it had humbled itself before God and the slave and asked forgiveness," she explained.[14] Although Sarah had developed a strong sense of independence by this time, Parker probably influenced her to leave the church. Throughout the first few decades of their marriage Sarah consistently adopted a modest and subservient tone in her letters to Parker, deferring to his superior knowledge. After fifteen years of marriage, she described herself to Parker as "uninformed and inexperienced," as well as "feeble and sick in body and oftentimes, faint in spirit," when she first met him. Although she had grown stronger "and *bolder* spiritually," over the years, she still craved his approval.[15] Parker often instructed her in his letters, adopting the tone of a gentle patriarch. When she complained about the pain in her face after having all her upper teeth extracted, for example, he chided her, concluding, "we have got to make the best of it."[16] Considering this teacher-student relationship, it is likely that Sarah learned to censure the church from Parker. Her courageous confrontation with the church leaders, however, reflects a strength of character which was all her own.

Sarah's rejection of traditional religion was not unusual among the Garrisonians; and for women abolitionists, the repudiation of orthodoxy often led to a feminist awakening. In rebelling against the authority and power of the entrenched clergy, many women felt empowered to question their subordination in other areas of life.[17] Feminist abolitionist Paulina Wright Davis was unhappy, she explained, until "I outgrew my early religious faith, and felt free to think and act from my own convictions."[18] But although Sarah supported women's rights and admired the movement's leaders, including Lucy Stone and Susan B. Anthony, she failed to publicly challenge the prescriptions of the women's sphere. Uncomfortable with public speaking and insecure about her writing ability, Sarah did not become a women's rights activist. She did, however, attempt to establish equality in the domestic sphere, insisting on partnership with her husband and an important role in their marriage and family.

During their first two years of marriage Sarah and Parker worked out a routine to accommodate the antislavery lecturing tours which pulled him away from home most of the time. Sarah often accompanied him as he traveled, visiting with friends and relatives and probably helping him prepare for his meetings.[19] During these early years Sarah and Parker managed to construct a relationship grounded in cooperation and respect and centered around their participation in the antislavery movement, not unlike many other radical abolitionist couples.[20] Sarah not only traveled with Parker and participated in his career, she also developed her own leadership role within the female antislavery movement. She participated in the Concord Female Anti-Slavery Society, hosting meetings and directing fund-raising efforts in coordination with other cities' women's antislavery groups.[21] As Parker developed his radical position in the movement, denouncing the church and state in meetings across New Hampshire, Sarah worked at the local level, cultivating antislavery sentiment among Concord women. Laboring toward a common end, Sarah and Parker produced a "partnership of equals."[22] And yet this partnership, from the onset, presumed a distinct separation of roles based on sex and it eventually developed into a gendered partnership of unequals.

Sarah's participation in the abolition movement changed after the birth of her only child in 1843. Accepting the responsibilities of the primary caretaker, Sarah and many other female abolitionists believed that women by nature would assume more involvement in the child-rearing process.[23] Abby Kelley Foster, for example, remained a full-time mother for the first year of her daughter's life, while her husband continued to lecture.[24] Although Sarah continued to support abolition through a variety of formal and informal activities, her participation was severely curbed by her domestic duties. She remained active in the Concord Female Anti-Slavery Society, but decided not to participate in the larger New Hampshire Anti-Slavery Society, even though that organization voted to allow women equal membership and officeholding opportunities. The more important and prestigious state society, therefore, became Parker's territory and Sarah limited herself to the small female organization. Many women preferred all-female organizations, which they found more comfortable and accessible. A long tradition of sex segregation existed within moral reform groups, based on presumptions about the differing capabilities and interests of men and women. Abolitionists followed this tradition during the movement's early years, beginning with the organization of the Boston Female Anti-Slavery Society in 1832, which developed as an auxiliary to the male-run Massachusetts Anti-Slavery Society.[25] Dozens of other female antislavery societies emerged shortly thereafter, often working closely with local men's groups.[26] Helping to raise funds through antislavery fairs and working to garner signatures for antislavery petitions, women abolitionists carefully maneuvered the boundaries of appropriate women's activity.[27] Although some women worked directly in the larger state and national associations, especially after the movement divided in 1840, many, like Sarah, continued to work through the female auxiliaries.

Sarah's involvement in the female society, though perhaps less acclaimed, proved important for her family's finances. The New Hampshire Anti-Slavery Society paid Parker a very small, and sometimes inadequate, salary as general agent of the organization.[28] Because the society depended entirely on donations, Parker received his earnings only if enough money was collected over the course of the year. Any contributions to the society, therefore, inevitably aided the Pillsburys' income. Through her contacts and experience in the female antislavery network, Sarah worked to ensure her husband's salary, focusing on antislavery fairs and public pleas for increased financial support. In a letter to the "Anti-Slavery Women of New Hampshire" published in the *Herald of Freedom*, for example, Sarah implored her virtuous sisters to donate goods and labor to an antislavery fair that she organized to support the field agents. "Some have families who look to them for daily bread," Sarah knowingly wrote of the lecturers. "Some of those who are devoted wholly to the work are fast wearing out, in their constant and energetic onsets upon the foe. . . . They need, they deserve, they will have the cheerful and hearty countenance and support of every enlightened and true lover of pure and virtuous liberty."[29] Thus Sarah managed to significantly influence her own household economy and the salary of her husband and yet remain comfortably within the domestic sphere.[30] Moreover, Sarah's efforts toward securing the family income initiated a long-term trend in which she filled in as head of the household while Parker saved the nation from slavery.

This readjustment of standard gender roles eventually became a source of frustration for Parker, who regularly regretted his inability to maintain a comfortable middle-class lifestyle for his family, and for Sarah, who resented her husband's lack of earning power and his failure to participate more fully in the domestic sphere.

Sarah's informal participation in the abolition movement also proved valuable to Parker in other ways. Although Concord failed to match Boston as a hub of radical antislavery activity, it did attract significant attention as home to the *Herald of Freedom*, Nathaniel Rogers's progressive antislavery newspaper, and most Garrisonians lectured there sporadically. Sarah became a popular host for these abolitionists who visited and spoke in Concord, including such luminaries as Antoinette Brown, William Lloyd Garrison, Theodore Parker, Wendell Phillips, and Lucy Stone.[31] While Parker boarded in the homes of abolitionists across the North, Sarah offered to house, feed, and entertain dozens of antislavery guests, in an informal extension of her reform efforts. "I like to have such choice people with me," Sarah cheerfully wrote her husband, "although it adds somewhat to my care and labor for the time being. But I can very well adapt myself to my circumstances and needs—and act the parts of both, 'Mary and [Martha].' "[32] Perhaps thinking of Parker's lonely nights spent in unfriendly local inns, Sarah made sure that visiting abolitionists felt comfortable and well cared for in her home. Her generosity undoubtedly benefited Parker's status in the movement by revealing the whole-hearted commitment of his entire family. Many abolitionists commented on Sarah's kindness and hospitality and she became well known in antislavery circles. "None know or appreciate more fully the heroic self-denial of your Sarah," wrote one grateful abolitionist to Parker. "When the historian of the anti-slavery movement makes up his jewels for the grand coronation of Liberty, I hope he will not forget these heroines of the fireside."[33] Neither of the Pillsburys, however, acknowledged Sarah's contribution to abolition to be as important as Parker's more public labor for the movement.

Although the work involved in entertaining visitors proved exhausting and sometimes expensive, Sarah enjoyed sharing her home because she was able to catch up on the latest developments (and gossip) in the movement and exchange ideas about related reform efforts. "Lucy [Stone] stopped with us . . . for one week," she wrote to Parker in 1854. "I felt happy every moment. Lucy gave me a copy of Henry [Wright's] work on Parentage and Marriage. I have read a part of it and, my reason and judgment acknowledge that Henry talks right."[34] Sarah not only learned more about the latest reform thought in regard to domestic life, she also discovered something about the private romance of her guest: "Lucy told me that she was expecting to be married in the Spring, to Henry Blackwell of Cincinnati!"[35]

Housing some of the nation's leading reform thinkers and activists, Sarah thrived on the exciting and stimulating conversation that buzzed throughout her home during their visits. She perceived her position among these famous lecturers, however, to be that of a humble servant. "Theodore Parker and Wendell Phillips are to lecture before the Lyceum here . . . and I intend to summon assurance enough to ask Wendell to come and stop with us," Sarah modestly explained to Parker. "I can furnish a neat simple supper, good clean bed and early breakfast, if I cannot converse with him much I do love to hear him talk with others who do know more than I do and I love to wait upon *such* men, and try to have them feel at home in our house."[36] She carefully negotiated a comfortable position among abolitionists, but she devalued her role in the movement. Whether hoping to reassure her husband of his superior expertise, or simply ill at ease in the spotlight, Sarah downplayed the significance of her domestic abolitionism.

As she worked out her role in the movement, Sarah also struggled to adjust to Parker's lengthy absences and the burdens this long-distance relationship entailed. Although the close proximity of her mother and siblings helped ease her loneliness, Sarah found the multiple full-time duties of household head, mother, and reformer exhausting and, at times, debilitating. In her effort to fulfill these burdensome responsibilities with little help from her husband, she found herself increasingly dissatisfied with her marriage.

On average Parker spent more than half the year away from home. In 1847, for example, he remained in Concord approximately three months over the course of the entire year. Moreover, because it often happened that antislavery meetings were not organized until the last minute, Parker often learned of his lecturing schedule only days in advance. Writing to his family of his uncertain summer plans, for example, Parker explained, "My doom and destiny are about as usual. I am to make a short jaunt to Cape Cod in June, shall be, perhaps at Lynn some in July, and on the first of August, shall probably go west. This is as far as I can report at present."[37] The unpredictability of Parker's schedule certainly increased Sarah's anxiety. In addition to regular absences, he also traveled to Europe in January 1854 and remained abroad for a full two-and-a-half years, returning in May 1856. Although Parker had originally planned only a brief trip abroad to regain his health, a number of unexpected developments, including a devastating illness, resulted in a lengthy stay. Sarah struggled with a deep and growing sense of abandonment during this long separation, especially after her mother and brother moved away from Concord in early 1855. Her long letters to Parker during his European sojourn reveal a woman still in love with her husband, but increasingly anxious over his absence. In describing her pleasure at writing to Parker while he was abroad, Sarah explained, "You seem to be so near me, so certainly in my presence, that I feel almost sure that I can reach my hand a little, and actually *touch* my dear beloved husband! Oh may it be my joy, dear Heavenly Father, to have my adored husband returned to my bosom in health and safety!"[38] As Parker stretched his short visit to Europe into a long-term absence, Sarah reluctantly reassured him that she approved of his decision to continue his stay abroad. "Should you remain away until another April or May, how quickly the time will pass"— and yet, she continued, "to think of it, it seems a long, *long* time." Sensing that perhaps she expressed too much hesitation, she immediately added, "But I want you to stay, until you have seen and learned all you had anticipated."[39] Unwilling to burden her husband with her unhappiness, Sarah constantly battled her own emotional inclinations.

Parker's long seasons abroad provoked other emotions in Sarah besides loneliness. "You know I am not disposed to jealousy," she reminded Parker in 1856, but, she added, certain "unjust remarks have sometimes made me weep for hours."[40] Reacting to a neighbor's suggestion that she should be concerned that the generous treatment Parker received while abroad would make him dissatisfied with his home life, Sarah unburdened her long-dormant feelings to Parker. "Ever since your connection with the A[nti-]Slavery movement, which has called you so much from home, I have had my feelings injured by similar remarks sometimes intimating to me that you . . . 'liked to be abroad where you could become familiar with other and many women,' or that you are fond of being noticed particularly by the romantic and visionary soul of women." Sarah claimed that she knew these accusations were *"unjust and untruthful"* and that Parker was *"every moment of his life at home or away unexceptionably faithful* to me *as his wife*!!" And yet these types of comments caused her much "embarrassment" and unhappiness.

After sixteen years of Parker's travels Sarah had become painfully familiar with such remarks. By the end of his long trip to Europe, however, she was vulnerable to these insinuations. During Parker's first year abroad he had developed an intimate friendship with wealthy (and single) English reformer Mary Estlin. She and her father had nursed Parker through a life-threatening illness in March 1854, and he remained in their stately home for several months. Parker often praised Mary Estlin in his letters to Sarah. "She is a darling creature," he gushed.[41] He even criticized Sarah's letters because they did not meet Estlin's high standards. "Your letter . . . was mostly *sentimental*," he chided, "which Miss Estlin has taught me to dislike more than ever."[42] Sarah responded with a cloying glorification of Estlin, which perhaps concealed deep jealousy and mistrust. "Parker dear," she innocently inquired, "do you ever give [Mary Estlin] an affectionate and friendly kiss? If so, just put one sometimes upon her cheek for me."[43] In the same letter Sarah, perhaps not coincidentally, expressed her opinion on a controversial reform movement called Free Love. "You have undoubtedly noticed much discussion . . . on the modern *ism* of *'Free Loveism'* or 'Promiscuous sexuality.' A very repulsive and forbidding ism as it appears to me."[44] Attempting to express her concern without risking his self-righteous rebuke, Sarah subtly questioned her husband's fidelity.

Parker's antislavery career distressed Sarah in other ways. His militant radicalism, for example, resulted in further isolation for the entire family. No moderate herself, Sarah understood and sympathized with her husband's radical positions. She risked the disapproval of her community when she and a few other rebel women dissolved their relationship with the Congregational church. Parker's iconoclastic tendencies, however, often caused her much pain. Because the Garrisonians endured social ostracism, the relationships they developed among themselves proved crucial to their emotional well-being.[45] The Pillsburys' closest friends were all radical abolitionists, and Sarah relied on the support and approval of these allies in order to continue to challenge the social order. Parker, however, relied primarily on his singular radical philosophy to guide and support his activism and this oftentimes brought him into conflict with everyone, including his allies. During the Civil War, for example, he and Garrison developed starkly opposing positions on the role of abolitionists in this time of crisis, and their personal relationship suffered as a result.[46] Although Sarah distanced herself from the disagreement, she could not sustain her friendship with Garrison while her husband publicly criticized him. Parker recognized the pain he caused his wife in this conflict. "My wild steps and opinions have been at times, [Sarah's] grief," he explained to a colleague, "and never more so than now, when I have to differ even with Garrison."[47] Alienated from her community, estranged from her more conservative and religious in-laws, Sarah agonized over her husband's inclination to push away their only friends.

She could sometimes forget these troubles, however, for the more pressing demands of running a household and raising a daughter. "I am *hurried* every hour with some useful business, or duty, on my hands," she explained in a missive to Parker.[48] Managing a household in the nineteenth century required a great deal of physical labor, especially on a limited budget. "I have been to work today with [a neighbor] out of doors, digging up roots, raking up the leaves, and various other chores, preparatory for the coming cold winter," she wrote. "It is hard work."[49] Sarah found herself constantly occupied with the responsibilities of food preparation, gardening, cleaning, sewing, correspondence, and innumerable other necessary duties. She also had the additional burden of boarders. Already lodging one young man, Sarah at first proved reluctant to accept any addition to her household, even when an abolitionist couple eagerly requested to board with her. "Oh! If *I* were only *strong* and *sound*!" she lamented, "I would surely keep such people in my family."[50] Apparently able to find the strength she sought, within a month Sarah was boarding the couple and boasting of her ability to keep a smoothly running home.[51] In addition to her household responsibilities, she also dedicated many hours to visiting neighbors and helping friends in need.[52]

Amid all of this labor Sarah suffered from any number of ailments and illnesses. While Parker traveled in Europe she experienced excruciating pain in her abdomen, suffered severely from menstrual problems, and even had her upper teeth extracted. The physical pain of this last experience was made more distressing by her anxiety that they could not afford false teeth to replace the ones extracted. "It doesn't seem to me as though our humble means would justify me in ever indulging the thought that I should have artificial teeth," Sarah sadly admitted. "But we may at some future time when Reforms are more proudly received, have an increase of worldly means."[53]

Financial difficulties constantly plagued the Pillsburys. "What little we have, has been gathered by hard labor, unceasing industry and close economy," Sarah reminded her absent husband. "We know something of self sacrifice and privation."[54] Valuing simple living, she expressed disdain for the expensive indulgences of her neighbors. "I mend and make our clothes," Sarah assured Parker, "and never spend an hour in superfluous dress, or fixing up, or putting on any of the trappings that most women ornament themselves with."[55] Never able to completely escape her Calvinist upbringing, Sarah celebrated sacrifice and suffering and denounced middle-class "trappings." And yet despite this shunning of worldly goods, Sarah did at times join the growing ranks of the middle class, expressing concern with fabric, furniture, trinkets, and fashion. Women played an important role in the developing consumer economy which exploded during this period. The purchasing of goods for the home "became a female function and prerogative" and a symbol of middle-class status.[56] Sarah could not fully enjoy this role as a consumer because, although her husband could claim a profession and an education, he earned too little to afford the luxuries of the typical middle-class household. Unable to fulfill this middle-class female role, Sarah strove to sustain her femininity in other ways.

Although she did not challenge the circumscribed position of women through public demonstrations, Sarah did attempt to widen women's domestic role. She often boasted of her independence and fortitude, but she always framed these achievements in a domestic and feminine setting. In reassuring Parker of her ability to endure his continued absence in Europe, for example, Sarah bragged of her household efficiency: "[Our boarders] are very much gratified with our home, complimenting me every day for my excellent judgment and arrangements in all that relates to good housekeeping, but say it is a perfect mystery to them how I keep everything in so good order, have such promptness in my hours of eating and rising, while I have so many interruptions."[57] Moreover, she continued, "I trouble no one, but look after all things myself, and I am proud to know that I am about the only woman in town who conducts so many kinds of business as I do." Perhaps fearing she expressed a bit too much independence and confidence, however, Sarah concluded her letter by reassuring Parker of his continued importance in her life: "I am *weak* and *woman-like*, and require encouragement and *deserved* praise from those I love, to buoy me up against all discouragements, and dark clouds. . . . But smiles, and words of cheer and gladness from my dear husband always . . . incite me to new energy and purpose."[58] Torn between glorying in her autonomy and acknowledging her "womanly" frailty, Sarah strove to be worthy of her husband without threatening him or exceeding the boundaries of her sphere. Despite the fact that many of Sarah's abolitionist acquaintances, including Lucy Stone and Abby Kelley, burst out of their confined "female" space to challenge not only slavery but also women's subordination, she chose to develop her skills, power, and independence within the prescribed limits of the domestic sphere.

From Sarah's perspective, Parker's career certainly proved problematic for their marriage in many ways. Although his absence allowed her the opportunity to develop a strong sense of self-sufficiency, the obstacles it created became, at times, unbearable. The ensuing resentment and even bitterness that quietly emerged in her letters became apparent to Parker over the years and he regretted his wife's unhappiness. Sarah, however, did not suffer alone. Parker's peripatetic lifestyle brought him grief as well. Torn as he was by gender expectations he failed to fulfil and frustrated by his inability to develop a satisfying marriage, home and family eventually became a source of heartache instead of harmony.

The birth of their daughter, Helen, in 1843 brought Sarah and Parker great joy. "Sarah is as tickled as a pussy with half a basket full of kittens," Parker playfully wrote his brother-in-law, after the child was born.[59] A healthy and energetic baby, Helen kept her parents busy during her first few months, but Sarah's mother and sister helped ease the young couple's burdens. With the additional financial expenses and emotional demands caused by the birth of a daughter, Parker could not afford to absent himself from the lecturing field and he quickly returned to his itinerant life.

Despite his support for innumerable progressive causes, including women's rights, Parker could not wholly escape the dictates of tradition. In theory, a woman might very well work and support a family; however, Parker felt strongly his duty to sustain his wife and daughter. His many masculine responsibilities, financial, intellectual, and even emotional, often preyed on his mind during his travels. Sometimes the call of his family forced him to limit his lecturing activity. In explaining why he refused a Western tour in the winter of 1847, for example, Parker wrote to Foster, "My [family] cannot go with me, possibly as can yours, and they are unwilling I should go so far in winter. . . . These wives, Stephen, must have a voice and some sway in matters of this kind."[60] In their admittedly reasonable demands, "these wives" sometimes resorted to more outspoken opposition to their husbands' absences. A letter from Parker to Sarah during a lecturing tour, for example, reveals indirectly her frustrations: "My health is as good as can be, covered as I am with biles. Your wish one evening at Lynn that I might have them, or something else while absent on this tour, is likely to be realized. If it affords you as much satisfaction as it does me suffering, you will be very happy indeed."[61] Clearly, Sarah had reached the limit of her patience when she wished painful boils on her husband as he left for yet another lecturing tour.

Not all male field lecturers experienced such family conflict. Pillsbury's traveling partner, Stephen Foster, developed a cooperative working relationship with his spouse, Abby Kelley Foster. Unlike Sarah, Abby Kelley earned a leadership position in the national organization after years of field lecturing alongside Foster and Pillsbury. When Kelley married Foster in 1846, they both agreed that Kelley would remain active in the movement. In a personal letter to Kelley after her marriage, Pillsbury anxiously inquired if she would continue her field work. "Though as Abby Kelley you have died, I hope you yet live, and live too to the Anti Slavery Enterprise as you have lived before," he declared. "I doubt if there was much joy in heaven, when Theodore Weld ran away with both the Grimkés and made one a mother, and both obscure and private women."[62] Angelina and Sarah Grimké had, with Kelley, forged the way for women antislavery lecturers in the late 1830s, but both retired from public speaking when Angelina married Theodore Weld.[63] Despite Parker's support for women antislavery lecturers like Kelley, more traditional gender roles predominated in his own family.

The financial support of his family was one such traditional masculine responsibility he took very seriously. "I have deprived my wife and daughter of many comforts" on account of antislavery commitments, admitted Parker regretfully.[64] Although he lamented the fact that his family sometimes had to make do with old clothes and simple meals, he did not consider this a sign of his failure as a husband and father. Even though masculinity had become popularly associated with individualism and economic success in the antebellum period, Parker rejected the notion that a man could be

measured by his pocketbook. He instead clung to the old measures of manhood, such as community involvement, virtuous behavior, and personal sacrifice.[65] Not completely impervious to the pull of middle-class materialism,
however, he sometimes indulged in the pure pleasure of consumer pur-
chases. Sarah could not hide her delight at these rare moments. "What shall
I say of the very beautiful watered BLACK DRESS! Oh! It is magnificent!" she
bubbled to Parker.[66] A full-fledged proponent of simple living, Sarah
quickly followed her enthusiastic response with a reminder to her husband
that she did not regret her modest wardrobe. "Never for once, have I felt in
the last fifteen years disposed to complain or feel hurt that I had no more,"
she assured him. "At the same time, I love to see and have *good* articles of
dress, plain but not showy, or gaudy, for you know dear one, *that I am a little
modest woman!*"[67]

Throughout his years in the antislavery movement Pillsbury managed to
garner a modest income, but certainly not enough to sustain a fashionable
wardrobe for his wife. Only with a few unexpected financial developments
after the Civil War, including a generous bequest from an antislavery colleague, an inheritance from a successful brother-in-law, and Helen's marriage to the publisher of the Concord daily newspaper, P. Brainard Cogswell,
did the Pillsburys become financially comfortable.

Brainard Cogswell proved important to Parker long before his marriage
to Helen in 1888, and for reasons other than his financial support. He began
boarding with the Pillsburys as a young man in 1848, while he learned the
newspaper trade from George C. Fogg, a reformer who published a Free
Soil journal.[68] Cogswell, who eventually developed a prestigious career as a
progressive publisher and local politician, remained in the Pillsbury household for the rest of his life.[69] Mentioned casually in letter after letter by
Sarah, Parker, and eventually Helen, Cogswell clearly acquired an important
and intimate position within the Pillsbury family. As Parker struggled to fulfill his role as father and husband at long distance, he found that Cogswell
performed efficiently as a surrogate "man of the house" during his absences.
Not only helping with strenuous chores and adding to the family income
with his rent, Cogswell became a close friend to both Sarah and Helen.
Writing to Parker of her recent illness, Sarah illuminated Cogswell's valuable presence in their home: "Sometimes when Brainard came in, he would
find me in tears and he always would sit down by me, rub my hands and arms
and head gently, talk, and read to me as long as he could stay, and almost always leave me feeling more hopeful and cheerful," she reported. "He said he
would try and wait upon me, as he knew Parker would, and he succeeded
well."[70] While Sarah and Helen developed deep feelings for Brainard, Parker
did not express jealousy or resentment. Quite the contrary, he appreciated

Fig. 2. Parsons Brainard Cogswell. From E. O. Jameson, *The Cogswells in America* (Boston, 1884).

Brainard's role in their life, probably because it alleviated his own guilt at his constant absence. When Cogswell died in 1895 at the age of sixty-seven, Parker lamented the loss to a friend: "I had resigned all that constituted me the head of the household to him and most admirably was he fulfilling the trust."[71]

Cogswell not only became the acting head of the household, he also developed a leadership position in Concord. A journalist and publisher, Cogswell established the first daily paper in town, the *Concord Daily Monitor*. He held innumerable elected and volunteer positions in the community, including as longtime member of the Board of Education, state printer, and state legislator. In 1892, he was elected mayor of Concord. An earnest social activist, Cogswell advocated a number of reforms, including abolition. He even reluctantly turned down an opportunity to work as Frederick Douglass's printer in 1854 due to other commitments.[72] Although never an outspoken radical like Parker, Cogswell devoted much time and energy to moral reform. As director of the lyceum in Concord for a number of years, Cogswell brought to the city many of the most progressive speakers on antislavery, temperance, and women's rights.[73] After listening to an African-American reform orator Cogswell had brought to town, Sarah explained to Parker, "She was very much liked—A great change has come over the people here, for Brainard's perseverance in bringing such people before the citizens in Lyceums here has greatly softened their feelings on subjects of Reform."[74] As the major stockholder of the progressive Concord-based Republican Press Association, Cogswell also helped to publish several of Parker's pamphlets in the 1890s.[75] Unlike Parker, who tended to alienate neighbors and even friends with his uncompromising radicalism, Cogswell enjoyed the respect and admiration of the citizens of Concord. He became for Sarah and Helen an ideal surrogate family leader.

Despite Cogswell's assistance, Parker nonetheless remained torn for most of his life between his responsibilities to his family and his commitment to radical reform. His frustration at leaving his family peaked during the years of his daughter's childhood and youth, when he believed his influence and support were most needed. While Parker never developed the kind of intimacy with his daughter that she shared with her mother, he still remained a strong and important influence in her life.

The customs of family life and child-rearing experienced distinct changes in the antebellum period, especially among the middle class. As the nature of the economy began to evolve from agricultural to industrial, middle-class Americans developed new patterns of family organization in order to adapt to this shift.[76] Determined to push their sons into the new white-collar jobs in order to maintain their class standing, the middle class provided their male offspring with a good education, kept them at home longer, and encouraged them to marry later. These tactics applied primarily to sons instead of daughters because class standing was determined by the male's status. Young girls, however, were not ignored. They were expected to learn the values of self-control and sacrifice and become experts in the area of household responsibilities. More and more girls also received an education in order to become better wives and mothers.

Americans were also beginning to have fewer and fewer children in the nineteenth century. Economic, religious, and social developments accounted for this declining fertility rate. With less land to bequeath to heirs, many couples decided they simply could not afford a large family. Moreover, for the increasing number of people who moved to urban areas, large families came to mean more mouths to feed instead of additional workers for the farm. The Second Great Awakening and new religious trends also may have led to a decline in family size. An emerging evangelical emphasis on individual control as opposed to faith in the will of God encouraged people to take the initiative in regard to limiting the family.[77] Finally, popular ideas about sexuality provided further justification for small families. Nancy Cott has documented the emergence of a new prevailing ideology of female sexuality in this period which declared women "passionless" and thus justified their decision to abstain from sexual relations and have fewer children.[78]

Parker and Sarah embraced several of these trends, including small family size. Although there is no direct evidence to explain why the Pillsburys had only one child, we can speculate about their motivations. They certainly recognized that they could not afford a large family on Parker's meager and unpredictable salary and they welcomed the religious conception of human mastery as against divine will. It seems unlikely, however, that they adopted abstinence as their solution to family limitation. Even though Parker—who publicly supported women's power to limit and control sexual relations within marriage—never referred to sexual relations with his wife in his extant letters, Sarah, on the other hand, often alluded to her physical longing for Parker during his absences. "I confess I am at times almost impatient for the moment that [I am] encircled in the arms of my absent one, *that* moment that will permit the *silent*, but *tenderest* expression *with* the lips, of those endearing emotions which true and loving hearts feel most, but cannot express by *words*."[79] As birth control devices, such as condoms and sponges, became more widely available in this period, couples like Sarah and Parker could continue to enjoy sexual relations without the fear of pregnancy.[80]

Because they had only one child, the Pillsburys were able to raise their daughter with particular care. They regularly discussed all areas of child-rearing, from diet to education, and they consciously chose to ignore many of the popular gender norms that predominated in the antebellum period. Although Sarah remained Helen's primary caretaker throughout her adolescence, Parker diligently endeavored to participate in his daughter's upbringing. Expressing disdain for the dictates of traditional womanhood, Parker ignored the topics of romance and marriage and instead focused on

self-control and education. He penned letter after letter to Helen throughout her childhood and youth, instructing her on almost every topic imagin-
able. Employing his career and travels as the foundation for his correspondence, Parker attempted to inculcate in his daughter the values of radical
reform.

In almost all his correspondence with Helen during her youth, Parker reminded her of the importance of physical, emotional, and intellectual self-
control. Reformers enthusiastically endorsed self-control in the antebellum
period, hoping that the careful internal regulation of individuals and institutions would lead to the development of a true Christian society. Self-control,
for these men and women, implied the ability to plan and determine the future. As they struggled to understand their world amid dramatic change—
from the introduction of the railroad to the explosion of urban areas—they
desperately sought ways to control whatever they could.[81] Their concern
with self-control manifested itself in a variety of popular reform trends, including vegetarianism, Graham diets, and water cures, each of which Parker
zealously endorsed.[82]

The topics of diet, clothing, and exercise appeared repeatedly in Parker's
letters to his daughter, as he instructed her in the dictates of good health.
Describing a family who raised their children in what he called the "true
way," Parker explained, "They wash all over in cold water, and they eat no fat
meat of any kind, and keep no pork in the house. . . . Then they never tasted
a drop of tea or coffee in their lives. . . . And they never make any but the
plainest of cake and pies."[83] Concluding his letter, Parker warned, "If we sin
against nature by eating and drinking improperly, we must suffer the consequence. . . . If you would have red cheeks, handsome teeth and sweet breath,
with a skin clear and beautiful as a carnation pink, you must understand and
practice these things." Good health, according to Parker, required more than
a restricted and simple diet, it also necessitated regular and intensive exercise. "Ever keep one principle in view and act upon it, and that is that a good
brisk circulation for the blood is absolutely indispensable to health," Parker
advised Sarah in regard to their daughter. "Exercise in the open air, a real
running, romping exercise is needed—not a staid prudish, old-maidish
mincing creep, with mouth puckered and arms as stiff as Presbyterian Principles."[84] Associating good health with "rough hard usage and coarse fare,"
Parker articulated the convictions of many reformers who believed that a
strong, clean body would lead to a purified and virtuous society.[85] In teaching his daughter about diet and exercise Parker also instructed her in the values he associated with a moral Christian society.

Emotional self-control proved just as important as bodily self-control in
Parker's lessons to his daughter. Too much of any emotion would lead to

both physical and intellectual difficulties, he explained. The countless heart-rending farewells with her father that Helen experienced quickly became a foundation for a lecture on the importance of emotional self-control. Writing to Helen from the Atlantic at the onset of his sojourn to Europe, Parker chastised his eleven-year-old daughter for her sentimental display at their separation. "I pitied you terribly and so did others, when they saw how badly you felt. . . . But you must learn to bear these things bravely."[86] Maintaining one's equilibrium and remaining in control not only allowed one to keep emotions private, according to Parker, it also proved very useful during crises and difficult times. "Did you ever think darling, how much we need courage and cool self-possession in these times? . . . When you see every body alarmed at some sudden noise or occurrence, keep calm yourself. Let them run and scream; but you had better walk, and keep cool. Then when you do get to the scene you can be of some service."[87] Perhaps thinking of his own experience using peaceful nonviolence in response to anti-abolition mobs, Parker wanted his daughter to develop emotional self-control both as a protective tool but also as an element of moral firmness and individual strength.

In addition to good health and emotional restraint, intellectual self-control warranted much discussion in Parker's correspondence. The development of critical thinking and writing skills, explained Parker to Helen, required regular study and relentless concentration. Writing to his daughter on Christmas Eve in 1851, Pillsbury asked, "What progress are you making in the New Spelling Book, the New Testament and Plutarch? It is time for you to make study a part of every day's business. . . . I hope by the time you are fourteen, you will have read all the books in the house that are worth reading and that you will have studied a great many things besides."[88] The frivolous play of young girlhood had to be sacrificed in order to develop one's intellect. "We must learn to make ourselves happy by reading, and if we have no books, by writing, and if we have no pen and paper, by thinking. . . . I have felt afraid that little girls of our neighborhood loved play and doll-dressing rather too well. You must try to set them good examples."[89] The ability to think on one's feet, develop a logical argument, and use evidence effectively proved absolutely necessary to the reform lecturer, and Parker hoped his daughter might acquire these skills. Moreover, intellectual self-control also helped mold young people into responsible and useful citizens and Christians. "You must remember *the business* of life, is *work* and *study*, that is, something useful," Parker reminded Helen. "Something that does more lasting good to ourselves and others, than play or sport."[90]

While self-control dominated Parker's child-rearing letters, he also reinforced the importance of scholarship by providing Helen with a variety of educational stories based on his travels and experiences. In 1850, when Helen was seven years old, Parker penned a letter in which he described in detail the landscape of Ohio, but also the meaning of physiology. Concluding the letter, Parker explained, "I have given you two lessons in this letter— Geography is a description of the earth or parts of the earth, and Physiology is a description of the bodies of the men and women who live upon it."[91] Parker also provided historical, cultural, economic, and political information on the people and places he visited. In one letter he described the cheese factories that dominated some towns in Ohio, and in another he explained the difficult labors of coal miners in Kentucky.[92] While Helen attended public school during her youth, illness and bad weather limited her education severely, and Parker attempted to compensate with his long-distance lessons. He hoped to send her to a private school for continued education, but neither his funds nor her health allowed for any extended academic endeavors.[93] His personal lessons became the substitute for Helen's unattainable private education.

Helen, in fact, never moved away from the home of her parents. The only reference to her activity outside the domestic sphere involved her participation in the Unitarian church (Parker, who disavowed any institutional religious ties, referred to Helen's associates as "Ewenitarians").[94] A progressive religion that attracted many reformers and educators, Unitarianism had emerged in the first half of the nineteenth century and many of its leaders became active in radical reform.[95] When Helen eventually married Brainard Cogswell in 1888, at the age of forty-five, the two of them continued to live in the Pillsbury household. We can only speculate why Helen delayed marrying for so long. Her close relationship to her mother may have made it difficult for her to abandon Sarah. Helen probably recognized that once she left home, Sarah would be alone. And when old age forced Parker to remain at home in the 1890s, Helen became a nursemaid to both her parents, making sure they were comfortable.

Helen's relationship with her father may also have influenced her to stay at home. Although Parker spent very little time with his daughter, she loved and respected him. As a child, Helen developed a playful relationship with Parker, boldly articulating her own interests and engaging her father on his own turf. At the age of twelve, for example, Helen corrected her father's spelling in an instructive missive: "In your letter to me yesterday I noticed you spelt one word wrong, it was puppies; you didn't put but two ps in. . . . There was also a word in mother's letter that you didn't spell right. . . . I believe this is all the criticism I have on that letter. I guess you will do better next time."[96] Mimicking his formal tone, she seems to express both a sense of humor and an impatience with his never-ending lessons. Later in life Helen would maintain this good-natured relationship with her father. Perhaps motivated by her parents' deteriorating relationship, Helen often acted as a bridge between Parker and Sarah, especially during his travels.

Helen never adopted Parker's uncompromising philosophy, and this disappointed her father. Describing Helen to a young woman abolitionist in 1860, for example, Parker wrote, "Taking everything into account my daughter is all, and even more, than could be expected. She is now seventeen, well grown physically, but not handsome except that she has fine eyes and a good expression. In study she is not up to the average, from your standpoint; though here, she rates very well. In music, she is my own child; loving it intensely, but with almost total inability to make it."[97] This painfully objective evaluation of his daughter barely hides some disappointment and regret, no doubt. Perhaps guilty that he had not provided Helen with a better education or more personal attention over the years, Parker would probably have preferred a daughter with the same untiring motivation and political and moral convictions that kept him away from home most of her life. Not surprisingly, instead of following her father's footsteps, she followed her mother's lead.

Very few couples, even among the radical reformers, were able to maintain a completely egalitarian household. Inevitably the women took on a greater burden of the domestic duties and child-rearing responsibilities. This does not, however, necessarily indicate the insincerity of male reformers. Parker, Sarah, and many other radicals found themselves subject to the overwhelming influence of middle-class values, prejudices, and presumptions, despite their earnest attempt to challenge and transform the social order. Even as Parker promulgated women's rights at conventions across the North, his own wife remained at home, raising their daughter and laboring to maintain a comfortable domestic sphere. And yet he consistently encouraged his daughter to look beyond the boundaries of traditional womanhood and develop a strong, independent, and virtuous identity. Indeed, gender notions strongly influenced Parker's family relations as well as many other areas of his life. As he struggled to build strong loving ties with the women in his life, Parker also developed very particular notions about appropriate male behavior and the meaning of true manhood. These ideas were strongly influenced by his role in the antislavery movement and also his support for women's rights.

3

Masculinity and Women's Rights

As an outspoken abolitionist, Parker Pillsbury endured many public abuses by his opponents, but when he and his colleagues began openly supporting women's rights in the antebellum period they were vilified with unusual vehemence. The press began to question the manliness of the radicals, often referring to them as "Aunt Nancy" men, "Miss Nancys," or "man milliners."[1] Profeminist men have often been represented as weak, impotent, and lacking in virility by opponents of women's rights and Parker Pillsbury was no exception.[2]

Pillsbury managed to endure this persistent impugning of his manhood because he had long since rejected popular definitions of masculinity. He developed his own sense of manliness during his career as a Garrisonian antislavery lecturing agent. Indeed, the Garrisonian strategy of moral suasion and philosophies of disunionism and anticlericalism greatly influenced many abolitionists toward an egalitarian masculinity and strong profeminist activism.[3] Men such as Frederick Douglass, Nathaniel Peabody Rogers, and William Lloyd Garrison participated in women's rights conventions and promulgated women's full and equal participation in antislavery societies.[4] Other abolitionist men, including Stephen S. Foster and James Mott, married feminist women and maintained relatively egalitarian relationships in which both partners continued their public work in antislavery.[5] All of these profeminist men rejected popular notions of manhood which glorified men's unquestioned predominance in the public world.[6]

Pillsbury's understanding of manhood was more than simply a reflection of Garrisonian egalitarianism, however. His masculine identity was influ-

47

enced by his rural upbringing and family background and it continued to evolve over the years, shaped by his experiences in the antislavery movement and as a husband and father. His vision of masculinity was a complex one that was as much a cause as a product of his activism in public life; indeed, his many reform causes had common roots in a masculine sense of self and morality.

When Pillsbury joined the antislavery movement in 1840 at the age of thirty-one, popular visions of masculinity were in flux. As industrialization and urbanization changed the political, economic, and cultural terrain of U.S. society, gender became an important tool for classifying and ordering a fluid population.[7] Indeed, numerous traditions of masculinity and femininity competed throughout the nineteenth century, differing according to race, class, ethnicity, geographical location, and a variety of other factors.[8] In particular, Euro-American middle-class notions of masculinity changed significantly during this period. The depth of a man's commitment to his community and the quality of his spiritual life provided the framework for judging manhood in the late eighteenth century. By the midnineteenth century, as industrialism led to an increased focus on individual economic success, physical courage and individual accomplishment furnished the new guideposts of manliness.[9] Despite this shift in middle-class notions of masculinity, one thing remained constant: the presumption of male dominance. Although Pillsbury's vision of masculinity included elements from both of these stages, he wholeheartedly rejected women's subordination and he subverted earlier traditions of manhood to create his own profeminist sense of masculinity.[10]

Friends and admirers frequently commented on Pillsbury's imposing physical presence and his family's rugged New England homestead, which Pillsbury described as "the hardest farm in the town."[11] Taking pride in his laboring background, Pillsbury made physical strength an important element in his masculine identity. In describing his decision to secure a formal education at the age of twenty-six, for example, he wrote, "With hands callused and irrecoverably bent, and shoulders bowed with the long and hard labors of the farm, I entered upon a course of Theological Study."[12] Pillsbury's brawny self-image also influenced his reputation within the antislavery movement. Ralph Waldo Emerson, for example, lauded Pillsbury's physical presence and his ability to dominate his opponents:

> Pillsbury, whom I heard last night, is the very gift from New Hampshire which we have long expected, a tough oak stick of a man not to be silenced or insulted or intimidated by a mob, because he is more mob than they; he mobs the mob. John Knox is come at last, on whom nei-

Fig. 3. Parker Pillsbury in Midlife. Courtesy of the New Hampshire Historical Society, F4664.

ther money nor politeness nor hard words nor rotten eggs nor kicks and brickbats make the slightest impression. He is fit to meet the bar-room wits and bullies; he is a wit and a bully himself and something more; he is a graduate of the plough and cedar swamp and snowbank, and has nothing new to learn of labor or poverty or the rough of farming.[13]

Pillsbury also admired physical hardiness in fellow abolitionists. He praised radical colleague Stephen S. Foster, not for his eloquent antislavery oratory, but for his farmwork—his "bending to rigorous field labor, with hands hard and callused," in which "he had come to his true dignity, his real greatness, as never when haranguing an admiring multitude in Boston."[14]

This emphasis on physicality reflected an older tradition of economic independence and of glorifying and romanticizing manual labor. Pillsbury often conflated "manly" economic independence with physical strength and activity. Such "physical" occupations, however, saw a decline in the nineteenth century as many young men moved into urban offices and the professions. Pillsbury regretted this transition because in his view it weakened men, both physically and morally. "The truth is," Pillsbury asserted in a letter to his daughter, "honest, productive industry has become despicable, all who can shirk it, do."[15] As occupations that required physical labor declined in status, Pillsbury's conviction that manhood necessitated brawn and vigor increased.

Many radical abolitionists had other reasons to be concerned with the body. Most who lectured in the field relied on bodily strength to endure the physical demands of a lecturing agency, including mob attacks. Traveling from town to town, often on foot, and lugging heavy loads of meeting notices and antislavery material, lecturers were regularly forced to endure meager meals, dingy accommodations, and limited comforts. Moreover, although avowed advocates of nonviolence, Pillsbury and other abolitionists recognized that bodily strength would aid them in enduring physical abuse by their opponents. During one meeting at Cape Cod, for example, Pillsbury and his colleagues were ejected from the platform "with many kicks, and blows" by a "brutal and ferocious mob" which then "dashed the platform all to pieces." In the course of the attack the abolitionists had their clothes literally torn from their bodies.[16] Not surprisingly, Garrisonians often referred to themselves as "soldiers" in the "war" against slavery. Nathaniel P. Rogers described the "pitched battles" of antislavery work and Pillsbury spoke of the "din and smoke of the entrenchments" during antislavery meetings.[17] Because Pillsbury spent twenty-five years lecturing in the field—more than any other Garrisonian—he expressed particular concern with the issue of physical endurance. Strong bodies, therefore, became symbolic among Garrisonian abolitionists of nonviolent resistance to those who supported the institution of slavery and employed violence to defend it.

On the surface this concern with physical sturdiness seemed merely to prefigure the growing nineteenth-century obsession with the male body.[18] However, Pillsbury and other Garrisonians, sensitized to the politics of gender because they themselves were so often accused of being weak and unmanly, strongly rejected the popular association of masculine strength with brute force. While the general public associated physical courage with the Davy Crockett myth, which, according to Carroll Smith-Rosenberg, offered Jacksonian men "an outlet for hostility and frustration in the violence of jingoism and racism," Pillsbury rebuked American men for their physical oppression of slaves, American Indians, and women.[19] He clearly differentiated his call for male strength from traditional chivalry, which he considered "an outrage and insult."[20] He denounced men's exploitative use of physical strength to subordinate women under the guise of protecting them. "The difference between man and woman in governments and in society is at last, one of brute force," Pillsbury explained in an equal-pay editorial. "It is the oppression of the weak by the strong."[21] He called for true men to resist popular notions of robust manhood and employ their physical strength to protect the downtrodden of society.

Pillsbury and other Garrisonian lecturing agents—who often witnessed the private lives of their host families while on the road—also developed a feminist critique of the meaning of able-bodied masculinity within the home. They highlighted the contradictions between traditional notions of men's strength and the unequal division of household labor. Lodging in the homes of hundreds of families during his lecturing tours, Pillsbury observed that despite men's supposed superior strength, women often engaged in the most difficult and labor-intensive chores in the household. In one editorial, for example, Pillsbury denounced the male members of a family with whom he had lodged for their failure to participate in household labor. While two "feeble-looking women" arranged a meal for ten men, "the husband, with his hired man and two large boys, sat comfortably round the fire, not lifting one finger to assist; not so much as to bring the water or wood, or hold the unkempt, uncomfortable, and, of course, noisy and troublesome baby."[22] Although the husband offered to take care of the children so that his wife might attend Pillsbury's lecture, the abolitionist considered this merely "insult added to injury" and he employed the incident as a text for his lecture. Pillsbury used traditional notions of masculinity and femininity—"two large boys" lounged while "two feeble-looking women" labored diligently. And yet he subverted these traditional gender stereotypes by employing them to call for a more equitable distribution of household labor. Brawn became a badge of unmanliness when associated with the exploitation of women—or any oppressed group.

In denoting men's superior strength as a source of women's oppression, not their protection, Pillsbury exposed the roots of patriarchy and called on men to reverse the meaning of their physical manhood. He employed traditional ideas about men's bodies to guarantee women's equal position in society. In coordination with the Garrisonian condemnation of violence among both anti-abolition mobs and slaveowners, profeminist abolitionists associated manliness with resistance to aggressive physical force.

If true manhood required a strong and healthy body, that body in turn required maintenance through prodigious self-control, the second element in Pillsbury's model of masculinity.

In espousing intelligent self-regulation as a requirement for true manhood, Pillsbury demanded both internal and external bodily restraint. For example, in a letter to his daughter in 1853, Pillsbury lamented the lack of virtuous teachers in the West, providing a revealing description of disheveled and dissolute manhood: "[T]he teachers in some cases, are most ferocious fellows—shaggy and ragged, dirty and uncouth, smokers and chewers of tobacco, swearing and swaggering, bearded and whiskered looking ruffians, I would as soon toss a child into a lion's den, as to trust him under their care."[23] These men appeared unruly in every way possible. Depicted as animal-like—ferocious and powerful lions—they represented a danger to virtuous humanity, as embodied by children. Clean, neat, and healthy, "manly" men ate, worked, and socialized with careful regularity and avoided excess of any kind—particularly intemperance.

Many social reformers perceived a distinct lack of self-control among American men and even within American institutions. The Garrisonians were especially disturbed with the lack of self-control they perceived among Southern men, who viciously abused slaves and also engaged in excessive drinking and violence.[24] Indeed, the entire South seemed to lack self-discipline, according to the Garrisonians. And this sinful and decadent Southern slave system had infiltrated the nation's politics and religions. Pillsbury expressed particular concern with "intemperate" American manhood as manifested in the nation's political institutions. He discovered intemperance not only among individual politicians, but within political parties and even in republicanism itself. He compared political parties to "the new fledged drunkard—every excess is a true and terrible prophecy of greater excesses to come, until the once gentle husband and tender father murders wife and children together, and then reels after them into eternity by drunken suicide."[25] Intoxicated political parties, represented by the "once gentle husband and tender father," threatened the existence of the nation, represented by "wife and children." Just as drunken men abused women, so a drunken government abused its people. Although Pillsbury appealed to the stereotype of women as defenseless in order to gain the sympathy of his audience, he used this vision of womanhood to oppose violent "masculine" public policy.

Pillsbury had good reason to be anxious regarding intemperance: improved technology, a booming economy, and an increased taste for whiskey led to an extraordinary rise in alcohol consumption in the first half of the nineteenth century. Americans drank more hard liquor between 1800 and 1830 than ever before or after.[26] Political celebrations were directly associated with public drunkenness and candidates relied on their ability to provide liquor as a powerful campaign tactic. This widespread alcohol abuse, along with tobacco fixation and other "unclean" habits, galvanized Pillsbury's conviction that manhood declined as impure bodily indulgences increased. "When men use tobacco as I saw some use it in New York," asserted Pillsbury, "dollars and cents lose their value. . . . It is not loss of money, but *manhood*, that is to be counted."[27] Moreover, Pillsbury and many other Garrisonians linked abstinence with the noble temperament they believed necessary for antislavery work. "Alcohol has no charms for the genuine abolitionist," explained Pillsbury, "and anti-slavery truth has less than none for the besotted drinker. Anti-slavery involves self-denial, and demands it, and self-indulgence will have no fellowship with our *stern anti-slavery fanaticism*."[28]

While historians have accurately emphasized the conservative tendencies of many male reformers concerned with self-control, Pillsbury and other Garrisonians consistently employed this element of masculinity to promote radical profeminist goals.[29] A full-fledged teetotaler himself, Pillsbury saw temperance as a means of improving women's lives—particularly women exploited by drunken husbands. However, he did not participate in the organized temperance movement of the 1830s and 1840s, because he believed it failed to address the real problems created by drunkenness and because many of its advocates proved to be exploitative and discriminatory themselves. Both Pillsbury and Frederick Douglass actively supported the creation of separate women's temperance societies because, according to Douglass, women were "cramped and denied an equal share in the activities of other Temperance organizations."[30] At a "Tee-Total Convention" in Concord, New Hampshire, Pillsbury introduced a resolution condemning all of the state's temperance societies.[31] Because Christian ministers, feminists' and abolitionists' most severe and persistent opponents, directed the early temperance movement, he maintained a critical position. Further, the language and focus of these temperance organizations highlighted the maintenance of sobriety among "respectable" middle-class men. Pillsbury and many female reformers, on the other hand, believed that temperance societies needed to directly confront drunkenness and its effects, such as wife and child abuse.[32] This focus on drunkenness tacitly singled out working-class men, especially immigrants, for chastisement and reveals Pillsbury's inability to escape the powerful pull of middle-class imperatives even as he tried to reconfigure middle-class manhood. Nonetheless, Pillsbury's concern with self-control and sobriety distinguished itself from other middle-class male reformers who seemed more interested in maintaining middle-class hegemony than battling women's oppression.

The Garrisonians' focus on self-control was strongly influenced by their experience advocating radical antislavery among the people. Persistently attacked by out-of-control opponents—mostly men—Pillsbury and his peers associated self-restraint with virtuous manhood. The most faithful male advocates of women's rights, including Nathaniel P. Rogers, Stephen S. Foster, and Pillsbury, were longtime field lecturers and nonresistants who learned the practical and spiritual benefits of controlling one's passions, especially when outnumbered by unrestrained opponents.

Physical strength and self-control guided many Garrisonians toward a pro-feminist position, but "civic morality" sealed their position as uncompromising champions of the women's rights movement.

> It *may be* that right and wrong, truth and humanity, are but the misty dreams of moralists and poets. It *may* be that the nation can annihilate every remaining tribe of Indians, as it has most of them already, enslave all Africa, and seize all the Western Hemisphere as its own, and no Supreme Power hold it accountable. But woe is unto it, if the visions of prophets, the preaching of apostles, and the inward convictions of all true and honest men, shall ever become reality.[33]

In this powerful and prophetic warning Pillsbury linked radical reform, true manhood, and political action with God, heaven, and the empowerment of the oppressed. Prophets and apostles, Pillsbury's preferred metaphors for radical reformers, vocally defended "truth and humanity," as represented by Indians, slaves, and the colonized. However, radical reformers required the aid of virtuous American manhood. In his subtle summoning of all "true and honest men" to act on their "inward convictions" and thus protect justice and humanity, Pillsbury grounded American manhood in, what might best be termed, a civic morality.

Relying on Revolutionary-era notions of republicanism, Pillsbury emphasized three elements in civic morality: self-sacrifice, virtue, and independence. This definition of civic morality represented a rejection of midnineteenth-century masculine values of self-interest and individualism and a celebration of earlier notions of community and spiritual manhood. However, Pillsbury modified these older visions of masculinity with a new progressive twist. He replaced the patriarchal and hierarchical elements of eighteenth-century society, which had accompanied community-oriented manhood, with a forward-looking vision of republican egalitarianism. Pillsbury firmly linked manhood and civic morality to a progressive political activism.

Distraught that young men seemed self-indulgent and politically apathetic, Pillsbury confided to his daughter his anxiety at the decay of American manliness: "What gives me profound apprehension as I travel is that so many native born American men seem growing up and getting old, without one noble impulse or aspiration, or apparent thought, to know any thing, to do any thing, to be any thing, or to suffer any thing beyond the most vulgar herd of rum drinking, tobacco chewing, blaspheming loafers and loungers, of fifty years ago."[34] Pillsbury, like most reformers, believed that men had a political and moral responsibility to improve their society. The key to this masculine responsibility and the linchpin of civic morality was self-sacrifice. Subordinating one's selfish interests to the greater good provided a virtuous foundation for political activity and American manhood. Garrisonians, in their willingness to set aside worldly success and endure the ostracism of their neighbors and communities, clearly set the standard for self-sacrifice. Pillsbury himself relied on the meager earnings of a lecturing agency—which often proved inadequate—to support himself, his wife, and daughter. Garrison regularly coaxed monetary "gifts" and loans from wealthy abolitionist patrons in order to support his family, while lecturing agents Stephen Foster and Abby Kelley Foster eked out a living on a small farm.

Just as most American men failed to practice self-sacrifice in their political lives, they also proved unwilling to exercise political independence, according to Pillsbury. Political participation in the nineteenth century changed dramatically in both practice and meaning. As political parties slowly discarded their reputation for corruption and incompatibility with republican government they emerged as powerful new organizing forces in American politics.[35] At the same time, party loyalty became associated with manhood and political leaders chastised nonpartisan reformers as unmanly.[36] This transformation in the meaning of political participation and the gendering of party loyalty challenged radical Garrisonian abolitionists in particular because they adopted both an antigovernment and an antiparty position, and thus became vulnerable to charges of effeminacy. In response to these accusations Pillsbury denounced the privileging of partisanship and associated masculinity and virtue with earlier republican traditions of political independence. He adopted eighteenth-century criticisms of political parties as evil and sectarian because they encouraged men to vote the party line with little independent consideration of "public virtue" or "private morality."[37] Only independent political activity, he argued, could "guard the old landmarks of truth, justice, honor and honesty" and thereby promote virtuous social reform. Independence, in this case, denoted the opposite of nineteenth-century ideals of individualism—instead it symbolized selflessness and concern with the social good. Most feminists, at least following the Civil War, also embraced this definition of independence.[38] Moreover, Pillsbury reversed the gendering of politics by denouncing partisanship as unmanly. "How much we need a host of independent, free, noble minded men, pledged to no party, no religious affiliation, no mere human ties of any kind—model men, in every high and divine sense of the word," explained Pillsbury to William Lloyd Garrison, Jr.[39]

Not surprisingly, American men in Pillsbury's view also failed to adhere to the final element of civic morality—virtue. Just as eighteenth-century statesmen had feared that as society "progressed" it would become vulnerable to the corrupting influences of "civilization," Pillsbury also bemoaned the corruption which he perceived as threatening society and manhood.[40] He located this corruption in part in the nation's political leaders, whom he described as "anti-republican, anti-human, and anti-christian—beasts of prey on the rights of man."[41] Greedy and selfish, these men personified the debilitating effects of individualism. Most Garrisonians agreed with Pillsbury, focusing particularly on the demoralizing influence of Southern slavery on political institutions and the nation itself. American politics (and manhood) desperately required an infusion of virtue.

Pillsbury's advocacy of civic morality, though distinctly radical for the period, reflected his class, regional, and religious background. Civic morality for Pillsbury, Foster, Rogers, and other profeminist men involved in part a paternalistic support for those disempowered by the institutions of American society. For example, Pillsbury employed a fatherly image of true manhood in his depiction of a fellow reformer: "A man with a conscience, singularly scrupulous and tender in behalf of justice and right for the lowliest and humblest of the human family, especially the colored race and women."[42] Real men understood and acquiesced in their obligation, as men, to protect, defend, and support "the lowliest and humblest of the human family." Garrisonians based their philosophy of human rights activism at least in part on a Euro-American middle-class understanding of uplift and improvement for the oppressed. They assumed that their definition of virtue, morality, and social justice had a universal appeal and that those exploited and marginalized groups in society desired their advice and aid.

Civic morality also proved very important in guiding Pillsbury toward a radical position on women's suffrage. In the antebellum period many Americans began to argue that women were, by nature, more virtuous and self-abnegating than men. Therefore, in connecting self-sacrifice and virtue, two strongly "feminine" traits, to political participation and, further, in documenting the failure of men to practice these values, Pillsbury set the stage for women's suffrage. As men abandoned their duties of self-sacrifice and virtue and political institutions suffered as a result, the nation required that women extend their influence to the public sphere. "Government languishes to-day for want of virtuous woman's influence and voice," argued Pillsbury in a women's suffrage editorial.[43] Many other Garrisonians also emphasized woman's higher moral nature as a reason to enfranchise her (this would become a popular argument later in the decade). Theodore Parker, in calling for women's political participation, claimed that while "men's moral action, at best, is only a sort of general human providence, . . . woman's moral action is more like a special human providence." Frederick Douglass claimed, "The vote of women is essential to the peace of the world."[44]

Even if men did adhere to civic morality in the political sphere, practicing virtue, self-sacrifice, and independence, these values obligated men to enfranchise women. Emphasizing paternalism and equality, Pillsbury contended that withholding suffrage from "the humblest human being" represented a "rebellion against the constitution of the moral universe."[45] "The question of suffrage is one of justice and right," he claimed. Although Pillsbury relied on an essentialist argument that assumed women's "natural" virtue and self-sacrifice, he also emphasized a moral argument that defined women as individuals who possessed political rights as independent citizens.

Civic morality provided the spiritual and moral foundation for Pillsbury's model of manhood. True men certainly required strong bodies maintained through vigilant self-control, but without a spiritual and political commitment to human justice manhood shriveled. Rejecting individualism because it lacked even the slightest concern with virtue, Pillsbury instead embraced a more cooperative philosophy. He designed civic morality using older traditional elements of masculinity—self-sacrifice, independence, and virtue—but he built into these values progressive notions of egalitarianism and used them in support of radical politics. Indeed, Pillsbury's vision of manhood led him to support women's equality in all facets of life, including the controversial arena of sexuality.

In March 1863, Samuel May, Jr., the general agent of the American Anti-Slavery Society, received a confidential letter from Charles Griffing, a Western abolitionist, accusing Parker Pillsbury of the most scandalous impropriety. Griffing and his wife, Josephine, had often traveled and lectured with Pillsbury across the West during the 1850s. Griffing explained to May that during these lecturing excursions Pillsbury advocated and acted on a "free love" sexual philosophy.[46] Although Griffing admitted that Pillsbury publicly denied any support for free love, he contended that Pillsbury's opinions regarding marriage and women's rights were identical to those espoused by "free lovers." To prove his point, Griffing quoted extensively from an article penned by Pillsbury on the subject of marriage. In this article Pillsbury articulated the implications of the women's rights movement for the institution of marriage:

Equally connected with the enterprise [women's rights], are the subjects of Courtship, Marriage, and Parentage, and whatever pertains to the birth of children, *who shall be their father, and* how they shall be reared and educated. *On none of these questions, has woman yet been really consulted.* Whatever be the physical or moral defects and deformities of the husband, society holds her bound to transmit all these qualities to another generation.[47]

What seems like a critique of women's subordination within marriage and a call for women's full control over their bodies appeared to Griffing a declarative statement of free love. "*It was an advertisement of his position*" on free love, claimed Griffing, with the intention of gaining the confidence of the "*Liberals on the marriage question.*" Pillsbury, continued Griffing, even boasted "that he knew Women in Ohio who would be very glad to have him become the father of children for them."[48] If Pillsbury's own words (as filtered through Griffing's pen) were not proof enough of his heresy, Griffing also had both evidence and rumor to further his argument. During their last tour together in Indiana, Pillsbury exceeded the limits of Griffing's forbearance: "Myself, wife and Pillsbury were under the necessity of occupying the same sleeping apartment. The room was large and contained two beds some distance apart. In the morning, about sunrise, or a little after, Pillsbury got out of bed, *stripped himself, naked, washed himself, and walked about the room in a perfectly nude state*, entirely regardless of the presence of myself and wife."[49] As if this outrageous behavior might not be enough to prove Griffing's point (that Pillsbury gave antislavery a bad name), Griffing concluded by repeating the rumor that Pillsbury had engaged in sexual intercourse with one married and one unmarried woman.

Interspersed throughout this long diatribe was a running commentary on Pillsbury's role in the breakup of Griffing's marriage. Griffing clearly blamed Pillsbury for his wife's refusal to "receive me as her husband" and her eventual decision to leave him permanently. Despite the obvious ulterior motives of Griffing, May decided to investigate the accusations. He wrote to the editor of the western *Anti-Slavery Bugle*, Marius R. Robinson, and requested his opinion on Pillsbury's moral character. Robinson dismissed Griffing's accusations, extolled Pillsbury, and added that Griffing had a history of condemning anyone who had befriended his estranged wife, going so far as to threaten those abolitionists who would consider hiring her as a lecturing agent.[50] With this backing, May explained to Griffing that he could not accept his accusations as reliable because he was not an unbiased observer.

This provocative incident raises the question of the function and status of sexuality for Pillsbury and its relation to masculinity. Like many reformers during this period, Pillsbury considered self-restraint in regard to the body absolutely necessary for individual and social improvement.[51] This concern with bodily self-control motivated Pillsbury to support only reasonably regulated sexual relations as an element of true manhood. Abstinence was acceptable—and much preferred to lasciviousness.[52] Certainly the demand for individual self-restraint, especially among men, reflected a general trend in antebellum American sexuality.[53] Pillsbury, however, moved beyond popular trends to support women's control in the areas of sexual relations, choice of marriage partner, divorce, and child-rearing—all of which views of his helped to stimulate Griffing's accusations. Long before moral educationists such as Lucinda Chandler advocated women's "self-ownership" and the "rationalization of sexual desire," Pillsbury, and a few other male and female radicals, called for the emancipation of women's bodies.[54] Clearly, Pillsbury's demand that men voluntarily yield such privileges to women frightened and enraged many—including Griffing, who found himself challenged by a wife who refused to engage in sexual relations and successfully sought a divorce.

Pillsbury considered the empowerment of women within marriage, particularly with regard to sexual relations, necessary for the progress and improvement of society. He articulated this conviction in an article written in 1853 (the same article Griffing cited)—complaining that women had no choice regarding sexual intercourse with their husbands. "To refuse compliance, is a violation of her marriage vows, even though she preserves herself as pure as vestal virgins."[55] The issue of women's sexual rights entered popular discourse in the early nineteenth century, as presumptions about women's supposed "passionlessness" seemed to entitle them to the right to refuse intimacy, even with husbands. Historians have interpreted passionlessness as a useful tool for women because it was employed to limit procreation and because women's power consequently became associated with their moral and spiritual nature, not their sexuality.[56] Women's empowerment in the arena of marital sexual relations also became popular as an element of the nascent temperance movement, especially in the postwar period. Wives, temperance advocates argued, were entitled to refuse intimate relations with drunken and abusive husbands (but presumably not entitled to refuse sex with sober, responsible husbands). By the last third of the century even the courts acknowledged "sexual cruelty" as a legitimate ground for divorce.[57] However, Pillsbury eschewed "passionlessness" in his defense of women's sexual rights; instead, following the dictates of civic morality, he argued that justice and equality required that women, like men, ought to have complete control over their bodies. True men, he believed, respected women's sexual choices, even if this required abstinence.[58] Parker's wife Sarah certainly seems to have embraced a passionate sexuality that made it unnecessary for Parker to practice his own advice.

Many male Garrisonian abolitionists joined Pillsbury in this vision of a feminist sexuality geared toward self-control and civic morality. Garrisonians emphasized the out-of-control sexual system that permeated Southern slavery and called for a restrained sexual system in the North. Slaveowners, they argued, engaged in illicit sex with black women and thus created a debauched system that affected everyone. Slave women had no control over their bodies or their marriages. Garrisonians asserted that self-control among men and self-ownership among women, in complete opposition to the sexual system that predominated in the South, was necessary in a democratic nation. Many radical abolitionists, therefore, proved to be sympathetic to women's sexual control.[59]

Pillsbury defended a controversial philosophy of sexuality, but he did not advocate uninhibited sexual relations between men and women, as Griffing seemed to believe. Pillsbury's position on appropriate sexual behavior drew upon that of free love advocates: he opposed the institution of marriage in its prevalent form because it subordinated women, and he advocated sexual intercourse only between two people in love and freely consenting. For example, in an editorial entitled "Swapping Wives," Pillsbury described two couples, living in Salisbury, Massachusetts, who, unhappy in their marriages, decided to exchange partners, divorcing their first spouse and remarrying their second. Both couples were "happy and harmonious" in their new partnerships. Bliss, however, did not last long: "A meddlesome community has just interfered and arrested all four, who, not able or willing to give sureties for appearance to court, are now in jail," Pillsbury explained. "The neighborhood could and did tolerate their matrimonial discords and contentions in a false union, for years," he continued, "but their felicity in the new and apparently real marriage, it could not endure."[60] Pillsbury's language resembled that of free love advocates who differentiated between "true" and "false" love. A marriage based on "false" love never received legitimization in the eyes of God or the experience of husband and wife. Any manifestation of "true" love, whether formalized in a first marriage or a second, was blessed with a virtuous legitimacy. Sarcastically pillorying the Calvinistic attitude of the community which disapproved of second marriages but approved unhappy first marriages, Pillsbury clearly dismissed any thoughtless adherence to unjust laws.

Pillsbury's notions of manhood imbued his understanding of sexuality. True men controlled their carnal urges and within healthy marriages sexual relations reflected the needs of both partners. Following the lead of progressive health reformers as well as women's rights activists, Pillsbury and his peers celebrated a "feminine" sexuality, based on romantic love, egalitarianism, and full exposure of the body's functions and desires. And yet, as Griffings's free love accusations suggest, even in the 1850s some Garrisonian men did not approve of Pillsbury's position on marriage and divorce.

Although abolition claimed most of Pillsbury's time and energy between 1840 and 1865, he considered himself a faithful and active women's rights ally. He sporadically penned articles condemning women's oppression and attended women's rights conventions.[61] Writing about the Worcester Women's Rights Convention in 1850, Pillsbury admitted, "I am not easily excited or moved, but it seems the circumstances by which I am now surrounded, exceed in interest and sublimity anything that ever passed before me. Description is out of the question."[62] He did not lack words, however, for describing his opposition to women's subordination in all areas of society. In 1853, he used a visit to the home of Abby Kelley and Stephen Foster to describe the physically demanding labor required of most women and also make a pitch for women's dress reform. Pillsbury arose very early and was surprised to find Abby already well into her daily duties. "The family Cooking Range was in full blast, on the heated top of which, floated her fleet of flat irons." Even before she had begun "woman's weekly blacksmithing," however, Abby had already milked four cows to have prepared for delivery to the city market at half past four o'-clock. After praising his host's cheerful work ethic, Pillsbury commented on her comfortable clothing: "She was drest all so free and easy, in loose Bloomer Costume, her constant working garb."[63] The bloomer costume was a loose-fitting outfit which combined pantaloons and a short dress or skirt. It replaced the heavy and long skirts worn by women, which restricted movement and collected dirt. This outfit became popular for a short time among women's rights activists in the early 1850s, but most eventually abandoned the costume because of public ridicule.[64]

Pillsbury considered most women's clothing to be just one more example of female subordination and restriction. He disapproved of changes of fashion and supported comfortable, quality clothing for women. He went so far as to explain his personal preferences in fabric to his daughter: "Were I a woman, it now seems to me I would always wear the *standard* articles—that is, those *always in fashion*. . . . I would no more notice all the styles that come up from year to year, then I do the shape of all the withered leaves round a caterpillars nest."[65] Fashion symbolized the uncontrolled and indulgent nature of popular visions of womanhood which Pillsbury hoped his daughter would reject. Moreover, as department stores increased in the 1850s and fashionable clothing became widely available to middle-class women, Pillsbury and many other radicals interpreted this rising obsession with stylish dress as a threat to feminism.[66] A longtime proponent of dress reform, Pillsbury argued that fashionable clothes reinforced women's dependence by defining femininity as consumption and artificiality.

In his support for women's equality in the antebellum period, Pillsbury did not avoid the more controversial topics. The issue of liberalized divorce laws, for example, divided even supporters of women's rights. Many believed that it would lead to increased opposition to the movement and should therefore be avoided. Pillsbury, however, eagerly supported the revision of divorce laws, disagreeing with many of his abolition colleagues. At the 1860 National Women's Rights Convention, Elizabeth Cady Stanton introduced a resolution supporting a progressive divorce law. Wendell Phillips and William Lloyd Garrison opposed Stanton's resolution because, Phillips argued, marriage and divorce were inappropriate issues for discussion at a convention intended to address women's legal inequities. Divorce, they asserted, affected both men and women equally. Even prior to this convention, however, Pillsbury bemoaned the failure of the women's rights movement to address the issue of marital injustices. In commenting on a women's rights convention in 1859, for example, Pillsbury explained to Phillips: "I longed to hear some one hurl a thunderbolt into our present marriage and Divorce Laws, and whatever else needs overhauling in the social system."[67] Male dominance within the institution of marriage, grounded in legal, religious, and cultural presumptions, ignited Pillsbury's singular opposition because it flew in the face of civic morality and true manhood.

In the antebellum period Pillsbury and a small but noisy group of progressive male reformers developed a profeminist masculinity that, while incorporating many traditional elements of manhood, rejected male superiority. In fact, Pillsbury's use of various characteristics of traditional masculinity allowed him to engage in a dialogue with his fellow citizens—he appealed to familiar meanings and practices while simultaneously subverting them to advocate a moral and progressive masculinity. He advocated manly vigor as a tool to defend the exploited; he employed self-control to support a profeminist temperance movement; and his call for civic morality included the championing of women's suffrage, sexual freedom, the right to divorce, and many other feminist issues.

Pillsbury's vision of manhood was strongly influenced by his first mentor in the movement, N. P. Rogers. An outspoken supporter of women's rights, Rogers instilled in Pillsbury his feminist convictions. Rogers' influence, in fact, proved to be deep and long lasting, affecting all areas of Pillsbury's reform experience.

4

Abolitionism Organized or Unorganized?

In 1844, Nathaniel P. Rogers wrote a heated editorial about the unappreciated work of abolition lecturing agents. "The turning-point-anti-slavery action," he declared, "is not in the New York or Boston Convention, . . . where the multitude shout to the eloquence of [Wendell] Phillips, or clap their hands at the demonstration or oratory of [Charles] Burleigh." On the contrary, he continued, "it is in the out-door, mobbed and unreported meeting, in central Rhode Island, or back in the district school-house gatherings in inland and *inmost* New Hampshire. There the decisive blows are struck, which touch the depths of the people, and sow the harvest seeds of the movement."[1]

In this acclamation of grassroots abolition N. P. Rogers had in mind his friend and colleague Parker Pillsbury, who, by 1844, was a veteran of the "out-door, mobbed and unreported meeting." Ever since Pillsbury's departure from the ministry in 1840, he had been employed as general agent of the New Hampshire Anti-Slavery Society, where he orchestrated the everyday activities of the organization and launched himself onto the lecturing circuit. Pillsbury had held hundreds of meetings in dozens of New Hampshire towns, often lecturing alongside Rogers and Stephen S. Foster.[2] By the mid-1840s, all three men had spent years inspiring supporters and riling opponents and, in the process, had forged strong ties of camaraderie.

But the independent direction taken by Rogers after 1844 would test these bonds to the breaking point. The editorial in which Rogers praised field lecturers also openly criticized the agenda of the Garrisonian antislavery leadership, thus initiating what would become a long internal dispute. Rogers

63

disparaged the "New York or Boston Convention"—the lively and well-attended spring gatherings of the national antislavery associations—for attracting too much attention and resulting in very little gain. Pillsbury, however, did not feel comfortable with his mentor's conclusions. Still only a local abolitionist, he remained in awe of the genteel and nationally recognized antislavery leaders and he felt uneasy criticizing the men and women who continued to inspire him. It would not be long before Pillsbury found himself forced to take sides in a bitter feud between Rogers and the Garrisonian elite that ended with Rogers's untimely death in 1846. As he struggled to negotiate common ground between his old New Hampshire friend and the powerful Boston elect, Pillsbury came to more clearly define his own personal philosophy of reform.

Nathaniel Peabody Rogers was a New Hampshire native, born in 1794, who lived his entire life in the Granite State. He attended New Hampshire's best school, Dartmouth College, graduating in 1816, and he eventually opened a law office in his hometown of Plymouth. Over the next decade Rogers built a successful practice, married, fathered eight children, and became active in the Congregational church. After moving to Portsmouth in the early 1830s, Rogers was converted to abolitionism by the writings of William Lloyd Garrison. In 1833, he and two friends formed the Portsmouth Anti-Slavery Society, the first immediate emancipation organization in New Hampshire. His interest in abolitionism grew over the years and by 1838 he had closed his law office, moved to Concord, and become editor of the abolition newspaper, *Herald of Freedom*.[3] Rogers quickly established himself as an uncompromising and radical thinker among abolitionists. He annoyed his more conservative New Hampshire colleagues with his hard-hitting attacks on the church, his support for women's rights, and his condemnation of "colorphobia."[4]

Rogers had a critical influence on Pillsbury's religious philosophy of reform. As the two traveled throughout New Hampshire in the early 1840s, holding antislavery meetings, debating "New" organizationists, and enduring mob attacks, Rogers helped Pillsbury to transform his loyalty to the church into zeal for abolition. Emphasizing the importance of two basic principles—perfectionism and agitation—Rogers guided Pillsbury toward the uncompromising philosophy that would shape his entire reform career.

In the 1820s, evangelical protestantism had popularized the doctrine of human perfectibility. Leading ministers including Lyman Beecher and Charles Finney moved away from a theology that preached "the inability and passivity of man" to one that emphasized free will, activity, and benevolence.[5] All individuals, they contended, had a responsibility to seek Christian per-fection within themselves and to create and sustain it in their society through good works. This benevolent activity was important as preparation for the coming millennium— "a thousand years of peace, prosperity, harmony, and Christian morality."[6] In working to welcome the millennium, perfectionists refused to tolerate any degree of moral ambivalence, from a sip of wine to an act of racial discrimination. Perfectionists—as the name implies—promoted absolute commitment to "uncompromising personal moral standards."[7]

Perfectionism, in Rogers's view, also required diligent moral agitation. Abolitionists, he insisted, should inspire "public disquietude" as they sought to revive the conscience of the people.[8] Such an awakening could not be achieved through the familiar routes of politics or violence, however. Political parties failed to sufficiently arouse the people, Rogers argued, and physical aggression was "at once met by physical resistance, and overpowered, and quelled." Public disquietude was best achieved "by touching the church, which is the apple of the community's eye." Pointing out the failures of religion, particularly its acceptance of slavery, would breed "commotion" in society. This tactic of moral agitation should be the goal of all reformers, Rogers contended. "The more [reform] disturbs and agitates a wicked proslavery quiet," he exclaimed, "the sooner the slave has his liberty."[9]

Armed with these precepts of perfectionism and moral agitation, Rogers developed an uncompromising position toward all of the important issues confronting abolitionists. At the time of the breakup of the major antislavery societies Rogers stood with the radicals. Attending the London Anti-Slavery Conference in 1840, Rogers, along with Garrison and Robert Purvis, refused to participate in the proceedings because of the exclusion of women. He eschewed political participation, arguing that politics inevitably required compromise, and he proved especially intolerant of the antislavery Liberty Party. Predictably, he was particularly unforgiving towards the American church for its refusal to fully embrace immediate abolition. "Somebody must startle the community, torpid and fettered as it lies, under sectarian delusion and despotism," he proclaimed. "While religion is sectarian, slavery is safe."[10] Pillsbury joined Rogers in his unsparing evaluation of those dishonorable political and religious institutions that compromised the millennium.

The Boston Garrisonians admired Rogers's fearless radicalism and in 1840 they attempted to lure him away from New Hampshire to edit their New York–based newspaper, the *National Anti-Slavery Standard*. Rogers refused this prestigious offer, preferring to remain in his home state. The Garrisonian elite soon had reason to be grateful for Rogers's decision, for between 1844 and 1845, Rogers and the Boston Garrisonians engaged in a bitter feud which resulted in Rogers's withdrawal from the movement.

Fig. 4. Nathaniel Peabody Rogers. Courtesy of the Trustees of the Boston Public Library.

On the surface, the conflict involved a simple disagreement over who owned the *Herald of Freedom*—the board of the New Hampshire Anti-Slavery Society or Rogers and his printer, John R. French. Below the surface, however, a much more important debate bubbled over Rogers's increasingly untenable antislavery policies and his refusal to toe the Garrisonian line. The Boston elite, including Garrison and his wealthy and powerful comrades, Wendell Phillips, Edmund Quincy, and Anne Warren Weston, eventually intervened to help resolve the dispute and also nudge Rogers back into line. They decided that the paper rightfully belonged to the New Hampshire Society, but they failed to convince Rogers to abandon his idiosyncratic views and remain the paper's editor. Throughout this painful conflict Pillsbury struggled to remain neutral. While his mentor stubbornly clung to his unpopular principles, Pillsbury eventually found himself forced to make difficult choices between Rogers and Garrison, New Hampshire and Massachusetts, second-tier abolitionism and the Boston elite, purity and practicality.

The most important source of the underlying conflict between Rogers and the Garrisonians was Rogers's espousal of the thorny policy of "no-organization." At heart, this policy involved a rejection of all forms of authority and a conviction that coercion was a sin. Rogers distrusted anyone in a position of authority, including ministers and priests, politicians and bureaucrats. He believed that change had to be voluntarily embraced—not coerced—for true legitimacy. Any political policy that "forced" an end to slavery, therefore, was unacceptable. Slave masters had to believe in their hearts that slavery was wrong for the institution to be eliminated. Legal limits on the expansion of slavery would do nothing, he believed, to change the real problem—which was that many Americans condoned the ownership of human beings.[11]

While many Garrisonians were wary of authority, few went as far as Rogers in denouncing all forms of organization and rejecting all antislavery legislation. Many abolitionists, in fact, considered Rogers' no-organization philosophy outlandish. Garrison himself was so strongly opposed to no-organization that he unsuccessfully tried to convince the New England Anti-Slavery Society to condemn it.[12] When Rogers began to openly advocate a policy of absolute "freedom" in antislavery organizations and meetings in 1844, Boston became even more anxious. Rogers opposed all forms of hierarchy, such as appointing a president, secretary, or business committee, and he refused to constrict anyone's freedom of speech with time limits. In describing what he considered an ideal gathering in Nashua, Rogers wrote: "Our meeting was of course, a *free* one, as all our meetings were. Not a word was offered, or attempt, to embarrass any of them with President, or Speaker of the House, and I never witnessed a better meeting or one I was happier to attend than this."[13] Titles and ranks merely reinforced inequality, according to Rogers, and he demanded absolutely egalitarian meetings.

When—in the spirit of no-organization—Rogers convinced the New Hampshire Anti-Slavery Society at its 1844 anniversary meeting to no longer name the *Herald of Freedom* as their "nominal organ," thus guaranteeing him full editorial control over the newspaper, he initiated the conflict that would lead to the demise of no-organization and his beloved paper. Although Rogers admitted that the society had always allowed him to edit the paper "independently," he demanded a written confirmation of this autonomy. "Editing, as well, as speech, ought to be unshackled and unrestricted," he preached.[14] In the same issue in which Rogers claimed editorial control over the *Herald*, its publisher, John R. French, who was Rogers's son-in-law, removed the name of the New Hampshire Anti-Slavery Society from the masthead and substituted his own name. This action—which seemed to imply that French now owned the paper—riled the board of the Society, which did not intend to relinquish entirely its connection to the *Herald*.

In the first public sign of a conflict, Pillsbury's lecturing partner Stephen Foster responded on behalf of the New Hampshire board to French's action in a severe letter published in the *Herald* in August 1844. Foster claimed that French had "assumed" control of the paper against the will of the society and that subscribers should withhold their support until French had dissolved his association with the paper. Foster and the board recommended that in the mean time, *Herald* readers should "circulate the *Liberator* and *National Anti-Slavery Standard* in its stead."[15] Foster's attack surprised Rogers: "I don't know what is going on in brother Stephen's spirit, that should revive in him this fancy for committeeship and form. He was among the first that taught us in New Hampshire to transcend it."[16] Surprise soon turned to anger, however, and Rogers countered by blasting the board for its stifling of "individual freedom" and called for the end to "organization" in New Hampshire antislavery. Organization, he claimed, "contracted debts,—and *contracted* the mind and spirit and effort of every agent it could control or influence,—and when it couldn't manage the movement and tame it, it metamorphosed. It organized over again."[17]

A few weeks later Rogers extended his anti-organization argument in another editorial. While appealing for contributions to a fund designed to purchase a home for Pillsbury, Rogers argued that all contributions to the abolition movement should be earmarked for a particular person or goal. "It is more anti-slavery-like to impart directly to a person with a soul and a heart, than to a corporation, which is without a heart—or to a committee, which, *at best*, is but a *representative* of humanity."[18] Rogers further contended that antislavery committees were not to be trusted and that the American Anti-Slavery Society Executive Committee had "squandered" large sums of money on such inefficient antislavery means as books and tracts, which simply sat gathering dust on shelves. As if that were not enough, Rogers concluded—in the remarks quoted at the beginning of this chapter—by commending the unrecognized hard work of backwoods New Hampshire abolitionists as against the applauded speeches of the Boston elite.

Rogers's public criticism of the finances of antislavery societies and his suggestion that inequality existed within the movement impelled the Boston leaders to act. Edmund Quincy, a Boston blue blood, immediately shot off an angry letter to Rogers asking, "Is it essential to foster the jealousy which is often felt in some degree by those who live in the country toward those who live in the cities?" He accused Rogers of hypocrisy by demanding that everyone adhere to his policy of no-organization and he warned Rogers that if he continued to attack and "cripple" the movement, "I will pitch into you with all my might."[19] Rogers ignored Quincy's warning and continued to publish editorials advocating no-organization.

While Quincy and Rogers quarreled, Stephen Foster, representing the New Hampshire board, engaged in a letter-writing battle with Rogers and French over the more tangible issue of who owned the *Herald*.[20] Foster claimed that the New Hampshire Society had always been the publisher of the *Herald* and thus clearly owned its subscription list and printing press. Rogers and French retorted that in 1839 the society had sold its "proprietorship in the subscription list" to its printers, Chace and Crosby, who then passed it on to French when he became printer in 1841.[21] This disagreement took on a more vindictive tone when Rogers and French began accusing Foster of pursuing warfare against themselves and the *Herald* for personal reasons.[22]

In December, the Boston leadership asserted its authority and sent a delegation to a special meeting of the New Hampshire Society to deal with the question of the ownership of the *Herald*. Although Quincy and Garrison vehemently denied that the controversy over the paper's ownership and the issue of no-organization were related, the two were very much intertwined.[23] The no-organization policies of Rogers threatened to unravel the already limited structure and discipline of the movement, and the Garrisonians refused to allow an iconoclastic New Hampshire editor to demolish their organization. Rogers understood this. "The *pretended* occasion on the part of the Massachusetts MANAGERS was, to settle the ownership of the Herald of Freedom," he explained several months later. "The *real* occasion was, to beat down the idea of volunteer press, and unincorporate anti-slavery action."[24] The special meeting appointed a small committee, which included local New Hampshire abolitionists Pillsbury, James Morrison, and David Folsom, but was dominated by Bostonians, including Garrison, Wendell Phillips, Edmund Quincy, and Anne Warren Weston. Predictably, the committee decided that the *Herald*'s subscription list, type, and press belonged to the society. Although they "urgently requested" that both Rogers and French stay on as editor and publisher, both refused.[25] Over the next year, Rogers and Garrison engaged in a heated battle, exchanging recriminations in public and private letters.[26] Their friendship ended on a bitter and angry note when Rogers died in the fall of 1846, after a protracted illness.

It was at the December special meeting that Pillsbury first publicly sided against Rogers and French, voting in favor of the board of the New Hampshire Society. Rogers was shocked by Pillsbury's decision to ally himself with those "who never had any respect for him, and who are assaulting me for the principles he himself professes to entertain."[27] Committed to neutrality,

Pillsbury may have surprised even himself with his decision, though he soon became convinced he had chosen wisely. When Rogers refused to continue as editor, Pillsbury was appointed as a temporary replacement. In response, French excoriated Pillsbury, who, he claimed, "for a year and a half has been my enemy." He accused Pillsbury of instigating Stephen Foster's warfare with "*whisperings* and *half-insinuations*" and thus causing the entire controversy.[28] These wild accusations served to further alienate Pillsbury from his old friend and make him confident in his difficult decision.

Historians have debated the significance of the Rogers conflict for the abolitionist movement and the Garrisonians in particular. Lawrence Friedman in his study of antislavery "cliques" interprets this conflict as an internal family squabble among the Garrisonians that resulted in the ostracism of a troublemaking relative. Rogers's exclusion, Friedman asserts, had a chilling effect on internal dissent, making all of the Garrisonian family members vulnerable to expulsion.[29] Lewis Perry, on the other hand, concludes that this dispute was in part a regional conflict. The rural abolitionists of New Hampshire, he avers, developed a "more personal, less conventional" antislavery outlook that disparaged the urban practices of "delivering addresses, publishing tracts, passing resolutions."[30] In his biography of Wendell Phillips, James Stewart concurs with Perry, adding a class dimension to the regional dispute. "Rogers had support in the New England hills and in Cape Cod, where abolitionists were countrified, poor, and anticlerical, and thus when he accused the Boston clique of abusing power, he struck a responsive chord."[31] Stewart quotes Wendell Phillips's patronizing critique of Rogers and his supporters as "half educated, [and] impertinent" and concludes that class certainly colored the dispute.

The Rogers conflict clearly did involve elements of family squabbling, regional antagonism, and class discord; and for Parker Pillsbury, it involved much more, besides. It forced him to take sides in a bitter family feud, to choose between his home state and the center of abolition activity, to clarify his reform philosophy, and to work out his personal feelings about his working-class roots. The dispute cost him and his wife a great deal, both emotionally and financially. He lost his mentor and dear friend, he found himself temporarily forced to give up lecturing in order to edit the *Herald*, and Sarah lost the support of Rogers's generous family, all of whom she had loved.

Neutrality was difficult. The two primary antagonists, Foster and Rogers, were like a brother and a father to Pillsbury. He had traveled across New Hampshire with both men, surviving crisis after crisis together and thereby building deep bonds. Pillsbury and Foster continued their lecturing partnership throughout the conflict and certainly they had ample opportunity to discuss Rogers and the *Herald*.[32] Foster probably attempted to convince his friend of the threat posed by Rogers's usurpation of the paper. Rogers, on the other hand, used the pages of the *Herald* to appeal to Pillsbury. He went out of his way to praise Pillsbury's "free" meetings as "just the thing wanted."[33] He also glorified Pillsbury for his self-sacrificing and virtuous antislavery "husbandry." As mentioned, the *Herald*'s public appeal for donations toward a home for Pillsbury's family, couched in no-organization arguments, could only have made Pillsbury's choices more wrenching.[34]

Pillsbury must also have felt some sympathy with his mentor's position. He had long been struggling with his ambivalent feelings about his backwoods upbringing and his outsider position among the Boston abolitionists. His years of antislavery service had gone unrecognized outside of New Hampshire and he certainly had sacrificed any pecuniary rewards for the movement. Already thirty-five years old, with a wife and young daughter to support, Pillsbury worried about their future if he remained a full-time abolitionist, and he may very well have resented what he perceived to be the inequality between Boston and New Hampshire abolitionists. Any bitterness toward Boston, however, was balanced by his admiration for the Garrisonian leadership and his desire to become a member of the elite inner circle. Boston held out the allure of an escape from rocky New Hampshire and his own lowly origins.

More important than his desire for acceptance among the radical Boston Brahmins, however, was a deep commitment to his own philosophy of reform. Though Pillsbury had developed a penchant for stubbornness and individualism under the tutelage of Rogers, his unique vision of abolition directed him to oppose Rogers on the issues of no-organization and ownership of the *Herald*. While surpassing Rogers in his unforgiving fulminations against the clergy and third parties, Pillsbury did not distrust all forms of authority. He discovered that his understanding of perfectionism did not demand forsaking practicality and that ultimately, Rogers's no-organization policy would not aid the cause of the slave nor help to create a more perfect society. A few years after the *Herald* crisis, Pillsbury would note that the remaining adherents to no-organization never called their own "free meetings," but regularly attended "organized meetings" and "swallowed down Presidents, Secretaries, Boards, and all, as easy as a Turkey can grasshoppers."[35]

While the conflict forced Pillsbury to refine his antislavery philosophy, it also resulted in a painful void in his family's social life. The large and cheerful Rogers tribe had been the heart and soul of the radical abolitionist contingent in Concord. Already decimated by the 1840 split in the movement, the Concord radicals suffered tremendously from the loss of the Rogers household. "We are few in numbers," wrote Sarah Pillsbury to Maria Weston Chapman, in explaining why the Concord Female Anti-Slavery Society sent so few contributions to the Boston fund-raising fair. "The members in dear bro[ther] Rogers family [have] refused to co-operate with us for several months past, in consequence of the most painful, and unhappy alienation of feeling that has been created among us."[36] Pillsbury wrote Garrison a few months later, "Rogers and his family treat us with cold neglect."[37]

The Rogers episode also stultified antislavery in New Hampshire. Many Granite State abolitionists sided with Rogers and persisted in their stand against Garrison.[38] These devotees of Rogers, according to Pillsbury, were "lost, and not good for anything, and don't wish to be, nor mean to be, without [Rogers] for Leader, or Priest." For someone who rejected all forms of authority, Pillsbury pointed out, Rogers certainly attracted a bevy of loyalists. "I think no poor, pious wight, ever worshipped his priest . . . more reverently, than do some of the abolitionists here, the late Editor of the *Herald of Freedom*," he reported to Wendell Phillips.[39] Many New Hampshire abolitionists remained stubbornly neutral in the affair and Pillsbury encountered much difficulty in gaining their support. "Almost every one said, 'go ahead, and if you get enough I will join you.' " He sardonically concluded, "If we can only live well enough without them, they will be our very best friends."[40]

New Hampshire abolition continued to be torn asunder over the Rogers affair throughout the following year. The annual meeting of the state society in June 1845 was characterized by disorder, as Rogers and his supporters used their policy of absolute freedom of speech to interrupt and distract their opponents.[41] The Garrisonian editor of the *National Anti-Slavery Standard*, Sydney Howard Gay, entitled his critical column about the meeting, "Annual Riot of the New Hampshire Anti-Slavery Society."[42] Not until Rogers' death in 1846 did abolitionists in the Granite State begin to close the rift.

The Rogers feud dramatically changed Pillsbury's role in the movement. Having reluctantly agreed to temporarily take over the reins of the *Herald* after Rogers's departure, Pillsbury was forced to abandon lecturing. Although it was a difficult and dangerous occupation, he had become a brilliant "field worker," attracting praise (and scorn from his opponents) wherever he went. But duty called and he found himself uncomfortably seated in the editorial chair once occupied by his estranged mentor. For his efforts, he found himself criticized from all sides. "We are not greatly cheered in our labors, except by the consciousness that we are doing our duty," Pillsbury lamented to Phillips. "The insult and abuse that is heaped upon us by correspondents, is too mean and vulgar to recite to you."[43] Moreover, adding injury to insult, Pillsbury did not receive a salary for his editorial labor. "I have consented for the present to perform my part as Editor *gratis*, which is probably about a fair price," he modestly wrote Phillips. "I can poorly afford it, but any thing for the cause's sake you know."[44]

Many of Rogers's supporters considered Pillsbury's decision to act as editor for the *Herald* an unforgivable betrayal. "When we see a boy brought up under the fostering care of a tender father, until he has arrived at mature age, turning round and treating him roughly, kicking him about, calling him hard names, . . . we not only feel sympathy for the good old man, but our indignation is roused to the very highest pitch," wrote one of Rogers's defenders in a letter to *The Liberator*. "And we speak out and say, if the old man has done a little wrong, we can't bear to see his son, that he has treated so kindly, become his executioner."[45] Although Garrison vehemently dismissed this characterization and defended Pillsbury's "manly yet tender" actions, the young New Hampshire radical must have felt distressed by such censorious claims.

When Rogers and French retaliated in February 1845 by printing a competing newspaper, *The Herald of Freedom*, Pillsbury's paper suffered.[46] "The subscription list is considerably below the *living* point," he informed Garrison, "and my idea is, we had better be taking measure to wind up."[47] And yet Pillsbury continued his work on the *Herald* during the ensuing months. Angered by Rogers's rival paper, Pillsbury dismissed it with uncharacteristic cruelty: "It is a tame issue of *weekly and weakly* twaddle. It is just like partly warmed water, too insipid to produce vomiting and yet to *nastily* sickish to be endured. But it makes me *feel pale* to notice the paltry *puke* at all."[48] Pillsbury's frustrations continued to grow and he summarized his sacrifices to Garrison in June: "My home is thirty miles and more from the press. And yet again, the compensation is likely to do almost anything but pay off my debts, and meet the clamoring calls that hunger and cold may put into the mouths of the three of us."[49]

As Pillsbury wearily traveled those long thirty miles from his home in Concord to his editorial chair in Nashua, he had time to ponder the emotional turmoil of the preceding year. While he had long since become hardened to the never-ending insults of his opponents in the antislavery battlefield, he remained sensitive to the indictments of his colleagues and friends. When two close acquaintances signed a letter accusing Pillsbury of "pirating" the *Herald*, he shot back a wounded response: "Is this the character I have earned in a five years life of wearying, prostrating toil in the Anti Slavery service? . . . My reputation and character with the *world* is a small matter," he assured his accusers. "They have called me fool, knave, insane, and any thing and every thing, but a true man. But I did hope to stand well with the abolitionists." He explained that he had reluctantly agreed to edit the *Herald*, always hoping that "bye and bye" Rogers would return to his post. "I knew it would be a *thankless* as well as an *unpaid* task to Edit it, with the divided feelings existing. But at the same time it seemed to me possible to save the paper." His sacrifice not only went unnoticed, it had been transformed into an act of greed! "I took the place of Editor to save the paper for him," Pillsbury concluded. "For so doing I am branded as a Pirate!!!"[50]

In the year following the conflict, it became clear that Rogers would not return to his post nor fully restore his friendship with Pillsbury. "I cannot please friend Rogers, nor can you," Pillsbury assured Garrison. "Nothing short of a perfect abandonment of the whole ground, a full retraction of all we have ever said or written . . . would be of any avail toward a reconciliation."[51] This was a painful realization for the young radical. Reacting at first with anger, he expressed little sorrow at Rogers's departure from antislavery. "After all I have heard and seen, my deliberate conclusion is that the cause of Anti Slavery and indeed of all true Reform will find no occasion to regret the separation of Rogers and French from the ranks of the abolitionists."[52]

At one point, in March 1845, Rogers published an editorial containing an overture toward Pillsbury. Unhappy at the demise of their tender friendship, Rogers expressed a willingness to forgive his young compatriot for his errors. Pillsbury, Rogers explained, was "overpowered" by the likes of the Boston elite. His "*slight self-esteem*" made him vulnerable to the machinations of the "field marshalls" of the movement.[53] "He could not, I think, have entertained any unfriendly feeling toward me or my anti-slavery course," Rogers concluded, "but he was overborne by the tremendous odds at that convention." Ignoring Rogers's condescending tone, Pillsbury responded by admitting that he still loved and admired Rogers. "My regard for friend Rogers has been greater than for any other man alive," he confessed in an editorial. "We ate, drank, slept, walked, rode, journeyed and conversed together, until, however he may have regarded me, he stole my affections. . . . It has ever seemed to me a matter of great condescension on his part, to bestow upon me the favorable regard he has." Pillsbury concluded, "My respect, therefore, has been mingled with gratitude the most heartfelt; and now to bear a testimony against him, fully realizes to me what is meant by plucking out a right eye, and cutting off a right hand."[54] Despite this attempt at reconciliation, the two men never restored their friendship. The wounds were too deep.

After Rogers's death some New Hampshire abolitionists, to Pillsbury's deep distress, accused him of contributing to their mentor's demise. At a meeting of the Rhode Island Anti-Slavery Society in December 1846, he spoke of the "suffering and sorrow" he had endured because of the "cruel charges" of his having been one of Rogers's "murderers."[55] Indeed, the conflict with Rogers proved so distressing for Pillsbury that he eventually acted as if the strife of those years had never occurred. In speeches and letters he consistently highlighted Rogers's dynamic personality and revolutionary ideas, and in his per sonal history of the movement he devoted an entire chapter to Rogers, never mentioning the bitter controversy.[56] Even twenty-five years later, working for the women's suffrage campaign, Pillsbury praised Rogers' early support for women's rights: "Woman also found in [Rogers] . . . a noble, brave, champion, demanding for her everywhere, in private and public, the same rights, civil, political, industrial, educational and religious which he claimed for himself."[57] In 1881, he reminisced to Rogers's widow on her birthday: "I can do little to day but give you assurances that my admiration for Mr. Rogers is as fresh and unabated as when it was my glory and pride, my delight and joy to do humble, honest service in the cause of liberty and Humanity at his side."[58] Occasionally, in his declining years, Pillsbury escorted old colleagues and new acquaintances up to the Concord cemetery to visit Rogers's grave. Few remembered the unmarked location of Rogers's burial. And yet, according to Pillsbury, there slumbered the "mortal remains of . . . the brightest, noblest, truest and every way most gifted son, not only of the Granite state, but of any state of this union."[59]

The Rogers affair did have a positive side for Pillsbury. After the *Herald* folded in 1846, Pillsbury found himself less of a local New Hampshire abolitionist and more a part of the national antislavery scene. He was appointed lecturing agent for several of the national antislavery societies and these organizations regularly elected him to important committees at their annual meetings. His name could be found next to those of Garrison and Phillips in their opponents' excoriations.[60] He began lecturing regularly in the West, where he developed a devoted following. Although his New Hampshire working-class background and his continued employment as a field lecturer excluded him from the highest positions in Boston, he became a respected colleague of the elite. Regularly exchanging letters with Garrison and Phillips and often boarding with one or the other when in Boston, Pillsbury had risen from a Granite state lecturer to a national figure. In breaking his ties with Rogers he escaped the confines of his home state and spread his wings.

Yet even as he gained national prominence, Pillsbury continued to advocate a uniquely anticlerical and antipolitical brand of abolition from the field. The Rogers imbroglio taught him that the antislavery movement was a worldly affair and that his reform philosophy could be both radical and practical. He rejected Rogers' no-organization ideas, but he retained his mentor's recipe for reform—perfectionism and moral agitation. During the decade following Rogers's death, Pillsbury became one of the most experienced and effective lecturing agents among the Garrisonians. He employed this expertise to build a committed following among grassroots abolitionists and radicalize the Boston leadership.

5

Grassroots Abolition

In late August 1853, Parker Pillsbury traveled to Salem, Ohio, to attend the annual meeting of the Western Anti-Slavery Society, as he had done every year for nearly a decade.[1] A darling of the radical abolition community in the West, Pillsbury was regularly bombarded with entreaties to give lectures.[2] He delivered the opening speech of the three-day gathering, and from this first presentation until the end of the convention he remained so fully occupied with meetings and speeches that he barely had time to eat or sleep.[3] The day after the convention he wrote Samuel May, Jr., "I did not write you during the meeting days, mainly because all the writing of the Resolutions, or almost all, fell as usual upon me—and then, no committee meeting was held without my presence, whether I belonged to that committee or not—and then the part I took in the speaking, together with the greetings of friends" permitted no time for personal correspondence.[4] Given all that had been accomplished, May could easily forgive Pillsbury's delay in writing. The audience passed resolutions of the most radical nature, including a critique of the church and the Free Soil Party.[5]

Pillsbury's leadership in the field, as typified at this meeting, was well established by 1853. His stubborn perseverance as a lecturer despite great personal and physical hardships impressed the reform community, but his dogged opposition to political antislavery and the church, themes which permeated every single meeting he conducted, provided the foundation for his reputation. Still committed to N. P. Rogers's reform recipe of perfectionism and moral agitation, Pillsbury sought and found a select audience of like-minded abolitionists who helped him push the Garrisonians toward an increasingly radical position.

Field-workers such as Pillsbury had a long history in the antislavery movement. From its inception in 1833, the American Anti-Slavery Society had focused much of its efforts on sending out lectures to champion immediate emancipation. Throughout the 1830s these traveling orators, rarely numbering more than fifty, helped build hundreds of local antislavery organizations across the North.[6] After the movement divided in the late 1830s, field-workers became even more important to the Garrisonians. While their competitors could rely on the church and the Liberty Party to attract new converts, the Garrisonians had little institutional assistance. The U.S. Congress had effectively destroyed the popular tactic of antislavery petitions with its 1837 Gag Rule, and Garrisonian newspapers consistently failed to attract large numbers of subscribers. Cheap and simple, local gatherings arranged by traveling speakers were an efficient means for Garrisonians to carry their message directly to the people, alternately "softening and subduing prejudice" and "cheering and encouraging supporters."[7]

Pillsbury expanded his field lecturing territory after the Rogers affair. At various times over the next twenty years he worked for the Massachusetts, New England, American, and Western Anti-Slavery societies, holding meetings throughout the Northeast and West.[8] Even his two-year trip to Europe in the mid-1850s was made on behalf of the American Anti-Slavery Society, and involved him in traveling and lecturing in England, Scotland, and Ireland.[9] Most abolitionists endured only a few years of full-time fieldwork, because antislavery lecturing often led to exhaustion and loneliness. "This is a hard, cold, stern life!" cried Henry C. Wright in describing the experience of field agents. "Does any one wish to become an iceberg, or a granite rock?—to become stern, severe as death?—to become hard, impervious, forbidding, repulsive?—let him enter the Anti-Slavery conflict."[10]

In strange and often unfriendly communities, these stalwart reformers had to rely on their own ingenuity to arrange meetings, find accommodations, and pay their bills. Too poor to afford cozy lodgings, lecturers often boarded at cheap taverns. Pillsbury described one such inn where he stayed during a trip to Ohio: "On entering the house . . . we ordered supper, in spite of appearances, with a temerity and desperation peculiar to anti-slavery agents. . . . Bad bread and worse butter constituted the principal dishes." He concluded with a description of his cramped sleeping room: "Our bed was too narrow for two and too short for one; but two of us occupied it, nevertheless; and, indeed, before morning, we found we were *but two of many*."[11] The general agent of the American Society sometimes arranged accommodations for lecturers at the homes of subscribers to the *Liberator* or *National Anti-Slavery Standard* by advertising their upcoming lecture tours and encouraging locals to provide food and shelter. However, foul weather or bad temper frequently dissuaded even staunch antislavery supporters from offering accommodations to these gypsy moralists. "The rough-and-tumble kind of a life the anti-slavery lecturer experiences is equaled by few," concluded Sallie Holley after her first few days in the field.[12]

Considering these conditions, it is not surprising that field agents like Pillsbury often suffered ravaging ailments. "No post is more dangerous than that of the Lecturing Agents," wrote Pillsbury in 1854. "Constant exposure to storms, to extremes of heat and cold, to continual change of diet and mode of life, added to the intensely exciting nature of the subject of their mission, all these together can account for their early departure, or broken and ruined constitutions."[13] Field agents understood the health risks their job entailed and often advised, warned, and aided one another through their sufferings. When Pillsbury fell ill in 1843 as a result of months of lecturing in the severe New England winter, his field colleagues sent him not only letters of good cheer, but—since he could not receive donations when he could not lecture—whatever meager financial assistance they could afford. Garrisonian lecturers Frederick Douglass and Charles Lenox Remond even solicited contributions for Pillsbury at their meetings.[14]

Sometimes lecturers managed to temporarily escape the treacherous conditions of itinerant life in the homes of local abolitionists. These generous hosts included laborers, farmers, tradespeople, and sometimes community leaders.[15] The arrival of antislavery agents often transformed these homes into frantic centers of abolition industry. While lodging with an active antislavery couple in Hyannis, Massachusetts, in 1848, Pillsbury was besieged by visitors. People arrived early in the morning and departed late in the evening, eager for antislavery news, political debates, and information on disparate topics. "Yesterday I came here . . . *to rest a day*," wrote Pillsbury to his daughter, but "was not without company a minute. . . . Folks would come in to know what I believed on almost every subject ever thought of."[16] Many people considered Pillsbury not only a moral agitator, but also a traveling pundit. His visits sparked countless informal gatherings at which he preached antislavery principles and also chatted casually about eating habits and raising children. Through this interaction Pillsbury became so familiar with the daily lives of his hosts that he found himself embraced as a member of many families. One couple in Ohio even named their son after him.[17]

The relationships he developed with local abolitionists benefited Pillsbury as well as his hosts. During one visit to Cape Cod he found himself kidnapped by a cadre of well-meaning local women who were determined to prepare a favorite local dish for him: "They set in like hammer and tongs, and declared we should all go to one of their houses and have some clam chowder. There was no escape and off we started—the Cape Cod ladies are earnest if *they do begin*. They heeled and sliced potatoes and onions, fried pork, shelled a bucket of clams, and in an hour, we had . . . the best clam chowder I ever saw. The table was elegantly set, and *we had a time* till midnight."[18] These moments of hearty good cheer offered Pillsbury emotional nourishment and he welcomed the respite from the intensity of the antislavery agitation.

His local supporters also helped to sustain him in the larger political debates within the Garrisonian community. In public letters to newspapers and at the annual conventions, they loudly and enthusiastically praised Pillsbury and endorsed his positions. "On Sunday Parker Pillsbury, that eloquent pleader for impartial liberty, delivered two lectures in this place," wrote "WHB" from Plymouth, Massachusetts. "I cannot conceive how any candid man, after listening to those words of 'truth and soberness,' could swear to support such a government, or continue his adherence to such a Church, as this country can boast."[19] Martha Barrett, an independent young working woman and abolitionist from Salem, Massachusetts, wrote in her diary, "Few men in my estimation come up to *Parker Pillsbury*. A strong, powerful intellect, well cultivated, a big warm heart, whose every throb is for humanity. He is a *man* indeed. . . . Since being with him I seem to be baptized anew into the antislavery gospel."[20]

Antislavery lecturers held meetings in any available location: churches (of all denominations), town halls, schoolhouses, courthouses, taverns, small shops, and wooded groves. In Carrollton, Ohio, Pillsbury held a gathering in a dreary, small, and uncomfortable courthouse. "The whole room presented a most *perditional* appearance, and were a person brought into it to be tried for life, I should think consistency with the gloomy place would require his counsel to advise him to plead guilty, and be hung and done with it."[21] Only a few days before Pillsbury had conducted a meeting in the shop of an artisan. "On Monday last, afternoon and evening, we met in a shoe-maker's shop; not a 'ten-footer,' but a 'seven by nine'. . . . The shoemaker—generous-hearted fellow!—not expecting us quite so soon, had not made ready. But he soon . . . covered it with rude seats and benches, so that, in a very few minutes, it was ready for DEDICATION."[22] Pillsbury frequently had to make do with such cramped quarters because most ministers, fearing his criticism of the church as well as potential property damage by an irate mob, refused to open their meetinghouses to him. Even the Quakers regularly rebuffed Pillsbury: "I have to hold my meetings, as in the case of the last two, in a flour mill, and in other instances in private dwellings," he grumbled, "while the whole country

Fig. 5. Parker Pillsbury in his Forties. This sketch was probably drawn by Martha Barrett, a young abolitionist from Salem, Massachusetts, who became a friend of Pillsbury in the 1850s. The drawing is interleaved in a copy of Pillsbury's book *Acts of the Anti-Slavery Apostles* (1883), owned by Barrett. Courtesy of the Peabody Essex Museum, Salem, Massachusetts.

is speckled with Friends' meetinghouses, not one of which can be opened for an evening meeting."[23] This persistent clerical obstruction of abolition meetings kindled in Pillsbury and other Garrisonian lecturers increased hostility toward the church.

The inconvenient location of many of Pillsbury's meetings in addition to the radical nature of his lectures sometimes resulted in poorly attended gatherings and limited accomplishments. "I have lectured to every body who came near me," Pillsbury assured the readers of the *Liberator*, "but . . . I have not procured one single subscriber to any of our papers. Such is the experience of one week."[24] Despite such dry spells, radical abolitionists often attracted large audiences. In 1846, more than a thousand people gathered in Ohio for an antislavery anniversary, in 1851, also in Ohio, no fewer than two thousand thronged a convention; and in 1852, approximately twenty-five hundred attended a meeting in Harwich, Massachusetts. In small communities Pillsbury estimated that many of his audiences ranged from fifty to a hundred.[25]

Regardless of size, Garrisonian abolition meetings followed a distinct pattern carefully designed to educate, persuade, and convert. At the outset, numerous resolutions were read to introduce the audience to the basic tenets of Garrisonian antislavery, usually tailored to local circumstances. Lecturing agents then argued in support of these resolutions, often for hours at a time. The audience responded with questions and comments. Inevitably a few opponents attempted to refute or attack the resolutions and their proponents. Occasionally they resorted to disruptive tactics, including distracting noises or even brute force; in the face of these attacks, Garrisonian lecturers consistently responded nonviolently. The meetings concluded with a call for contributions as well as subscriptions to antislavery newspapers.

The resolutions which lecturers presented to their audiences set the tone for their meetings and strongly influenced the nature of antislavery politics which developed in each community. Pillsbury's resolutions inevitably centered around the destructive influence of politics and religion on the movement. Probably more than any other Garrisonian lecturer, Pillsbury concerned himself with battling the opponents of radical antislavery, particularly those ministers and politicians who he believed embraced abolition only tepidly. As a result, the areas most influenced by Pillsbury's meetings developed unusually uncompromising, anticlerical, and antipolitical abolition societies.[26] These societies, in turn, further influenced the Garrisonian leadership to maintain its independence from political and religious abolitionists.

Pillsbury was not the first to condemn the church as abolition's most persistent opponent. The Garrisonians had a long history of contention with the Northern clergy.[27] While evangelical religion had originally stirred support for emancipation, ministers soon realized that radical stands against slavery would hopelessly divide their congregations, so they avoided the topic altogether.[28] When the Garrisonians recognized that the seminaries training young ministers also opposed antislavery activism, they launched an unrelenting campaign to denounce the church for its "unchristian" position.[29] While many abolitionists stayed within the church, the radicals insisted that as long as Northern churches continued their fellowship with Southern slaveholders and remained opposed to immediate emancipation, membership in such institutions constituted support for slavery.[30]

Pillsbury believed that the clergy, because they controlled "the mind and will of the people," were particularly responsible for the lack of antislavery sentiment in the nation.[31] His own tenure as a Congregational minister provided him with first-hand evidence of the church's opposition to antislavery. "The church and ministry *as a body*, are the most fearful and powerful obstacle to the anti-slavery cause," he declared in 1841.[32] While Pillsbury joined

his radical New Hampshire colleague Stephen Foster in dramatically inter-
rupting religious services and calling on audiences to "come out" from their
proslavery churches, he ultimately preferred to expose the church's apostasy
through his abolition gatherings and the letters he published in antislavery
newspapers.[33] Whether as a central topic or a sideline, he persistently castigated the ministry, thus helping to keep anticlericalism a burning issue
among abolitionists. "My situation as a traveling agent gives me an opportunity to become well acquainted with the character of a large portion of our
churches and ministry," explained Pillsbury in a letter to the *Herald of Freedom*. "Finding them the strong-holds of our slave system, I deem it my duty
to expose the enormity of their wickedness."[34]

In this effort to "expose" the church, Pillsbury focused on such issues as
the failure of any major religious denomination to disassociate itself from its
Southern counterpart, prejudice within the church, and clerical efforts to
hinder abolitionists. The language he used to develop these accusations often surpassed the severity for which Garrison was famous. Pillsbury once declared the eminent professors at Andover Seminary to be "too vile to be
reached or judged by human indignation."[35] He regularly described his opponents at local meetings and conventions as "cubs" of the proslavery
church and he depicted the entire Northern clergy as an unscrupulous band
of "thieves." In Georgetown, Massachusetts, for example, the local minister
was "a sleek looking little fellow," who "signified his love of sect and hatred
of truth, by refusing to read a notice of our meetings."[36] He even compared
the church to the "deepest den of drunkenness, the haunts of the gambler, or
the festering putrescence of the brothel."[37]

Because Pillsbury lumped all churches together as proslavery institutions,
even his own colleagues occasionally expressed concern that his unrelenting
anticlericalism alienated potential supporters.[38] In an 1853 letter to Anne
Warren Weston, British abolitionist Mary Estlin regretted the tendency of
Pillsbury and others to belittle "the most sacred subjects." She feared that
Pillsbury's comments would be used to "prove the irreligious tendencies of
the *American Society*." She concluded with obvious frustration, "It is a standing wonder to me that respect for the feelings of their associates and regard
for the interests of the Cause do not check their indulgence of such mis-
placed levity."[39] Pillsbury responded to such reprimands with stubborn disregard. He continued to denounce the church, suggesting that a few decent
ministers did not change the overall "proslavery" position of the church. "I
never have doubted the purity and the piety . . . of large numbers of the
members of the American Church," Pillsbury admitted. "And yet I stand
here to affirm that the position of . . . this Church, as held and defended by
the leaders . . . is an entirely false and wicked pro-slavery position."[40]

While Pillsbury's hard-hitting religious denunciations proved shocking enough to irritate his colleagues and agitate the general public, it was the misrepresentation of one of his antislavery meetings that gave him his nationwide reputation as a heretic. It is unclear which paper first carried the apocryphal story, but it quickly made the rounds in July 1851, especially among the nation's religious newspapers. The New York *Tribune* attributed the following version to various other newspapers:

> Parker Pillsbury, the notorious abolitionist and come-outer in Massachusetts, in his ridicule of the Church, lately held a mock meeting on Sabbath, in Salem, and went through the ceremony of taking several dogs into the church, propounding doctrinal questions to them, and baptizing them, using the words—I baptize thee, Bose, I baptize thee, Tiger, &c. We presume his new members will never equal their pastor in depravity.[41]

The *Tribune* went on to defend Pillsbury, even though "[he] is not one of our sort of anti-slavery men," asserting that the story was "essentially and grossly untrue." On the occasion referred to, according to the *Tribune*, Pillsbury "was endeavoring to present in as striking a light as possible the truth that God has put a difference between men and brutes, and that any institution which disregards this fundamental distinction is a gross insult to the Almighty." Just as it was wrong to treat people like animals, so it was wrong to treat animals like humans. "To impress this idea upon his hearers with the greater force he supposed the case of a clergyman gravely going through the ceremony of taking dogs into the Church; 'I baptize thee, Bose.' " He concluded by asking his audience if "they ought not to be even *more* shocked at seeing men . . . degraded to the condition of mere brutes."[42]

The "dog story," as it became known, continued to circulate despite the *Tribune*'s rebuttal. The Oberlin *Evangelist* even added a new twist to the story, claiming that Pillsbury had done the very same thing four years earlier.[43] Garrisonians found that they had to correct this false tale at all their gatherings and in their papers.[44] At a convention in Barnstable, New York, for example, four speakers, including Stephen Foster, Austin Bearse, George Putnam, and Garrison, all felt compelled to refute the outrageous charges against Pillsbury and denounce the newspapers that carried the story.[45]

When the dog story first started making its rounds, Pillsbury was busy lecturing in the West with Sojourner Truth, the well known ex-slave from New York, and other Garrisonians. They held numerous successful antislavery meetings across Ohio, leaving little time for anything but lectures and travel.[46] By late October, however, Pillsbury found time to pen his first public reaction to the—by now, infamous—dog story. His letter was in response to a retraction of the story printed in the Oberlin *Evangelist*. Pillsbury claimed that normally he would not bother to respond at all to the story, for he was familiar with such "shameless and unblushing falsehoods, which the religious as well as political press of the country" circulated about him. The *Evangelist*'s retraction, however, charged that the tale originated with a Southern slaveholder attending the meeting and Pillsbury wanted to correct this error. The story, he explained, "was made up and set on foot in the Salem (Mass.) *Register*, by some devout church-going people, who were not at the meeting, and knew nothing in reality about the affair."[47] Pillsbury thus laid the blame at the door of the church, portraying himself as the victim of a vicious religious plot, instead of the perpetrator of an appalling heresy. He also made clear that the slaveholder charged with initiating the story was quite innocent, and that despite his own personal hatred of slavery, he refused to falsely accuse others. "For myself, slander and abuse are all I expect," he admitted. "But I must not and will not be accessory to such treatment of others, be they slaveholders or what they may."[48]

As the weeks passed, the story became more outrageous. It also continued to hinder Garrisonian gatherings. In late October, still lecturing in Ohio, Pillsbury and his colleagues arrived in the small town of Andover to find their audience locked out of the meetinghouse. The local minister had apparently warned the owner to "beware" of the abolitionists because "Stephen S. Foster . . . had . . . gathered, baptized, and given the sacrament to a church of cats and dogs!!" Although Pillsbury responded with humor—"we were not told . . . whether any conversions followed" —he was clearly frustrated. "Do you not think the devil will get ashamed of lying by and by, and throw up the business, when he sees so many ministers, that can lie him all out of countenance, and take the premiums at every Fair?"[49] A few months later, at Fairfield, New York, Pillsbury and Lewis Ford were refused permission to hold a meeting at the Methodist Episcopal church until Pillsbury proved he had not "baptized and received to the church communion three dogs."[50] Only several days later, at a meeting in Salisbury Corner, a member of the local Baptist church loudly demanded to know if "Mr. Pillsbury was the man who baptized the dogs."[51]

By the spring of 1852, nearly a year after the story first emerged, it finally seemed to fizzle out. And yet the tale of an abolitionist who baptized dogs was too fantastic to languish for long—or to remain within the confines of the United States. At the end of Pillsbury's two-year European tour in the mid-1850s he discovered that the story had followed him across the Atlantic. "The old dog story is . . . in Scotland," he wearily wrote Samuel May, Jr.[52] In 1857, after his return to the United States, the story resurfaced yet again when a columnist for the Boston *Transcript* dredged it up to condemn the "wickedness" of abolitionists.[53] Pillsbury finally responded. "After the stunning vollies of slander and abuse of my humble self which have filled the atmosphere of both hemispheres about a monstrous 'dog baptism' that, it is alleged, I performed, several of my friends have desired me to make a statement of the affair."[54] He explained that the lecture in question was an attempt to illustrate the sentiment that " *'Slavery degrades man to a level with the brute.'* " In order to help his audience feel the force of this iniquity, he reversed the "terrible proposition" and described an attempt to "lift the brute up into that 'Holy of Holies,' where only man has right to stand!" The thought of this "God-defying depravity" produced a look of "solemnity" on every face that was "proof positive that for once we had begun to see and feel what it was to sink the image of the invisible God into a chattel slave."[55]

Before the dog story became deliberately distorted, it was just the kind of speech N. P. Rogers would have applauded. Pillsbury's dramatic attempt to make his audience feel the horror of slavery through vivid illustration— "Tiger, I baptize thee in the name of the Father, of the Son, and of the Holy Ghost" —resulted in a moral uneasiness that stunned his listeners. The dog baptism example also emphasized the intimate connection between the church and slavery and the failure of the church to challenge this depraved institution. Although the illustration was distorted by the press and used to ridicule radical abolitionists, as the true story eventually emerged it offered Pillsbury another opportunity to point to the apostasy of the church—both in its falsification of the story and in its complicity in the institution of slavery.

Undaunted by the treacherous tactics of his opponents, Pillsbury found other arenas for proselytizing on behalf of his anticlericalism. Lecturing agents' field work included participation at the annual conventions of the major Garrisonian abolition organizations. These three-day meetings, usually held during late spring, provided abolitionists with the opportunity to share their experiences, renew old friendships, and recharge for the coming year, as well as to attempt to resolve differences concerning strategy and policy. The first order of business at most conventions involved appointing a select group of men and women to the all-important Business Committee. Usually composed of wealthy Bostonians, a few field lecturers, and a handful of state representatives, this exclusive group, representing all four major Garrisonian organizations, met privately to determine the resolutions to be presented and debated at the larger convention. Although resolutions could be introduced from the floor, the Business Committee generally dictated the range of issues to be discussed during the meeting. By the late 1840s, Pillsbury had earned a coveted seat on the committee, and he used this position to publicize the experience of field lecturers and highlight the apostasy of church and political opponents.

At the 1847 New England Anti-Slavery Convention, for example, Pillsbury introduced a controversial resolution that congratulated the North "on the declining state of American religion, the absence of its revivals, and the decline of the supremacy of its clergy over the people."[56] The resolution also celebrated the "reviving of pure religion, through the Anti-Slavery and other reformatory movements of the age." Pillsbury used his field experience to support this resolution, describing for his audience numerous personal encounters with church corruption, including an unflappable man who freely confessed that he had joined the church simply to gain political office.[57] Other local abolitionists also took to the floor to denounce the church and support Pillsbury, as they often did, including Seth Sprague of Duxbury, who employed a more "moderate" approach.[58] Pillsbury's uncompromising anticlericalism had already influenced many local antislavery activists and they were not afraid to voice their opinions at the national and regional gatherings. Although the convention tabled Pillsbury's resolution, his speech, made effective by "apt illustration," convinced many of his colleagues: similar resolutions found acceptance at smaller antislavery meetings throughout 1847.[59] Even as the popular press publicized Pillsbury's celebration of the decline of American religion as "infidelity of the worst kind,"[60] and wondered "can fanaticism go further?"[61] the New Hampshire Anti-Slavery Society passed a resolution congratulating "the whole human family on the rapid declension of *American* religion, as inculcated by the great orthodox denominations of religionists in the land."[62]

Antislavery political parties also received Pillsbury's condemnation at major conventions and, indeed, at all his public gatherings. "May Heaven save the Anti-Slavery movement from the contamination of politics, no matter of what party," he declared early in his career.[63] While most Garrisonians agreed with Pillsbury about the negative influence of politics, many radicals nonetheless eventually joined one of the three moderately antislavery third parties. Even Stephen Foster, Pillsbury's closest radical ally during the 1840s, turned to political antislavery in the late 1850s.[64]

Beginning with the Liberty Party in 1840 and continuing with the Free Soil and Republican parties, Pillsbury inveighed against antislavery politicians for failing to maintain their commitment to abolitionism once elected to office.[65] His critique proved only partly accurate. Most Liberty Party supporters and politicians advocated not only immediate emancipation, but also an end to discriminatory laws and practices in the North.[66] As the Liberty Party declined, however, a disparate group of more moderate antislavery politicians initiated the Free Soil Party in 1848, and eventually the Republican Party around 1854. Both of these parties focused more on the rights of white laborers and the "tyranny" of the slave South than on the moral issues of abolition and racial equality.[67] Eschewing radical antislavery, party leaders simply opposed the extension of slavery into the new territories, arguing that if limited to the South, slavery would eventually die a natural death.

Garrison himself had long understood that political parties survived through compromise, and so, choosing to influence individual politicians through moral suasion and public pressure, he distanced himself from formal politics.[68] Pillsbury agreed with Garrison but went further. Antislavery third parties were more detrimental to the "true" abolitionist movement than the two major parties (both of which were openly opposed to immediate emancipation), he argued, because they diluted the effects of radical antislavery by "paralyzing the public conscience" with specious solutions.[69]

Even the Liberty Party, probably the most faithful to antislavery of all the parties, proved itself "destitute of manly independence" and a most "insidious foe," according to Pillsbury.[70] Drawing on his experience in the field as a compelling reminder, he admonished his colleagues, "We have encountered no opposition half so bitter, so malignant, as from men claiming to be the very elite and elect of the Liberty Party."[71] But whatever the failings of the Liberty Party, the Free Soilers posed a greater threat. Pillsbury had witnessed the dangers of the new group at firsthand, and he enumerated them in 1849. First, subscribers to Garrisonian newspapers were switching to conservative Free Soil papers. Furthermore, Free Soil abolitionists, who had "lost all interest and faith in the moral movement," had influenced many former Garrisonians to cancel Pillsbury's visits to and meetings in their towns. Finally, Free Soilers drained Garrisonian reserves by siphoning off contributions that otherwise would fuel radical antislavery. Pillsbury had good reason to be concerned. Free Soilers had gained some power in New England and Ohio by toning down their abolitionism, stressing nonextension of slavery, and neglecting equal rights for blacks. While most Free Soilers were as dedicated to abolition as the Garrisonians, they believed tactical compromise was necessary.[72] Pillsbury ardently disagreed. "We can do better things," he declared, "than to send good or bad men to Congress, to swear fealty to tyrants, and fidelity to a union with slaveholders."[73]

Pillsbury continued his war against the Free Soilers during the early 1850s. At a Massachusetts gathering in 1853, he attacked abolitionist and Free Soil Senator Charles Sumner for his "overcautious" policies and timid leadership. Sumner's sudden conservatism, according to Pillsbury, proved that "in all political associations, it will be found that whatever of love for truth and freedom there is in them, it gradually declines, till it is swallowed up in a reckless strife for party success."[74] He also introduced a resolution that reemphasized the moral integrity of the Garrisonian movement, and reminded the audience that any increased antislavery sentiment in the nation was a direct result of "our faithful and inflexible adherence to our original and fundamental principles."[75] Pillsbury's colleagues passed his resolution unanimously.

Such "faithful and inflexible" adherence to radical principles often resulted in heated conflicts at Pillsbury's local meetings. Sometimes his adversaries preferred to engage in more physical battles, especially when their debating skills failed them. Indeed, the antislavery movement had a long history of encountering violent opposition. "Gentlemen of property and standing"— often catalyzed by fear of social change, greed, and racism—led hundreds of brutal anti-abolition mobs in the 1830s.[76] In later decades opposition came from other quarters. It was the clergy and conservative political abolitionists who encouraged the opposition to Garrisonian lecturers by the 1840s. After all, these two groups had the most to lose if the policies of the Garrisonians found a receptive audience. Radicals had declared themselves the true religious and moral leaders of the nation, thus co-opting the role of the clergy and putting them on the defensive.[77] Political abolitionists desperately needed the vote of every single antislavery supporter, but Garrisonians, convinced that the Constitution and the government provided a foundation for Southern slavery, encouraged their membership to abstain from voting![78] Although these religious and political opponents proved less violent than earlier mobs, they found other, more creative tactics for obstructing antislavery meetings. Pillsbury had to resort to sustained sarcasm to hide his frustration at the work of a few industrious souls in Dorset, Ohio, who sneaked into the meetinghouse where an antislavery gathering was to take place and held a "Love feast," as he called it. "By the aid of an *outhouse vault* near by, they contrived to cushion over all the seats in the room, *with an upholstery peculiarly their own*—the odor of which was, no doubt, *sweet incense in the nostrils of the deity they adore.*"[79]

Occasionally Pillsbury did encounter more violent opposition led by what he described as "religion and politics." These experiences hardened his conviction that Garrisonians must remain independent of both church and party. One violent outbreak occurred at a meeting in Harwich, Massachusetts, attended by Pillsbury, Foster, and William Wells Brown, a fugitive slave. Following the usual intransigent criticisms of the church by Pillsbury and Foster, a large mob attacked the three men and savagely threw them from the platform.[80] "I was immediately seized with great violence," Pillsbury wrote, "and hurled with blows and kicks to the ground, tearing the but-

Fig. 6. Stephen Foster. From Wendell Phillips Garrison and Francis Jackson Garrison, *William Lloyd Garrison, 1805–1879: The Story of His Life Told by His Children* (Boston, 1894).

tons from my coat, and otherwise injuring it, and was then dragged and pushed some distance from the stand, where I was at length rescued."[81] He accused members of the "Orthodox and Baptist Churches" interested in defending their institutions, of leading the mob. "The severest things had been said of the government and the political parties," he explained, "but it was not until the character of our religion had been questioned that there was any serious outbreak."[82]

At another meeting in Bridgewater, Massachusetts, as Pillsbury and his lecturing partner Lucy Stone discussed the "crimes, as well as absurdities and inconsistencies, of the church and political parties," they were pelted with a variety of objects: "Dried apples, smoked herring, beans and tobacco quids, were a part of the logic with which, in great profusion, they met our arguments," explained Pillsbury.[83] The opposition did not confine itself to small objects, however. One of the "cubs of the church," he explained, "hurled a large prayer book with great violence at the head of Miss Stone, from the serious effects of which she has not yet recovered. If the force of the blow had not been abated by one end of the book striking her shoulder, it would have prostrated her on the floor."[84] Women antislavery lecturers attracted a particularly strong reaction from many audiences because they challenged not only the political status quo, but also gender norms. Often labeled Jezebels, they were subject to vicious verbal and physical attacks.[85] Pillsbury made sure to publicize the violence against women abolitionists, hoping to startle the community with the grossly inappropriate actions of his enemies in the church.

Mob violence was just one more motivating factor that kept Pillsbury committed to the uncompromising philosophy he first adopted during his early travels in the backwoods of New Hampshire. His experiences as a field lecturer in the late 1840s and early 1850s reinforced his perfectionist disregard for any form of compromise, and he loudly denounced those who failed to adhere to his standards. With barbed accusations and vivid examples drawn from his travels, Pillsbury constantly reminded his colleagues of the costs of cooperating with church and political abolitionists. Cheerfully he endured his own vilification by the popular press as a necessary sacrifice for the "truth."

While Pillsbury's persistent denunciations helped to further radicalize some of his colleagues, others responded with disapproval. "Pillsbury we think goes too far," wrote a Western abolitionist after attending one of the radical's meetings. "There is no doubt, but that the political parties are corrupt, and . . . the American church too, needs reproval. . . . But is this any reason why those that are honest should be denounced?"[86] Many abolitionists agreed that Pillsbury stepped beyond the boundaries of civility and fairness. After all, he saved his most savage words for those who considered themselves abolitionists. But the Garrisonians tried to offer an alternative to third party and church abolitionists, and field agents like Pillsbury gave voice and life to this goal, challenging their foes, face to face, year after year, for the hearts of the people.

By the mid-1850s, however, even the formidable Parker Pillsbury began to feel the physical and emotional effects of more than a decade of full-time fieldwork. Looking across the Atlantic to the shores of the Old World, Pillsbury sought rest and revitalization in a sojourn abroad. Even as he excitedly explored the British Isles, however, he soon found himself drawn back into the complicated politics of the antislavery movement.

6

An American Abolitionist Abroad

In the fall of 1853, after thirteen years of unrelenting labor, exhaustion finally caught up with Pillsbury. His voice cracked, his body ached, and fatigue settled in to stay. Dreading the terrible hardships of the coming winter, Pillsbury decided to take an extended leave of absence from his antislavery position. He wrote to the general agent of the American Anti-Slavery Society discontinuing his lecturing agency for the next few months. Before he could begin to prepare for his respite, however, he received a perfectly timed and tempting offer. A friend in Massachusetts invited him on an extended trip to the Mediterranean, even proposing to pay the bulk of his expenses. "The offer seemed almost a special Providence," he cheerfully professed.[1]

Fearing the Boston elite might prefer a more sophisticated ambassador to Europe, Pillsbury decided to discuss the proposed trip with Executive Committee member Wendell Phillips. He was delighted to find his worries unfounded. "You can hardly conceive the joy it gave me, to find you favorable to the undertaking," Pillsbury happily replied to Phillips after receiving his friend's blessing.[2] He immediately worked to garner additional financial aid from other wealthy abolitionists and finalize arrangements for this much-needed voyage.[3] Although his traveling companion eventually decided not to make the Mediterranean trip, Pillsbury doggedly proceeded with his plans to cross the Atlantic.[4]

"My hope and expectations are to visit Britain, France and Italy, and to do something for the cause of Freedom and Humanity," he explained to his Western colleagues. However, he concluded, rest would take precedence over labor, "for my object in traveling will be by no means achieved, if both body and mind are not greatly strengthened for the work to which I have consecrated my life."[5] Even as he assured his friends of his intention to relax, he detailed for Wendell Phillips the important antislavery issues he intended to address while in Europe. Focusing especially on the need to defend the Garrisonians against "calumnies and allegations" circulating in the British Isles, Pillsbury assured Phillips that he would destroy the arguments of their enemies.[6]

Throughout his unexpectedly long European trip, Pillsbury remained focused on these two goals of personal recovery and the promotion of Garrisonian antislavery. By the time he returned to the United States two and a half years after his departure, he had experienced tremendous personal growth, including improved mental and physical health. He had also learned much about the complex politics of British antislavery and built significant support for Garrisonianism. Pillsbury's experiences in Europe reinforced and refined his perfectionist philosophy and fortified him to return to the divisive debates that characterized the abolition movement during the second half of the 1850s.

As his trip unfolded, Pillsbury learned that relaxation did not come easily to one who had spent the previous decade laboring day and night. Unable to remain sedentary even for the duration of the voyage to England, he found himself giving an antislavery lecture on the ship! Even as he struggled with seasickness, Pillsbury refused to waste any opportunity to promote the cause. "My remarks were received with the profoundest respect," he assured his Boston colleagues, "and at the close, loudly cheered."[7] Pillsbury also learned that antislavery sentiment engendered a different response outside the United States. "It was a British ship, a British Captain, and a British company," he remarked in explaining why his lecture was so eagerly demanded and welcomed.

Pillsbury arrived in the damp, cold city of Liverpool in February 1854. Excited but also a bit anxious, he first attempted to deliver letters of introduction to local abolitionists. After an exhausting and fruitless search across the unfamiliar city, Pillsbury gave up and decided to look to Dublin, where he hoped to find the Irish antislavery leader, Richard Webb.[8] A longtime supporter of radical abolition, Webb had hosted many Garrisonians as they traveled through Ireland, including Frederick Douglass, Henry C. Wright, and Garrison himself. Webb enthusiastically welcomed Pillsbury to his home and encouraged him to recover his health in an extended visit. "The longer he stays the better we shall be pleased," Webb wrote Garrisonian insider Maria Weston Chapman.[9] After resting in Dublin with the Webbs for several weeks, Pillsbury returned to England, this time headed for Bristol to visit esteemed reformers John B. Estlin and his daughter Mary. By the time he arrived, however, his health had taken a turn for the worse.

Suffering from "an indescribable pain in the chest left side and difficult breathing," Pillsbury hovered close to death for the next two months.[10] "Never before for any cause [have] I been kept so long in undress," he admitted in his private journal.[11] His affluent hosts provided the best medical care available, including daily visits from a local physician and biweekly consultations with a respected surgeon. Pillsbury's road to recovery, however, proved slow and painful. "Had my two doctors this morning and was sentenced to another blister and various other equally agreeable applications," he complained to his journal.[12] This devastating illness did, however, have the beneficial side effect of forcing Pillsbury to abandon his antislavery work for an extended period of time and learn to relax. By April, he began to show signs of recovery as he shared casual meals and long walks with Mary Estlin and her father. "Since dinner, (which by the way was a funny one, and gave us great sport, on account of the mutton having got tainted) Mary and I have walked to the Old Clevedon Church and the hills beyond," he pleasantly recalled, "where we had a great sight in the way of scenery, both by sea and land."[13] He even allowed Mary Estlin to instruct him in dancing, abandoning at least temporarily his self-conscious seriousness.[14] So remarkable was this frivolity that Eliza Follen commented to Estlin, "the picture of you teaching Parker Pillsbury to dance [was] too much for me."[15]

The image of Parker and Mary whirling in one another's arms was perhaps too much for Sarah Pillsbury also. Agonized at her inability to care for Parker during his life-threatening malady, Sarah felt both grateful and apprehensive to learn that the sophisticated Mary Estlin was tenderly nursing her husband. "I never felt such drawing toward any person whom I never saw, as I do toward Miss Estlin," she enthused to Parker.[16] And yet, struggling with her own insecurities and self-doubts, she certainly felt threatened by the well-educated and cultured Estlin. "She improves any space by writing *very* fine," Sarah assured Parker. "What a gem of perfectness she is!"[17] When she learned that Estlin sometimes affectionately kissed Parker, Sarah responded with perhaps too much enthusiasm. "I am gratified that Dear Miss Estlin manifests her fondness for you by sometimes kissing you," she wrote Parker. "I hope she may often feel moved to do so. Call some of them, dear one, Mine, for could my lips touch your sweet face and neck—(for I always admire to kiss your neck under your ears) you would almost fear they might be made sore." Perhaps hoping to remind Parker of their own passion, Sarah did not openly reveal any jealousy. But the kisses between Estlin and Parker certainly became a topic of conversation in the family. Young Helen followed her mother's lead in approving the friendly salutes: "Miss Estlin writes Mother dear Papa that she has sometimes kissed you, we are glad she has; and I want you to give her in return some kisses for me; for I love her most dearly."[18]

While Pillsbury's infirmity distressed his wife, it also revived his self-confidence. Throughout his illness Pillsbury received dozens of concerned and hopeful letters from friends, colleagues, and family. These emotional expressions reassured him of his continued importance to the movement. In a large packet of letters from Boston, which Pillsbury described as a "casket of jewels," the Garrisonian elite shared their solicitude.[19] "Humanity, cannot spare you, yet," cried Henry C. Wright. "I would gladly exchange places with you, if that would prolong your stay and opportunity to labor, a while longer."[20] Garrison also expressed his deep feelings for Pillsbury: "If I could fly, like a strong eagle, I would soon be by your side, in bodily presence, as I am now, and shall be continually, in spirit."[21] Even famed English writer Harriet Martineau—who would later censure Pillsbury for his radicalism—invited him to visit her countryside home "to be nursed and to enlighten her at the same time on [antislavery] politics and drink in the fresh air and lake scenery."[22]

Buoyed by a newfound self-confidence and a deep appreciation of the precariousness of life, Pillsbury left Bristol in May to travel for a few weeks with his friend and patron, Charles Hovey. For the next few months Pillsbury absorbed the art, history, and beauty of France, England, Scotland, and Ireland, as an eager tourist. Traveling with the wealthy and generous Hovey, Pillsbury stayed in the finest hotels, dined in exclusive restaurants, and met with eminent people. This first-class tour, which he described as a "pilgrimage of pleasure," amazed and thrilled him.[23] A farm boy from the granite hills of New Hampshire, he found London especially remarkable. "I love to revel in its beauties," he gushed, "to admire its wonders, and to be overwhelmed with its stupendous greatness."[24] Still recovering his health, Pillsbury shunned antislavery lecturing throughout this summer sojourn, meeting only informally with abolitionists wherever he traveled. Not until the annual London conference of the British and Foreign Anti-Slavery Society (also known as the Broad Street Society) in November did he speak publicly. But his participation in this conference immediately embroiled him in the complicated politics of British antislavery.

When Pillsbury arrived in England in 1854, the British and Foreign Anti-Slavery Society had just experienced a change of leadership. Founded in 1839, this abolition organization represented a new generation of antislavery activists in England. Having already successfully pushed the British government to pass the Emancipation Act of 1833, Broad Street abolitionists turned their focus more toward the antislavery movement in the United States. As a result of their close ties to the U.S. movement, however, they could not avoid taking a position toward the schisms that divided American abolitionists in 1839 and 1840. The British and Foreign Society made clear its preference when it excluded American female representatives from the London Anti-Slavery Conference in 1840, causing Garrison and other radicals to sit in the balcony with the ostracized women. Broad Street's leading voices, Joseph Sturge and John Scoble, openly criticized the Garrisonians and actively supported the more moderate American and Foreign Anti-Slavery Society (which deliberately modeled its name after the Broad Street Society). Many other abolitionists in Britain, Ireland, and Scotland, however, favored the Garrisonians and withdrew their support from the Broad Street Society. This weakened the British and Foreign group and by the mid-1850s they expressed interest in a reconciliation with the Garrisonians both abroad and at home. They elected a more conciliatory leader, Louis Alexis Chamerovzow, in 1853, and the Garrisonians had some hope of a better relationship with their former opponents.[25]

When Pillsbury arrived this optimistic atmosphere still prevailed, but circumstances shifted quickly. His first interaction with the new British and Foreign leader proved a portent of things to come. During Pillsbury's Parisian excursion with Hovey in the summer of 1854, he received an invitation from Chamerovzow to speak at the British and Foreign anniversary in May on the topic of the Nebraska Bill.[26] British radical S. Alfred Steinthal expressed optimism at this conciliatory move on the part of the new leader. "It is an encouraging sign to find that the British and For[eign] are really taking steps to cooperate with out and out abolitionists," he hopefully concluded.[27] Pillsbury, however, immediately wrote back to Chamerovzow, "declining positively" because of his still delicate health.[28] He sent this letter to his American colleague William Wells Brown, who was lecturing in London, and asked him to forward it to Chamerovzow. Somehow the letter did not reach its destination until long after the conference, and as a result, Chamerovzow proceeded to publicize Pillsbury as a speaker.

Although Pillsbury attended the May anniversary with Brown, Hovey, and British radical George Thompson, he declined to speak. It was not until Pillsbury and Chamerovzow finally met at the conference that each learned of the missing letter, but this did not dispel the distrust that the incident inspired. Chamerovzow accused Brown of deliberately holding up the letter, and Pillsbury doubted Chamerovzow's claim that he had not received it.[29] To make matters worse, Pillsbury penned a scathing review of the anniversary for publication in the *Liberator*.[30] "Most of the speakers exhibited an utter ignorance of the whole subject for which the meeting professed to be called," he haughtily explained. "To me, it all appeared a farce, a mere make-believe. . . . The only real obstacle to the spread of anti-slavery light and thought on this side of the Atlantic," he concluded, "is the British and Foreign Anti-Slavery Society."[31]

Despite Pillsbury's unsparing critique of the Broad Street Society, Chamerovzow invited him to speak at the London Anti-Slavery Conference to be held in November. This meeting was advertised as an effort to mend fences and build a united British-American antislavery movement, and Pillsbury reluctantly agreed to participate.[32] Already skeptical of Chamerovzow's intentions, Pillsbury doubted the possibility of unification at the conference. "What I fear," he predicted to Samuel May, Jr., "is . . . that at the London Conference even George Thompson will oppose, or not advocate, a Resolution endorsing or recognizing the Am[erican] A[nti] S[slavery] Society."[33] George Thompson was a longtime friend of Garrison, but he lately seemed more interested in reconciliation than in sustaining the radicals. May concurred with Pillsbury: "The idea of obtaining strength from an alliance with those who have been seeking our ruin, and in every mean and covert way, too, for fifteen years, is to me simply preposterous."[34]

Both Pillsbury and May were prophetic in their dire expectations. While the conference attendees eagerly passed a resolution condemning American churches for their position on slavery, they balked when it came to a resolution approving the Garrisonians. Pillsbury angrily spoke about the years of "infidelity" on the part of Broad Street and its continued dismissal of the American Anti-Slavery Society, but he received little support. As he predicted, even George Thompson tried to avoid controversy by refusing to advocate Pillsbury's resolution of "sympathy" with the American Society.[35] Moreover, Pillsbury delivered a speech spotlighting the apostasy of the Quaker church, which was omitted from the official reports of the meeting. "I overhauled the . . . Whiggism of American Quakerism . . . for nearly half an hour . . . but not one allusion" to it is made in the report, he complained.[36] Chamerovzow, a Quaker, objected to Pillsbury's speech and ensured its exclusion from the report. "His attack on delinquent *American Friends* was not in good taste, nor was it to the point, because their shortcomings had nothing to do with *us* as a Society, though it was clear the object was to saddle us with the responsibility of them," he explained to John Estlin.[37]

A few months following the conference Chamerovzow and Pillsbury exchanged a flurry of letters that led to the demise of their precarious relationship. The former initiated the correspondence with a friendly inquiry regarding some numbers Pillsbury used in one of his speeches at the conference and an expression of regret that time and circumstance did not allow for "a more personal acquaintance" between the two.[38] This letter infuriated its recipient, who considered Chamerovzow's offer of friendship mere sophistry. "It is to me a most impudent, insulting, unbearable piece of palavering, diplomatic, dissimulation, deception, hypocrisy," he sputtered to the Estlins.[39] Fearing his response might be rash, Pillsbury sent it first to the Estlins, who suggested several changes. The final version, however, remained hostile. "You pretend to some regrets at not seeing me more in London," he wrote. "I was a whole week ready to be seen, two days of which were spent in the same room with yourself." Pillsbury accused Chamerovzow of adopting "false positions," which revealed him to be "*weak* if not *wicked* to a most surprising degree." After this thorough flogging, Pillsbury curiously signed off, "your true and firm friend and constant well wisher."[40] Chamerovzow, clearly unaware of the Estlins' role in Pillsbury's response, forwarded this harsh letter to them and also sent his reply for their perusal! This sixteen-page document detailed all of Pillsbury's errors and misinterpretations and accused him of writing a most "insulting, ungentlemanly and coarse rejoinder."[41] Although this concluded the direct correspondence between Pillsbury and Chamerovzow, more defensive letters passed between each antagonist and the Estlins, who occupied an uncomfortable and perhaps insincere middle ground. Neither Pillsbury nor Chamerovzow ever fully understood the extent to which the Estlins influenced their correspondence.

This explosive encounter raises several significant issues for understanding Pillsbury's experience in Europe, including the question of self-identity. Pillsbury spent much of his time in Europe with people of wealth, privilege, and social standing. He stayed for months at the home of John Estlin, a famous ophthalmic surgeon, socializing with the gentry of western England, and he traveled in style across the continent and the British Isles with Boston Brahmin Charles Hovey, fraternizing with the elite.[42] And yet Pillsbury remained painfully cognizant of his own lack of social charm and grace. His conflict with Chamerovzow was a vivid reminder of this defect. Both the language and the style of their interaction reflected a stark contrast of social expectations. Early in their association Chamerovzow adopted the tone of a forgiving patriarch, while Pillsbury fell into the role of an angry and rebellious subordinate. For example, Chamerovzow reacted to the misunderstanding at the May anniversary by eventually apologizing to William Wells Brown for his unfair accusation and graciously inviting Pillsbury to the November conference, while Pillsbury responded by writing an excoriating denunciation of the anniversary and the British and Foreign Society.[43] Even several Garrisonians judged Pillsbury's censorious review to be in poor taste. "A wise discretion," commented Philadelphian Sarah Pugh, "would have dictated silence."[44]

Pillsbury continued to display a lack of "wise discretion" in his ferocious reply to Chamerovzow's courteous though perhaps calculating correspondence. Pillsbury preferred provocative language—referring to Chamerovzow as "weak" and "wicked." Chamerovzow quickly honed in on the "ungentlemanly" and "coarse" character of Pillsbury's letter, employing a patronizing tone in response. He highlighted Pillsbury's lack of education by pointing out his "eccentric . . . interpretation of Saxon English" and haughtily revealed all of Pillsbury's ignorant errors. "It is not my habit to argue with a man who has come to a foregone conclusion," Chamerovzow declared, "and I shall not condescend to it in this case with Mr. Pillsbury."[45] Both antagonists persistently appealed to the Estlins—because of their social standing and power within the movement—for validation and advice. The Estlins, instead of brokering a compromise, reinforced class and cultural differences. Mary Estlin suggested to Chamerovzow that the argument reflected "style" differences between the refined British and the blunt Americans: "[Pillsbury's] style of thought and language may be at times so peculiar and unlike our own, as to be unintelligible."[46]

The Estlins also transformed this private conflict into a public debate by copying all of the correspondence between the two men, as well as their own comments, and sending it out to several key figures in the movement. The reactions of Richard Webb and Francis Bishop clearly reflect the strong underlying context of social status and cultural differences. Webb praised Chamerovzow's "long and fluent letter" and his "remarkable good humor and forbearance," and criticized Pillsbury for "making such a fuss." He argued that it was "foolish" for the two men to interact because of their obviously contrasting personalities. "Pillsbury is a rough, earnest man, with his heart in his work, not over courteous, or precise in obeying the requisitions of exact taste." On the other hand, "Mr. Chamerovzow is gifted with great self restraint, evenness of temper, and good humor." Webb gives Chamerovzow a title, where Pillsbury gets none, and applies to him all of the characteristics of the gentle patriarch dealing with an unruly servant.[47]

Francis Bishop also read class differences into the conflict between Pillsbury and Chamerovzow, but instead of celebrating Chamerovzow as the benevolent patriarch, he praised Pillsbury as the forthright commoner dishonored by the wily aristocrat. Bishop, a Unitarian minister and longtime radical Garrisonian, explained in a letter to Mary Estlin that at the London conference Chamerovzow had treated Pillsbury as a "great troublesome child to be coaxed and humored, rather than a *man* to be consulted and listened to with respect."[48] This would surely outrage a man of Pillsbury's "honest and earnest character." In light of this previous behavior, Chamerovzow's letters, according to Bishop, were "most uncandid and sophistical" and "especially false in spirit."[49] Bishop concluded that though Pillsbury might do better while in England to display some of the " 'wisdom of the serpent,' " certainly none of the Garrisonian abolitionists had achieved any of their successes through "what some call 'good taste.' "[50]

Although Pillsbury was unaware of the public dissemination of his private correspondence, he certainly recognized the criticism he received from Mary Estlin. She wrote Pillsbury a chiding letter following the conflict, to which he responded with both humility and resentfulness. "It was a great mistake that I ever came to this country," Pillsbury complained after receiving Estlin's reprimand. Recognizing that Estlin presumed to judge him as a social superior, he claimed to appreciate her wisdom. "Criticize me to the extreme verge of necessity or propriety," he humbly wrote, "I will love and reverence you all the more." He also admitted that his uncultured background was the source of his problems: "Do not embarrass me by expecting more of me than I am capable of."[51] And yet the undertone of resentment was unmistakable. Pillsbury simultaneously depicted himself as a clumsy simpleton unaware of the complex rules of social grace, but also as a trusting man capable only of forthrightness. Conflicted over the implications of his low social standing, Pillsbury wavered between rejecting the class and cultural hierarchy and embracing it with humility. His stay in Europe, and particularly his interaction with Chamerovzow, made him painfully aware of the importance of social standing. He enjoyed socializing with the upper class, but he became increasingly disgruntled at his inability to discard his lowly roots.

The Chamerovzow conflict also raises the issue of Pillsbury's perfectionism and his confrontational tactics. Several American and British abolitionists worried that his uncompromising positions and strategies would not be well received in Europe. Sarah Pugh wondered how the British and Foreign Society would "bear Pillsbury's outspoken opinion of their society" and his "fearless assertion of what he believes."[52] Webb even predicted that an "uproar" would result if Pillsbury gave rein to his anticlerical sentiments in Britain.[53] Despite the concerns of his colleagues, Pillsbury made it clear that he would not soften his style or words to accommodate his new audience. At the May anniversary and the November conference he openly advocated his perfectionist philosophy and agitational tactics. Not mincing words or wasting time, Pillsbury blasted his hosts at the anniversary for their refusal to acknowledge the American Anti-Slavery Society and their "tame" resolutions.[54] As long as the British and Foreign Society balked at openly recognizing the Garrisonians as the legitimate American abolitionists, according to Pillsbury, they revealed themselves as mere halfway reformers, more dangerous to the cause than its opponents. "We [must] not let the enemy get advantage by another act of pretended friendliness," he warned

Samuel May, Jr. "It is far better for Anti Slavery, to keep these people in a hostile position or attitude toward us, until their repentance is far less equivocal than any we have seen yet."[55]

He continued his denunciation of Broad Street at the London conference, adding a dash of antichurch sentiment by highlighting the apostasies of the Quaker church. Even as the radical George Thompson tried to broker a compromise that would have united the British and Foreign Society and the Garrisonians, Pillsbury refused to advocate any such policy. He demanded that Broad Street prove its newfound virtue by admitting its past mistakes and embracing the American Society.[56] His unsparing criticism of the Quakers was also a test of Broad Street's sincerity. The deliberate omission of his speech from the official report merely reinforced Pillsbury's certainty of the British and Foreign Society's dishonesty. By the time he received Chamerovzow's letter in early 1855, he was already convinced that this new leader was as unacceptable as the old one. His depiction of Chamerovzow as "weak" and "wicked" was merely his perfectionist response to sin, as he saw it. In the end, nothing aggravated Pillsbury more than those "halfway" reformers whose pretenses always hurt the movement.

The Chamerovzow controversy, combined with his long and severe illness, made Pillsbury's first year abroad a difficult one. He was particularly frustrated with his lack of achievements. "My life seems spending to little purpose," he complained to his journal in late 1854. "Hosts of Americans come over the water, . . . all doing something good or ill, and *I do nothing*. Alas! for such a record."[57] As he fully regained his strength in early 1855, however, he began to increase his antislavery activism and establish clear goals for his continued residency in Britain. The purpose of his visit abroad had always involved not only regaining his health, but also promoting Garrisonian abolitionism. Once he felt physically restored, he immediately looked to develop strategies for achieving the latter goal. Pillsbury recognized that Britain differed significantly from the U.S. and he wisely modified the old familiar patterns of field lecturing that had dominated his life during the previous decade. Working closely with the general agent of the American Society, Samuel May, Jr., and the accepted leader of Garrisonianism in Europe, Maria Weston Chapman, Pillsbury developed a three-pronged battle plan for advancing uncompromising antislavery in the British Isles. As always, raising financial support proved an important issue and Pillsbury focused particularly on women's groups to achieve this goal. In order to advocate the radical policies of the Garrisonians without raising the ire of conservatives, Pillsbury also initiated a campaign of countless small, private gatherings, combined with many well-orchestrated larger public meetings. Finally, hoping to counter the growing influence of non-Garrisonian American abolitionists in Europe, Pillsbury initiated an offensive of letter writing and private conversations attacking and undermining the offenders.

Long before arriving in England, Pillsbury had established a rapport with women abolitionists. Supportive of their full and equal participation in the movement, he earned their trust and enjoyed their companionship. He often traveled with women lecturers, including Abby Kelley, Sojourner Truth, Sallie Holley, Susan B. Anthony, and Josephine Griffing, and he learned to appreciate their skillful advocacy of the cause. It is not surprising, therefore, that Pillsbury quickly worked to earn the approval of women abolitionists in Britain. Even during his first few months abroad, as he recovered in Bristol from his severe illness, he established friendships with numerous local women abolitionists. "Have had Collections of beautiful Pictures and rare Autographs sent me to examine by Miss Phelps and Miss Carpenter," he proudly wrote in his journal, "with beautiful flowers from Mrs. Stephens and Mrs. Armstrong."[58] Such gifts were followed by numerous personal visits and long rides in the countryside. By the time he left Bristol, Pillsbury had fostered the admiration of a committed group of women abolitionists.

British women had a long history of antislavery activism. Though often overlooked by historians who tend to focus on the achievements of male politicians, women's local activity proved very important to the success of British abolitionism.[59] Moreover, as the movement began to change following the elimination of slavery in the British colonies in the mid-1830s, women established an even more pivotal role. Formal political activism was replaced by the tactics of moral suasion, boycotts, and fund-raising, areas in which women predominated. By the 1850s, women's antislavery societies outnumbered men's groups and American abolitionists in Britain found themselves competing for the support of women. As Garrisonian J. Miller McKim explained after his 1854 visit, "The most active abolitionists were, with few exceptions, to be found among women."[60] Pillsbury concurred, adding that British women boasted a remarkably thorough understanding of the movement: "Few I fear, among our best supporters at home, East or West, have so full and correct a knowledge of the history and the philosophy, the genius and spirit of the Anti Slavery enterprise" as British women.[61]

Women abolitionists in England, Scotland, and Ireland were exceedingly skillful in raising funds for the U.S. movement. Harriet Beecher Stowe certainly understood this when she toured Britain, amassing over $20,000 through the women-organized "Penny Offering," which was supposedly intended to aid the Christian education of black Americans.[62] British women were especially active in supporting the annual fairs of American antislavery groups. Some women's societies were entirely devoted to collecting goods for a particular bazaar, working year-round to attract donations as well as sewing, knitting, and otherwise producing sale items of their own. Boston Fair organizer Maria Weston Chapman labored diligently to garner the support of these women's groups for her annual bazaar. She maintained a regular correspondence with dozens of women in the British Isles, encouraging them in their antislavery activity.[63]

Pillsbury recognized the importance of women's activity, and he worked closely with many groups. During the 1850s, however, there were many other Americans traveling throughout the British Isles trying to raise money for their particular antislavery cause, and Pillsbury found that he had competition wherever he went. Calls for the support of fugitive slaves and the education of free blacks were especially effective during the mid-1850s, when Pillsbury was attempting to gather contributions for Chapman's Boston Bazaar. He battled these competitors by cultivating warm and friendly relations with women's groups. "Last night we had a grand Sewing Circle for the Boston Bazaar," he wrote in his journal. "I *read* and *talked* Anti Slavery, and the ladies *worked* it."[64] This close interaction had a strong effect on both Pillsbury and many women. Pillsbury became increasingly impressed with the determination and effectiveness of women's groups. "It is most delightful to see the zeal and fidelity of a few peerless antislavery women in some of the towns in my travels," he wrote to his wife. "It is not a little *sewing circle work* with them; but in some cases it is day after day, *stitch*, *stitch*, . . . worsted work, embroidery, bead work, and every thing else, all beautiful offerings, brought and laid cheerfully on the altar of Humanity."[65] Meanwhile, dozens of female antislavery societies gushed over Pillsbury's lecturing talents and his untiring commitment to the cause. After he spoke before the Edinburgh Ladies Emancipation Committee, the women expressed their "appreciation of Mr. Pillsbury's long tried, zealous and self-sacrificing labors on behalf of the slave."[66] The Bristol and Clifton Ladies Anti-Slavery Society praised his "gentle Christian spirit, his singleness of purpose, and remarkable self renunciation, and devotion to the cause of the Slave."[67] Pillsbury also managed to help create several new women's antislavery groups. "Mrs. Chapman will be glad to hear that last evening we organized in this city a Ladies Anti Slavery Committee," he reported from Nottingham in February 1856. "About twenty enrolled their names and paid the admission and annual fee of half a crown."[68] Women also established antislavery organizations after Pillsbury's visits to Liverpool and Jedburgh.[69]

Pillsbury used the same tactics that worked so successfully with women's societies—small, private gatherings—to promote the larger aims of Garrisonian abolitionism, especially during his first year abroad. As he struggled to regain his health, he discussed American abolitionism regularly with new acquaintances, at social engagements, and while traveling. The Boston elite encouraged him in this strategy, thrilled that he managed to recover his health while promoting emancipation. Wendell Phillips exhorted Pillsbury to "mingle with abolitionists, know them and be known of them. . . . [All] you are still able to do in society [through] conversations," he concluded, "helps the cause most essentially."[70]

Pillsbury's years of traveling and attending meetings made him comfortable with new people and an expert at advocating the cause. As he recovered in Bristol with the Estlins, Pillsbury not only forged ties with women abolitionists, he also participated in social affairs, persistently conversing about antislavery, the American clergy, the Bible, women's rights, and American politics.[71] These informal interactions resulted in "a great work," according to Mary Estlin. "Mr. Pillsbury . . . has touched more hearts and given more light than we can ever have the power of doing," she wrote Anne Warren Weston. In recommending Pillsbury's continued stay in England to the Boston leadership, Estlin described his dynamic influence at a recent antislavery gathering. "The light which a short conversation shed over the circle, the strengthening of their hands for the work before them, the deep sympathy awakened for himself, and for you all, . . . these are the things worth ministering to, and it is not confined to this place."[72]

Pillsbury also used his informal activist techniques to build very strong relationships with several leading abolitionists in Britain. The Estlins became deeply attached to Pillsbury during his extended stay at their home and he repeatedly visited them throughout his two years in Britain. Both Mary and John Estlin enjoyed enormous influence over the abolitionist movement in England and Pillsbury's intimate access to them proved extremely beneficial to the Garrisonians. He also developed strong ties to another dominant figure in British reform, Harriet Martineau. Although a few years after his departure from Europe Martineau would disparage Pillsbury for his agitational tactics, the two radicals initially admired one another. After learning that Pillsbury had received an invitation to spend a few weeks with Martineau at her country estate, Wendell Phillips entreated Pillsbury to accept the offer. "Her deep interest in the cause, her wide influence and uniform readiness to use it in our favor entitle her to the best sources of information, and you could give her the very latest and best," explained Phillips. "Go by all means to see her if you possibly can."[73] Pillsbury did visit Martineau a few months later and during his stay the two reformers worked together writing antislavery articles. "Yesterday Miss Martineau and I wrote all day to publish something against the infernal slave catching business in America," he confided to his journal.[74]

In 1855, Pillsbury began to extend his antislavery activism to include large meetings and conventions. By this time, the Boston elite, which had worked hard to convince Pillsbury to remain abroad for another year, officially appointed him a lecturing agent for the American Society in Great Britain and Ireland.[75] Perhaps feeling the need to earn his agency, Pillsbury embarked on a rigorous lecturing schedule throughout 1855 and early 1856 that rivaled his U.S. routine. He did, however, modify his speeches to appeal more directly to his foreign listeners. He focused more on educating his audience, especially in regard to the horrors of slavery and the recent history of such political events as the Kansas-Nebraska Bill and the Fugitive Slave Law. He also often vividly described his antislavery adventures in the United States, including dramatic mob attacks and other turbulent attempts to undermine his lectures. These personal narratives appealed to foreign listeners, who comfortably denounced those Americans responsible for such behavior. Pillsbury astutely emphasized slavery as an *American* blight, encouraging his audiences to use their moral power to influence the United States. Following the lead of many black abolitionists who lectured in Europe, he sometimes even disclaimed his U.S. heritage: "I am not an American citizen, for the reason that I would not be voluntarily recognized as properly associated with a crew of pirates," he declared at one meeting. "I have voluntarily disfranchised myself, and only live in my own country a stranger and a foreigner there. For the price of citizenship, in the United States of America, is too high for me to pay."[76] Pillsbury's careful reshaping of his lectures paid off. "His presence has done the cause an immense amount of good; people have seen the true light who would otherwise have remained in darkness," declared S. Alfred Steinthal.[77]

In his attempt to appeal to English audiences, however, Pillsbury did not moderate his commitment to perfectionism and moral agitation, nor did he avoid "touching the church." Some Garrisonians in Britain and the United States questioned the advisability of these tactics. Richard Webb, for example, complained to Boston that Pillsbury "expects everyone to be a good Garrisonian abolitionist and does not know how to make proper allowances for people's circumstances."[78] And yet at meeting after meeting Pillsbury's denunciation of American religion failed to ignite the same kind of outrage he provoked in the United States. Because he skillfully distinguished American churches from their British counterparts, his speeches did not arouse deep-seated resentment. After one of Pillsbury's first lectures following his illness, Francis Bishop described his friend's success "in contrasting *American* religion with the Religion of Christ." Bishop expressed astonishment that Pillsbury "carried his whole audience with him, Orthodox ministers and all, when he declared himself proud in being called and in being deserved to be called, an 'Infidel.' "[79] Even when Pillsbury characterized the American

Board of Commissioners of Foreign Missions as proslavery and pro-polygamy at the 1854 London conference, the audience did not rise in as-tonished protest. Although the American Board was defended, the issue failed to arouse anywhere near the same excitement as the resolution to ac-knowledge the American Anti-Slavery Society.[80]

The reaction at home, however, proved much more explosive. Appalled to see the missionary efforts of American churches impugned at an interna-tional conference, the New York *Independent*, a religious newspaper, pilloried Pillsbury as "foul-mouthed and reckless."[81] Although the Garrisonians had long since agitated against the Board of Foreign Missions because it admit-ted slaveholders into its congregations, Pillsbury's accusations proved par-ticularly vexing because of the cosmopolitan nature of the conference.[82] Irate at the U.S. churches being humiliated abroad, the *Independent* attempted to nullify Pillsbury's allegations by questioning his sanity and integrity: "We have no occasion to judge whether he speaks under the hallucination of frenzy, or with a full consciousness that he is lying." The Garrisonians re-acted by publicly denouncing the *Independent* and justifying Pillsbury's orig-inal charges.[83] When the *Independent* refused to publish Pillsbury's rebuttal, the Garrisonians passed a resolution at their annual meeting regretting the "lame and impotent effort" of the *Independent* to defend the Board of For-eign Missions.[84]

These very different reactions to Pillsbury's criticism of a prestigious mis-sionary organization reveal the reason that he managed to sell his anticleri-calism so successfully in the British Isles. Unthreatened by Pillsbury's de-nunciations of American churches, British audiences could feel superior when they listened to these disturbing allegations. After one of Pillsbury's lectures in England, a Baptist minister claimed that "he had always gloried in the name of Baptist, except in connexion with American slavery; in that connexion he was compelled to feel ashamed of it."[85] Pillsbury finally found an audience who appreciated his abrasive condemnation of American religion.

Pillsbury's commitment to perfectionism and agitation also manifested itself in the final component of his European agenda—battling non-Garrisonian abolitionists. He had always saved his most unforgiving attacks for individuals and institutions advocating only "halfway reform." He be-lieved moderate abolitionists misled earnest and naive citizens, resulting in a loss of potential converts to "true" antislavery. His perfectionism convinced him that any moral ambivalence, no matter what the reason, was both spiri-tually bankrupt and functionally dangerous. He devoted the bulk of his ca-reer to battling what others considered to be legitimate reform efforts.

Among these "halfway reformers," according to Pillsbury, were many

African-American ministers who disagreed with the tactics and policies of the Garrisonians. "The anti-slavery cause has no worse foes, none more dangerous," he warned his British audiences, than these "clerical pretenders."[86] While Garrison attracted intense support among most Boston blacks, he also alienated many other African-American abolitionists with his antipolitical, anticlerical, and disunion policies, and his unwillingness to accept disagreement.[87] Most black abolitionists were interested in a practical and broad approach to abolition, which included fighting to end not only slavery in the South but also racial subordination in the North. They embraced political as well as moral efforts to fight slavery and some advocated physical resistance. Moreover, most African-American abolitionists considered *all* efforts to promote the black community, including economic opportunities, social equality, civil rights, and political rights, to come under the rubric of antislavery activity.[88] While the Garrisonians supported such efforts, they did not consider them to be within the realm of "true" abolition.

Black abolitionists had successfully promoted antislavery throughout the British Isles since the 1830s: Frederick Douglass himself had made a two-year tour in the mid-1840s.[89] When Pillsbury arrived in England in 1854, African-American Garrisonian William Wells Brown was in the final stage of a three-year lecturing agency, having given over a thousand speeches across the British Isles.[90] While Brown had long supported the Garrisonians and had even lectured with Pillsbury, some of his decisions during his British tour irritated his Boston colleagues, including his cooperation with non-Garrisonian black abolitionists. The Boston elite regretted, for example, Brown's support for Henry Highland Garnet's Free Produce Movement, arguing that such "extraneous" issues merely took attention away from legitimate antislavery efforts.[91] Other black abolitionists in Britain during the 1850s successfully sought financial support for a variety of causes, including fugitive slaves, black schools and churches, and antislavery political parties. One of Pillsbury's most important goals included dissuading British abolitionists from supporting these efforts.

He wasted little time in attempting to undermine his opponents in Europe. Using the familiar tactics of informal meetings, small gatherings, and public letters to warn his audiences about the illegitimate goals of non-Garrisonian abolitionists, Pillsbury initiated a campaign against his enemies. "I give some public Lectures, but rely very much on little committee meetings of a more social character," he wrote his wife. "I give special information about . . . Canada Missions, vigilance Committees, . . . and all the spurious coins that now circulate here, in the name of Anti Slavery."[92] During these private gatherings Pillsbury admitted that the goals of these pseudo-abolitionists "are very well and proper in their way," but, he concluded, "they will not abolish the slave system, nor even weaken it."[93] In an attempt to convince British abolitionists to give their money to the Boston Bazaar instead of these other organizations, he wrote a public letter to a local newspaper: "Anti-Slavery is not merely a 'Vigilance Committee' aiding a few slaves to Canada under cover of night," he explained, "but a bold and daring onset upon the great Bastile [*sic*] itself, demanding immediately the deliverance of every captive."[94]

In addition to carefully defining legitimate antislavery efforts, Pillsbury also warned his British audiences about the confidence tricksters who pretended to support black churches and schools, but had no intention of following through on their promises. The Garrisonians were convinced that many such frauds were being perpetrated in Britain and they clearly spelled out these concerns to Pillsbury: "The darker the picture you draw of the hypocrites and sheepskin-wolves who have undertaken to make a living out of British sympathy for the slave," instructed Wendell Phillips, the better.[95] Pillsbury not only publicized well-known instances of chicanery, but also introduced a few dubious accusations. During a "tea party and public meeting" in Broughton, he "set matters right about Dr. Pennington," according to his journal.[96] J. W. C. Pennington, a fugitive slave, was one of the "coloured ministers" in Britain who opposed the Garrisonians. He had become a special target for Pillsbury because it was suspected that he had pocketed funds raised to purchase his freedom.[97] Pillsbury made sure the entire British public was awakened to these suspicions, by denouncing Pennington in a public letter to the Glasgow *Sentinel*: "He prevents or perverts the gifts that would be cheerfully laid on the altar of humanity, by representing things to be anti-slavery which are not, and runs away with the sympathies of a generous people, who really wish well to the cause of the slave."[98]

Because many of the African-American abolitionists who traveled through Britain in the 1850s were ministers or closely associated with the church, including Pennington, Alexander Crummell, Henry Highland Garnet, and Samuel Ringgold Ward, Pillsbury proved especially unforgiving in his criticism. Indeed, Pillsbury was probably more concerned with the religious ties of these men than with their conflicting interpretation of abolition. He considered it particularly unforgivable for black abolitionists to embrace the church and he attempted to point out what a contradiction this involved. "At the very time when Dr. Pennington was in the New York Presbytery, advocating and voting for a resolution to stifle discussion on slavery, his own brother and his brother's two young sons were being pursued by kidnappers," he exclaimed. How could any African American remain committed to such a church, "one of the most corrupt pro-slavery bodies this world of wickedness has produced"?[99] Most Northern blacks, however, joined separate black churches and these institutions served a critical role in African-American communities. Independent of white society, black churches provided a central location for religious, political, and social interaction. They also promoted and sustained black leadership, since ministers often doubled as community leaders.[100] Although Pillsbury regularly lectured in black churches and understood their importance as a refuge from racist white society, he remained skeptical of such black ministers as Pennington, who maintained ties with mainstream churches like the Presbyterians.

Pillsbury's campaign against the non-Garrisonians in Europe escalated in late 1855, as he began to focus on the influence of the indomitable Frederick Douglass. Ever since Douglass's celebrated tour of Europe in the mid-1840s he had become increasingly alienated from the tight-knit Garrisonian clique. Buoyed by his growing sense of independence, Douglass determined to publish his own newspaper upon his return to the United States. His Boston colleagues, however, protested this decision, arguing that Douglass's contribution to the movement lay in his oratorical skills. Besides, any additional newspaper would compete with the already struggling *Liberator* and *Standard*. Throughout the late 1840s and early 1850s relations between Garrison and Douglass remained strained. Garrison patronized Douglass, treating him like a rebellious son and eventually an ungrateful inferior. Douglass could not endure Garrison's inability to respect his decisions and treat him like an equal. When Douglass openly began supporting political antislavery in the form of the Free Soil Party and opposing the Garrisonian policy of disunionism, Boston branded him a traitor and declared war.[101]

By the time Pillsbury arrived in England the battle lines between Boston and Douglass had been drawn. This conflict deeply pained Pillsbury, who had worked with and admired Douglass for years. "The present spirit and position of Frederick Douglass has filled us all with regret and sorrow," he lamented to Maria Weston Chapman in early 1854. "Nothing so odd has transpired since the alienation of N. P. Rogers."[102] This interesting comparison to Rogers suggests that Pillsbury empathized with Douglass, just as he had with Rogers, though for different reasons. Pillsbury and Douglass both felt a sense of discomfort among the elite Garrisonians, each man painfully conscious of his inadequate educational background and social status. Moreover, Pillsbury's unsparing anticlericalism and Douglass's refusal to toe the party line further alienated them both from the Boston leaders. Despite this bond between outsiders, Pillsbury did not openly support Douglass. He concluded that Douglass, like Rogers, was an earnest and dedicated abolitionist who had made a disastrous decision. Unlike in the Rogers conflict, however, Pillsbury managed to avoid the Douglass divide as much as possible. He and Douglass remained on fairly good terms throughout the 1840s. Douglass wrote favorable editorials about Pillsbury's meetings and speeches, while Pillsbury's close friend and longtime boarder, P. Brainard Cogswell, even considered working for Douglass as his printer.[103] Not until Pillsbury traveled to Europe did he devote much attention to Douglass and even then he primarily focused on Douglass's English partner, Julia Griffiths.

Douglass and Griffiths met in England during his 1846–47 European tour and quickly developed a close friendship. In 1849, Griffiths moved across the Atlantic to work alongside Douglass in Rochester, New York. A young single white woman with great intelligence and energy and an open worshiper of Douglass, Griffiths ignited much gossip during her six-year stay in the United States. While the Garrisonians worried that this partnership would lead to accusations of miscegenation and damage the movement, they deliberately stoked the fire by questioning the nature of Douglass' relationship with Griffiths and suggesting that he was humiliating his illiterate African-American wife. This gossip became so ruthless and widespread that Griffiths returned to England in late 1855, where she initiated a campaign to raise funds for Douglass's newspaper. Her homecoming worried the Garrisonians, who feared that she would rekindle the tremendous enthusiasm Douglass had attracted during his earlier visit and effectively diminish their own support.[104] Their concern proved justified. Between 1855 and 1859 Griffiths organized twenty new female antislavery societies and dramatically increased financial support for the Rochester Bazaar, rival to the Garrisonian Boston Bazaar.[105]

Griffiths's arrival in England in late 1855 resulted in a change of plans for Pillsbury. "My mind was fully made up to go home in October," he informed Maria Weston Chapman. "But Julia Griffiths has just arrived with a labor on her hands, in the performance of which she may do us much mischief."[106] Pillsbury decided to remain abroad until the spring of the following year in order to counteract the influence of Douglass's skillful partner. Throughout these last months in Britain, Pillsbury became obsessed with Julia Griffiths. He constantly tracked her activities, wrote about her to Boston, and spoke about her during his private gatherings. Griffiths certainly was a first-rate antagonist; she worked with political abolitionists, promoted church antislavery, and castigated the Garrisonians. The epitome of compromise, according to Pillsbury, Griffiths threatened his vision of antislavery. "Julia Griffiths," he pronounced to Samuel May, Jr., "is the most devilish as well as most despicable of all the present foes."[107]

Pillsbury's denunciation of Griffiths, however, took on a curious dimension. He often referred to her in demeaning terms, usually emphasizing her single status by including "Miss" before each unkind or sarcastic characterization. Clearly angered by the sexual relationship he suspected between

Griffiths and Douglass, Pillsbury's favorite sobriquet for Griffiths became "Miss Jezebel Douglass."[108] Although well known for his abrasive and exaggerated language, he did not often employ such personally insulting adjectives. Hoping to thoroughly disparage this middle-class white woman, Pillsbury aimed for the most vulnerable point, her sexual purity. By using the term "Jezebel," a stereotype usually applied to African-American women, Pillsbury also indirectly suggested racial improprieties.[109] The sexual and racial undertones of Pillsbury's slurs suggest that he was willing to employ popular notions of female sexuality when convenient. While he could perhaps forgive Douglass his apostasies because of their personal friendship and common sense of alienation, Pillsbury had no such relationship with Griffiths and so let loose the full force of his disapproval.

Pillsbury's conflict with black non-Garrisonians and Julia Griffiths in Britain forced him to confront his own position on issues of racial inequality and prejudice. Since the beginning of his antislavery career in the late 1830s, Pillsbury had advocated full political and social equality between blacks and whites, as did most Garrisonians. One of his first major tours outside of New Hampshire involved lecturing in Rhode Island against the new state constitution because it disenfranchised black men.[110] In his denunciation of the church he often included a segment decrying "Jim Crow pews" and other examples of racial inequality in religion.[111] He addressed the predominance of racial prejudice across the North, focusing on segregation in transportation and education and the exclusion of blacks from well-paying jobs.[112] Pillsbury also developed strong personal relationships with many black Garrisonians, including Frederick Douglass, William Wells Brown, Sojourner Truth, and Robert Purvis. Although he sometimes patronized his black colleagues—for example, instructing Douglass to include more of the "plantation manner" in his lectures—he did not display the racism of some of his white colleagues.[113]

As he criticized black non-Garrisonians in Britain, he clearly attempted to acknowledge the worthiness of their goals. Often deeming it a "painful necessity" to discuss this topic, Pillsbury made sure to point out the real needs of fugitives, vigilance committees, and black schools, even as he distinguished these issues from "true" abolition.[114] Perhaps as a result of this forced acknowledgment of the concerns of black abolitionists, Pillsbury increased his discussion of racism and inequality in the years after his return to the United States. For example, he vividly highlighted the depth of American racism in a speech following the infamous 1857 Dred Scott decision of the Supreme Court: "We hate him for the color of his skin. We hate him for the crisp of his hair. We hate him for the form of his features, we hate him for the odor from his body. We hate him that he is ignorant when we have made him so; we hate him that he is degraded, when we keep him so."[115] In speeches throughout the Civil War, Pillsbury discussed the need for the North to eliminate racist laws and practices. He recognized that emancipation would not end Jim Crow, nor affect the general conviction among whites of black inferiority.[116]

Europe offered Pillsbury many important political lessons that would serve him well throughout his career, but his foreign travels also allowed him to develop numerous dormant artistic and intellectual interests. Pillsbury enjoyed the sights and scenes of many of the great cities of Europe, especially during his first year abroad. These traveling experiences helped him to satisfy a deep yearning to become culturally literate and thus earn a place of esteem among his well-educated Boston colleagues. His travels, however, also raised some complex and painful class issues for Pillsbury, especially as he witnessed the contrasts of poverty and affluence so prevalent throughout Europe. While his years abroad certainly helped to increase his self-esteem, they also made him more sensitive to the contradictions of his desire to climb the ladder of social status.

Pillsbury's first introduction to the art and history of Europe came during his tour of Paris in the spring of 1854. He and Charles Hovey visited innumerable museums, churches, gardens, and palaces. Overwhelmed with the beauty and history of this city, he tried to learn everything he could about each location, always picking up guidebooks and reading them carefully. He still felt inadequate to the task. "I begin to see that to *graduate* handsomely and honorably from Paris, a *Master* or even *Bachelor of Arts* in a knowledge of its works and its wonders, would require more time and severe study than to pass regularly and creditably through any University in America," he quipped in his journal after several days in Paris.[117] For Pillsbury, Paris was indeed like a university, where he hoped to earn degrees in culture, art, and history, but also overcome the deficiencies of his working-class New Hampshire background and develop a more respected position among the Boston antislavery elite. Being immersed in this cosmopolitan city, however, reminded him of his inadequacies, even as it helped him to overcome them. After visiting the Louvre he spelled out this contradictory effect. "O that Louvre—how it has captivated, bewitched, overpowered me, body and spirit. And yet I know nothing of the different schools of painting, and probably am no judge at all of the real merits of a picture or a statue." He did not conclude on this dispirited note, however. Instead, he asserted his right to his own opinion, uneducated though it might be: "But I can tell when a piece of work appeals to my every sense, and compels my admiration."[118]

Pillsbury continued his sightseeing in London, openly embracing his role

Fig. 7. Parker Pillsbury. Courtesy of the New Hampshire Historical Society, S1998.519.03.

as tourist. His journal reflects an increasing sense of comfort with this life of traveling observer. Visiting famous sights during the daytime, Pillsbury and his hosts filled their nights with plays, concerts, and dances. Amidst all of this sophisticated recreation, Concord, New Hampshire, must have seemed a distant dream to Pillsbury. Indeed, he conveniently forgot his teetotaling past as he surrendered to this new lifestyle. "Bought a Bottle of wine for the first time in my life," he casually mentioned in his journal, "and drank a glass with dinner—shall due [*sic*] the same while it lasts."[119] Fully committed to adopting the cosmopolitan manners of his European associates, Pillsbury willingly neglected the strict code of behavior that dominated his life as a staid New England reformer. His European friends approved of his efforts to embrace their culture and habits. "I took him to see the ruins of . . . our oldest Abbey," wrote Alfred Steinthal to Pillsbury's American supervisor, Samuel May, Jr., "and he was very properly pleased. I do not like a man who is not touched by looking upon the remains of days."[120] Pillsbury must have sensed such evaluations of his behavior and he probably felt even more compelled to appreciate and adopt the ways of his hosts. His wealthier patrons, however, made Pillsbury's job very easy. Visiting the spacious homes of upper-class reformers, he sunk into reverence: "All that wealth could procure or ambition covet . . . seemed to surround us," he wrote in his journal following a visit to the home of an Irish philanthropist. "The house, grounds, groves, gardens, the furniture, the pictures and other adornings were all that could be enjoyed, all that should be desired."[121]

Although he admired the luxuries of many of his European colleagues, Pillsbury did not ignore the dire poverty that surrounded him. Disturbed by the contrast between the ornate sights and scenes he visited and the poor people who lived nearby, Pillsbury often found it difficult to appreciate the beauty and history of these tourist attractions. "St. Patrick's Church, the most venerable and massive pile I have yet seen seems to have sapped all the wealth, vitality and life for a long way round," he declared after a visit to Dublin, "to rear itself into a domination and despotism, under whose weight and in whose shadow, no flower nor fruit can evermore flourish."[122] His visit to Versailles also disturbed him: "No wonder a Revolution grew out of its creation," he exclaimed. And how abhorrent that "the labor of so many *poor*," would be "lavished on a few *rich* and worthless creatures living only for themselves."[123]

Pillsbury considered the class problems of Europe much more serious than those in the United States. "Society has petrified itself into a most cheerless, hopeless form, for the poor of Great Britain," he explained to his family. "And to work out a solution from poverty and peasantship, and to become honored, or even respected by the more elevated spheres and circles, is a work of almost super-man power."[124] Pillsbury did not, however, often proclaim such opinions in his public speeches. He understood that involvement in labor issues in Britain would not facilitate his antislavery appeal. Labor activists criticized Pillsbury for his failure to address the issue of class inequality in Britain. "He stood on the platform in Manchester face to face with the English capitalists who grow rich by the toil of the oppressed poor, and if he could speak an hour or more upon American slavery, could he not devote ten minutes to English oppression?" asked American labor and abolition activist George Putnam.[125] Although Pillsbury continued to privately address and discuss class inequality in Britain in his letters and journals, he did not take the advice of Putnam and "devote ten minutes to English oppression" in his public speeches. This was not because he considered it an unimportant topic, or because it was unrelated to antislavery, but because he knew it would alienate his listeners. He had given many lectures connecting the oppression of "free" and slave labor in the United States, even in mill towns like Lowell, Massachusetts. His failure to continue making these connections reveals that issues of practicality sometimes subdued his perfectionist philosophy.

Pillsbury returned to the United States in the spring of 1856, his suitcases full of guidebooks and many other reminders of his European sojourn. His homecoming sparked not only tears of joy from his family, but also a large and lavish welcoming celebration organized by his antislavery colleagues.

"With deep feeling," Pillsbury addressed the crowd of over six hundred who had come to honor him that night in Faneuil Hall.[126] He had been back from Europe for less than a week and this was his first public appearance. "I could not have calculated, in the beginning of my connection with the great anti-slavery movement, on a result so flattering to myself as this," he softly explained, "and you must sympathize with me in the embarrassment I feel at this moment." Looking out at the countless familiar faces of those who had come to welcome him home from his two-and-a-half-year sojourn in Europe, Pillsbury did what came naturally—he launched into an antislavery speech, complete with allusions to the recent events that were turning Northern opinion against the South, Preston Brooks's assault on Senator Charles Sumner in the Senate Chamber, and the burning and looting of Lawrence, Kansas, by proslavery raiders from Missouri. "When the blood of your noblest, bravest Senator is flowing at his desk in the halls of Congress, and when the new towns in the frontier settlements are sacked and burned, . . . it almost seems to me that our sympathies should be turned in other directions than here," he passionately advised. After excoriating the apathetic American public, the church, and the political parties, Pillsbury described his antislavery experiences in Britain, emphasizing his fidelity to perfectionism and agitation. Although he had encountered similar obstacles abroad as at home, he did not back away from his uncompromising antislavery radicalism. "Whatever of success I may have had there, . . . not one jot of it has been at the price of any letting down of my own testimony," he assured his audience. "I stand acquitted at the bar of my own conscience . . . and I shall rejoice . . . if I stand approved by you also."[127]

Pillsbury's European tour affected the development of his political philosophy and personal identity in many ways. Most important, it allowed him to balance perfectionism with practical strategizing, flattering his European audiences even as he advocated the most uncompromising and anticlerical positions. When he returned to the United States he immediately employed his newly refashioned perfectionism to challenge his colleagues over their tendency toward moderation. Maintaining this position throughout the Civil War despite the opposition of the Boston leaders, Pillsbury developed the self-confidence and courage of his convictions to endure the ostracism of his colleagues.

7

Perfectionism and the Civil War

Rejuvenated and brimming with confidence after his trip to Europe, Pillsbury wasted little time before diving back into his work as an antislavery field laborer and uncompromising perfectionist. Within weeks following his homecoming celebration in Boston he began a campaign rebuking his fellow abolitionists for their welcoming attitude toward religion and politics. "Let us not be troubled, or lured from our noble purpose by the wiles of priests and political parties," he advised. "Our testimony is a diviner testimony, our mission a holier mission than theirs."[1]

This campaign against evangelicals and Republicans, combined with disagreements over tactics, caused a rift between Pillsbury and the Boston elite that would widen throughout the war years. Although the battle lines sometimes shifted, the division solidified. Pillsbury found strong allies among his fellow field lecturers, who had long since harbored feelings of frustration toward the Executive Committee. As with the acrimonious Rogers affair of 1844–45, the Garrisonian leadership tried to assert its authority over the dissenters. This time, however, the Civil War and a divided Boston made any simple resolution impossible.

Pillsbury's political differences with the elite spilled over into his personal life. Defying Garrison and other respected figures in the movement was painful for the Granite state reformer. He felt increasingly lonely and misunderstood. He desperately attempted to find a balance between compromise and perfectionism that would satisfy his own standards and appeal to his peers.

115

Field lecturers and the Boston elite (as reflected in the Executive Committee of the American Society) had always maintained a complex relationship characterized by a blend of respect and resentment, cooperation and competition. The Garrisonian leadership appreciated the work of the lecturing agents but often found it difficult to control them. In theory, the Executive Committee assigned agents lecturing duties and paid them. In practice, agents often arranged and accepted their own meetings and earned enough in donations and subscriptions to cover the cost of their salaries. Given the meager pay and burdensome nature of antislavery field work, most agents could easily have found more lucrative and less stressful careers.[2] Therefore, especially for experienced lecturers, the authority of the Executive Committee rested more on respect and personal relationships than financial ties. A delicate balance developed between these two groups over the years, but the coming of the Civil War catalyzed tactical and philosophical differences that would eventually tip the scales.

Tensions increased in 1857, when the Executive Committee canceled a well-publicized national Disunion Convention in Cleveland at the last minute because of a "financial crisis" in the nation. Prior to the cancellation Pillsbury reported optimistically from Cleveland, "Our extremest doctrines never found so ready response as now. Our contemplated Disunion Convention in this city seems to find only favour, in the eyes of all who have any real love or regard for liberty."[3] He was, therefore, deeply disappointed when he learned the meeting would not be held. "It is not for me to question the action of the Committee," Pillsbury conceded, and yet he was prepared to do just that. "You have little idea, I think, what an interest this proposed Convention has awakened."[4] He maintained that the postponement had damaged the cause and undermined the efforts of the field-workers who had encouraged all their audiences to attend this important meeting.[5] Angered and frustrated, Pillsbury and the other field lecturers (who had already arrived in Cleveland by the time they heard of the postponement) held an impromptu meeting and decided to host a convention despite the official postponement.[6] The movement's most outspoken lecturers, including the Fosters, Joseph Howland, Charles Remond, Lucy Coleman, and Charles Burleigh, gathered with such Western radicals as Elizabeth and Benjamin Jones, Martha Tilden, James Barnaby, and Abraham Brooke. In a speech before these friends and colleagues, Pillsbury freely expressed his disdain for the Executive Committee: "Those who announced the postponement of that Convention will never know, in the world, the extent of the evil they have done. . . . The foe was before us;—we were ready for the struggle; victory was about to perch upon our banners;—when our leaders sounded a retreat, and we were compelled to yield all to our enemies!"[7] Although Pillsbury backed away from this attack after his vituperative speech was published—to his dismay—in the *Anti-Slavery Bugle*, the rift between leaders and lecturers could not so easily be repaired.[8]

In 1858, relations deteriorated even further. A group of field lecturers, led by Pillsbury and the Fosters, insisted on continuing to denounce religious abolitionists despite the more vocal role certain popular evangelicals had adopted in their battle against slavery. Inspired by the roiling Northern resentment of the "Slave Power," famed Congregational minister Henry Ward Beecher spoke at antislavery conventions in the late 1850s and his colleague George Cheever formed the Church Anti-Slavery Society in 1859. Orthodox church officials and many in the popular press castigated these men for their abolitionism.[9] But Pillsbury and other antislavery lecturers remained critical of these "death-bed conversions." Why, asked Pillsbury, had it taken so long for the converts to antislavery to find their consciences? Garrison and several Executive Committee members, on the other hand, welcomed these popular and powerful adherents, arguing that their support would help to widen the ranks of committed abolitionists. This increasing reconciliation with the church worried Pillsbury and others, who feared that the Garrisonians would sacrifice their independence. After two decades of preaching against such compromises, Pillsbury felt that his entire life's work was threatened.

In his letters and at meetings and conventions Pillsbury increased his criticism of George Cheever and Henry Ward Beecher.[10] He warned his colleagues that they must not allow themselves "to be captivated by fair appearances, by specious promises, and by outside indications of a better tone of anti-slavery than actually exists."[11] Beecher and Cheever hypocritically "laid one hand on the Anti-Slavery movement and the other on the heads of the slaveholders," he asserted, and thus did more harm to the movement than Southern slaveholders themselves.[12] Citing his extensive field experience to support his unpopular opinions, Pillsbury concluded, "I know this sounds harsh and unreasonable, but if you will go into the field with us three months, we will convince you that the logic is good, the argument sound and unanswerable."[13] While several lecturing agents stood by Pillsbury at the annual conventions (Aaron Powell, Andrew Foss, and Joseph Howland), Garrison and the Executive Committee repeatedly prevailed with a more favorable assessment of Beecher and Cheever.[14]

Pillsbury's conflict with the Boston elite intensified as the Civil War drew near. Even as they continued to disagree regarding evangelical antislavery, the rise of the Republican Party caused a breach that rivaled the N. P. Rogers debacle.

The Republican Party had emerged as a powerful political force in the 1850s, aided by several key episodes that fostered anti-Southern feeling in the North.[15] This tumultuous decade began with the passage of the controversial Fugitive Slave Act, adopted as a part of the Compromise of 1850. The spirited response to the act in the North was a prelude of things to come. Because the act empowered federal marshals to require that all citizens help to enforce the law—that is, return fugitive slaves to their owners—many Northerners felt their government was compelling them to personally support slavery. Abolitionists used these concerns to inflame the Northern public and build resentment toward the South.[16]

As the initial uproar over the Fugitive Slave Act diminished, another development, this time in the literary world, helped to maintain anti-Southern sentiment. Harriet Beecher Stowe's tale *Uncle Tom's Cabin; or, Life among the Lowly* captivated its audience when it appeared as a serial in the *National Era* in 1851, and sold out immediately in book form in 1852. This sentimental novel about the miseries of slave life ignited widespread—albeit moderate—antislavery sentiment like nothing before.[17] Just about the time *Uncle Tom's Cabin* sold over a million copies, the 1854 Kansas-Nebraska Bill was pushed through Congress by Illinois Senator Stephen A. Douglas and aroused the Northern public even further. Determined to legally organize the territories in order to facilitate a Pacific railroad, Douglas nullified the Missouri Compromise and infuriated the North. Concerned that this rash disregard of the 1820 covenant—which had limited slavery to below 36°30'—was an act of treachery on the part of the South, many Northerners began to take seriously Republican Congressman Joshua Giddings's warning that Southern "tyrants" planned to make slavery a national institution.[18]

Two explosive events that occurred within a twenty-four-hour period in late May 1856 guaranteed a receptive Northern audience for the Republican party's indictment of the "slave power." When proslavery Missouri "ruffians" burned and looted the antislavery Kansas town of Lawrence, Northerners were stunned.[19] One day later, South Carolina Representative Preston Brooks entered the U.S. Senate chamber seeking revenge against Massachusetts Senator Charles Sumner for his "libelous" speech attacking the South as well as Brooks's relative and friend, Samuel Butler. Brooks brutally beat the defenseless Sumner over the head with a cane, continuing even after his cane broke and the senator lay bloodied and unconscious on the floor. Brooks only ceased flogging Sumner when he was physically restrained by another politician. Although the Senate ignored the attack and the House failed to expel Brooks, the Northern public reacted with outrage, holding protest meetings in nearly every city. Meanwhile, the South crowned Brooks its new hero and a Baltimore court merely fined him three hundred dollars for the assault.[20]

The Republicans, desperately trying to construct a unified party out of disaffected Whigs, Democrats, and Free Soilers, took advantage of the "sack of Lawrence" and the "caning of Sumner" to attract support and affirm their viability. They used Northern fears of a threatening "Slave Power"—as embodied by Preston Brooks and the Missouri ruffians—to generate enthusiasm among the voters.[21] Even as its constituency grew, however, the party continued to experience internal disagreement. Abolitionist Republicans like Joshua Giddings, Charles Sumner, and Henry Wilson called for more attention to the moral issue of slavery, while conservative Republicans focused on the rights of white laborers in the new territories and the tyranny of the Slave Power.[22] Conservatives outnumbered abolitionists, since the Republican party proved weak in its support for emancipation and racial equality. Some conservatives, like Frank Blair, Jr., even advocated the forced colonization of blacks.[23] Time and again throughout the late 1850s, the party failed to support efforts to enfranchise African-American men, desegregate schools, and eliminate exclusionary laws in the Northern states.[24]

Despite these failures, many moderate abolitionists (both African-American and white) supported the Republicans, seeing them as the best practical alternative to the Democrats.[25] Some Garrisonians even worked cautiously with the Republicans in the late 1850s.[26] For the radicals, this foray into partisan politics represented a significant change of tactics. But the explosive developments of the 1850s which strengthened the influence of the Republican Party also affected the Garrisonians. They experienced a transition in this decade—including an infusion of younger reformers—which made new strategies seem necessary. The new generation of abolitionists were now more likely to be converted to the movement by political events, like the Fugitive Slave Act, instead of through religious experiences. Many of these new activists were more interested in practical political change than in perfectionism or the millennium. Moreover, as antislavery attracted greater support in the 1850s, some of the old guard began to favor a more pragmatic approach as well. British abolitionist Harriet Martineau argued that the times required changes and that the position of American abolitionists should be to "secure . . . an ample following."[27] Garrison himself mellowed during this decade, favoring "the company of his children" over "barnstorming around the countryside with Pillsbury and Foster."[28]

Pillsbury, on the other hand, stuck to the old perfectionist philosophy centered on political independence and uncompromising standards. This position required that the radicals remain separate from the Republican Party. "My ideas have been that Mr. Garrison and the moral agitators can best aid you, by standing outside the arena of party strife," wrote Pillsbury to leading antislavery Republican Charles Sumner, "and *in the spirit of the ancient prophets*, boldly proclaiming and defending the absolute, ultimate truth."[29] Unbound by the compromises of politics and elections, "moral agitators" could adhere to perfectionist standards and more effectively pressure public opinion. As the Garrisonians became increasingly associated with the Republicans, he argued, they lost their ability to openly criticize the party. "Our mighty moral power is gone!" lamented Pillsbury.[30] Convinced that during this period of crisis the nation needed "the utterance of stern and important truths" instead of "congratulatory resolutions," Pillsbury decried the premature celebration of the Republican Party that seemed to dominate antislavery meetings.[31]

By 1859, Pillsbury's insistence on political independence and his subsequent confrontational position towards the Republicans caused an internal division among the Garrisonians. At the annual meeting of the Massachusetts Anti-Slavery Society in February, Pillsbury offered his by now familiar resolution which condemned "the subtle and fiendish spirit of hostility to the Anti-Slavery cause" exhibited by the Republican Party and professed it to be "far more dangerous to the cause of freedom" than the Democrats, who had "a more open policy and course of action."[32] He was supported by several lecturing agents whose field experiences led them to distrust the Republicans. Abby Kelley Foster seconded Pillsbury's provocative resolution, contending that the "Republican party is stealthily sucking the very blood from our veins." Thomas Wentworth Higginson also agreed, proclaiming that "the quiet of the present period forebodes great and imminent danger." Pillsbury's resolution, however, drew a spirited rebuttal from Garrison, who declared the remarks of his colleagues to be "unduly desponding and lugubrious." He argued that the Republicans should be judged not by the standards of abolitionists, but by the standards of political parties. The Republicans, he explained, claimed to be a nonextension party. "The Republican party has certainly been consistent in its efforts to prevent the extension of slavery," he continued. "Let the party have the credit of it. . . . Tell me that it is to be put in the same scale with the Democratic party."[33] Garrison's invitation to judge political parties by their own standards flew in the face of his previous stern condemnation of all political parties and showed his willingness to employ new strategies in the late 1850s.

The election of 1860 forced the radicals to continue confronting their differences over the Republicans. The Garrisonians had been caught off guard by Abraham Lincoln's victory in the Republican nominating convention— they had expected William Seward, a well-known political abolitionist, to win the nomination. As they scrambled to ascertain Lincoln's position toward slavery, they were increasingly disappointed. The Illinois lawyer's speeches and writings made clear that although he was morally opposed to slavery and would fight its expansion into the Western territories, he would make no effort to eliminate the institution where it already existed. Although most Garrisonians discouraged their audiences from voting for Lincoln, they nonetheless privately hoped for his victory.[34] Pillsbury, on the other hand, passionately condemned Lincoln and the Republicans in public and private, asserting that "but for the Republican party, we might ere now have had slavery abolished."[35] Even as his colleagues decried such inflammatory comments, Pillsbury continued to dramatically articulate his opposition to the Republican candidate. "I stand here to-day to give it as my deliberate opinion," he declared at an antislavery meeting in July 1860, "that in voting for Abraham Lincoln, you as effectually vote for slavery as you would in voting for [Democratic candidate] Stephen A. Douglas."[36]

This growing division soon began to affect all areas of the movement, including the question of the need for continued public meetings and field lecturing. Pillsbury was convinced that abolitionists should continue to rely on the same agitational tactics they had always used, and he encouraged the American and Massachusetts Anti-Slavery societies to increase the number of lecturers they employed during the growing national conflict. Still confidant that the Garrisonians offered the best hope for achieving abolition, he begged for more agents to be assigned to the field: "Was there ever such a harvest with so fearfully few Reapers?" he asked Garrison. "We need every man and woman, now in the field, in New England alone. New York needs as many more; and then, this world of a west, what can be done for it?"[37] Pillsbury also wanted more field lecturers because of their success in promoting anti-Republican sentiment. Indeed, his extensive fieldwork in Ohio and other Western states resulted in the Western Anti-Slavery Society adopting the most uncompromising resolutions toward the Republicans in the years preceding the Civil War.[38] In September 1860, the Western Society passed Pillsbury's resolution condemning the Republicans as the most "dangerous obstacle" to the antislavery movement—a resolution vigorously opposed by Garrison at the earlier annual meeting of the American Society.

Pillsbury's hope for more field lecturers was unexpectedly fulfilled in 1860, when Charles Hovey's will revealed that he had earmarked a large sum of money for progressive causes. Pillsbury had grown close to the elderly radical during their extensive travels together in Europe and he was deeply saddened by his friend's death, but he was also grateful for the infusion of cash. He was among the eight abolitionists named by the uncompromising Hovey to choose how to spend this reserve of forty thousand dollars.[39] Predictably, Pillsbury persistently pressured the other Hovey Committee members—Garrison, Phillips, Stephen Foster, Abby Kelley Foster, Henry C. Wright, Francis Jackson, and Charles Whipple—to commit more money and bodies to field work, especially in the West. "It seems to me," Pillsbury wrote Wendell Phillips in 1860, "that I, or some one, should go to the West, and, so to speak, *explore the field*. Some Conventions should be called at the most favorable points for bringing abolitionists together and making them better acquainted."[40] The Hovey Fund would, in fact, finance most of the field lecturing that occurred during the Civil War. With the largest fund of cash among all antislavery groups, the Hovey Committee also garnered significant influence. Even though Pillsbury and fellow radicals Abby Kelley Foster and Stephen Foster were excluded from the Executive Committee of the American Society, their position with the Hovey Fund gave them a stronger voice in the movement.

The financial aid provided by the Hovey Fund allowed Pillsbury to step up his lecturing efforts, especially after Lincoln's election. As the South began threatening secession and the Congress debated various Union-saving bills, many abolitionists followed Pillsbury's lead and worked diligently in the field pressuring politicians not to compromise with the South. Even as angry mobs desperate to avoid war interrupted Pillsbury's meetings, he lectured across the Northeast and West, reminding his audiences to stay focused on emancipation.[41] "The present condition of our National affairs does not affect our labors in the least, except to augment both their amount and importance," he declared at an antislavery celebration in Rochester, New York. "We must demand the abolition of slavery; and if we do not make the government obey, then we must abolish the government, and hang Abraham Lincoln as well as Jefferson Davis."[42] Pillsbury's uncompromising resolutions found enthusiastic support among the active contingent of radical abolitionists in Rochester. Local leader Amy Post labored diligently to guarantee a large audience for this important gathering.[43]

Even after the Southern states began to secede from the Union, mobilizing their armies and finally firing on Fort Sumter in April 1861, Pillsbury continued to advocate the importance of field lecturing. Many Garrisonians, however, believed that they should cease their agitation during the crisis and watch the " 'salvation of God' " at work.[44] Several societies, including the American Anti-Slavery Society, consequently canceled their annual meetings in 1861.[45] "In the existing circumstances of the country, and with a view to do nothing to divert public attention from the course which the U.S. government is now pursuing," the Executive Committee explained, "the Annual Meeting of this Society . . . [is] postponed."[46] Pillsbury fumed at these cancellations and the subsequent cessation of moral agitation. "The country is not yet half awake," he cried in a letter to the *Standard*. "Not a slave is to be rescued, not one fugitive sheltered, not one free colored man permitted to go up to battle. . . . [W]hat can a war, waged by such men, on such principles, achieve towards the 'salvation of God?' "[47]

Pillsbury also continued to condemn the Republican Party. He tried to convince his peers that war with the South did not mean that the North had suddenly become opposed to slavery, pointing to Lincoln's continued resistance to even small acts of emancipation. When General John C. Fremont declared martial law in Missouri, for example, and freed all the slaves of rebels in the state, Lincoln quickly revoked Fremont's order. Pillsbury used the president's subversion of General Fremont's proclamation as an example of his "cowardly submission to Southern and border slave state dictation."[48] He described the Lincoln administration as the "weakest" and "wickedest" in the history of the United States because it had the power to declare emancipation and it did nothing. He bitterly concluded, "I rejoice in defeat and disaster rather than in victory, because I do not believe the North is in any condition to improve any great success which may attend its arms."[49] This treasonous proclamation was precisely the kind of provocative rhetoric the radicals had always employed. Garrison, however, regretted Pillsbury's call for Northern defeat and instead cheered Lincoln's military victories. He focused on the encouraging signs, including Lincoln's actions in the South Carolina Sea Islands where several thousand fugitive slaves were under the protection of the North.

Pillsbury continued to warn his colleagues of the "danger of compromise" throughout the war.[50] Convinced that the spirit of moderation that seemed to permeate the Garrisonians was profoundly misguided, Pillsbury publicly accused his associates of "reposing on past laurels" and relaxing their standards.[51] "Until the Abolitionists restore themselves to their former integrity," he declared, "and demand Liberty instead of Lincoln, and Justice instead of Generals, and Repentance and Righteousness instead of Reconstruction . . . we shall continue to fail."[52] Central to his worries was the issue of how emancipation should be achieved. Many Garrisonians tried to stimulate abolitionist sentiment by insisting that emancipation would help the North to win the war.[53] This tactic proved successful; as military triumph and abolition became intertwined, the Northern public slowly began to embrace antislavery. And yet, according to Pillsbury, the victory was pyrrhic. Still strongly influenced by perfectionism, he refused to support the abolition of slavery as a military necessity, calling it "the most god-insulting doctrine every proclaimed."[54] Such a policy, he asserted, would not address the culpability of the North and the existence of racism across the nation. Emancipation had to come from moral, not military, necessity. Otherwise, the "humanity of the African race" would not be recognized and the nation would continue in its

Fig. 8. William Lloyd Garrison. Courtesy of the Trustees of the Boston Public Library.

sinful state. Perfectionism and racial equality demanded that all Americans recognize the sinfulness of discrimination as well as slavery, and repent of both. Garrison and many of his colleagues considered Pillsbury's uncompromising insistence on the moral foundation of emancipation ill-conceived and foolish.

Although some contemporaries dismissed this debate as merely a division "between the laughing and weeping philosophers," it represented a significant philosophical and strategic divide. Pillsbury and a few others adhered to a vision of the reformer as an agitator standing apart from society, committed to uncompromising standards of justice. In depicting the Republicans as "more dangerous" than the Democrats, for example, they clearly advocated an "all or nothing" perfectionist philosophy that rejected partial moral reform. Garrison, on the other hand, believed that the changing times required a more diplomatic and flexible leadership role for abolitionists. While Pillsbury's camp became more entrenched in radicalism, Garrison and others began to change their tactics in a distinctly more moderate direction.

The heated disagreements over philosophy and strategy that dominated Garrisonian meetings in the late 1850s and 1860s eventually spilled over into the abolitionists' private lives. As the debate became increasingly acrimonious, political differences became personal attacks. For example, after Garrison made light of a foreboding speech by Abby Kelley Foster at one gathering, hoping to "give a more cheerful tone to the meeting," Pillsbury rose and offered a dramatic "defense" of his field colleague.[55] This rebuttal astonished Garrison, who felt that Pillsbury's speech aimed "to excite for [Abby Kelley Foster] the deepest sympathy of the audience," while provoking "the most indignant feelings against" himself.[56] Pillsbury admitted that perhaps he was "all wrong" in his hasty rebuttal, but he was also shocked that his speech let "loose so many bolts and set them flying round my head."[57]

Still healing from this misunderstanding, Pillsbury was devastated when, a few months later, the *Standard* published Harriet Martineau's controversial editorial criticizing him for his "fretful, narrow spirit."[58] Urged by Oliver Johnson and Maria Weston Chapman, both members of the Boston elite, Martineau wrote a column accusing Pillsbury and other lecturers of obstructing the mission of abolitionists with their unnecessary "criticizing" and "censuring."[59] Although Pillsbury usually accepted the reprimands of his high-placed colleagues with a defensive humility, he now allowed his resentment to bubble to the surface. "I know how absurd it is for the like of me to attempt to stand up before such unequal odds," Pillsbury sullenly wrote. "With the Board [Executive Committee], with H[arriet] M[artineau] and almost everybody else against me my position must appear preposterous in the extreme." Still, he stubbornly concluded, "I . . . do not plead guilty to HM's charges!"[60] Although Pillsbury was encouraged by the public condemnation of Martineau's editorial by fellow lecturer Joseph Howland and his strongest Executive Committee ally, Wendell Phillips, tensions between the committee and the field workers continued to mount. When Oliver Johnson responded to a charge that the antislavery movement was too radical by passing the blame on to a few errant lecturers, Pillsbury fumed to Wendell Phillips: "We who are, and have long been lecturers, are too sensitive, no doubt. But when every fault, and blunder, and culpability, incident to the cause seems so wholly ours, it leaves our condition as unenviable as can well be conceived."[61]

Some of those who favored a more diplomatic approach to abolition even began to question Pillsbury's state of mind. After one of the New Hampshire rebel's lectures in 1862, Samuel May, Jr., wrote Richard Webb, expressing his concerns about Pillsbury's "fanaticism."

> We hold the Government, the parties, the churches, as ever, to their highest duty. But we hope not to part with our common sense (I had almost said our sanity), as I think we should, did we say with P. Pillsbury (and some others) that the present administration is the worst one we have ever had; 2. That Jeff. Davis would be preferable as a President to Abraham Lincoln; 3. That Emancipation would be a curse, if decreed as a political necessity, or as a war-measure, and should only be accepted or desired on the ground of repentance and absolute right.[62]

Other Garrisonians agreed with May's assessment of Pillsbury's eccentric positions (which May accurately summarized), especially after the stubborn radical's gloomy reaction to the emancipation of slaves in Washington, D.C. "When [Pillsbury] heard of the President's signing the Bill for Abolition in the District of Columbia," Samuel May, Jr., wrote Elizabeth Buffum Chace, "he said he dreaded to give way to any rejoicing, for he had noticed that any *good* thing in the government was quite sure to be followed by some extraordinary baseness!" May concluded, "P[illsbury] is . . . not in a quite healthy state of mind."[63]

Pillsbury recognized that some of his colleagues considered his course "somewhat erratic," and he diligently tried to dispel this notion.[64] Maintaining copious personal correspondence with leading Garrisonians, he slowly and doggedly worked to persuade his associates of the virtue of his position. He focused particularly on his old friend Wendell Phillips, a powerful Garrisonian and one of the most popular lyceum lecturers in the nation. Though Phillips had referred to Lincoln as the "slavehound of Illinois" prior to the 1860 election, he reversed himself with the onset of the war, supporting the Republican president.[65] By 1864, however, Phillips reversed himself again, agreeing with Pillsbury and criticizing Lincoln for his reluctance to declare full emancipation.[66] Pillsbury recognized the importance of this powerful and well-respected Bostonian's support, and he regularly praised his friend to all who would listen. "I sit at [Phillips's] feet, with profoundest respect," he wrote Charles Sumner.[67] Other Garrisonian leaders also understood the importance of Phillips's defection. In discussing the impact of the rebels on the movement, Samuel May, Jr., wrote to Richard Webb, "Wendell Phillips . . . is mainly to blame—because the sympathy and countenance he has given [Pillsbury and Foster] has magnified their self-importance and encouraged their petty plots."[68]

As the war dragged on, more Garrisonians followed Phillips's lead, and by 1864 a new coalition had developed among abolitionists. While Garrison continued to support the administration, former rivals of the Garrisonians like Gerrit Smith began to join the anti-Lincoln forces.[69] When General John C. Fremont decided to challenge Lincoln for the presidency, abolitionists including Wendell Phillips, Stephen Foster, and Frederick Douglass endorsed him. Fremont's controversial decision to free Missouri's slaves in 1861 had made him a star among abolitionists.[70] Pillsbury was thrilled by the new criticism of Lincoln, but he did not fully trust Fremont and hesitated to endorse his candidacy. After decades of denouncing all politicians as corrupt, he approached the party system with deep suspicion. When he received a special invitation to attend Fremont's nominating convention in Cleveland, Pillsbury asked his friend Wendell Phillips for advice. "Will it be too late to take the *back track*, when the Platform is made, if it is too weak to bear full grown men?" he inquired.[71] Pillsbury struggled over his decision to attend, but finally concluded that his experience and radicalism might have some influence. "I have a *feeling*," he explained to Phillips, "that these new-fledged-fowl, need old birds to teach them to fly." Pillsbury tried to radicalize the Fremont platform by making it more friendly to African Americans—calling for a strong endorsement of black suffrage and land for freed slaves—but he failed miserably. Even worse, he was attacked by some Boston leaders for his participation in the convention.[72] Oliver Johnson wrote an editorial in the *Standard* condemning the Fremont movement and denouncing Pillsbury for escorting the "unscrupulous and slippery" vice-presidential candidate, John Cochrane, to his chair.[73] Pillsbury was outraged at this accusation: "I never spoke *a monosyllable* to [Cochrane] in my life," he cried to Phillips, "and was not in the hall when he went to the chair."[74] His participation in the convention—motivated by an uncompromising opposition to Lincoln—resulted in moderate colleagues accusing him of hypocrisy and compromise! "I went to Cleveland at an expense of forty dollars, . . . made a radical speech, wrote three newspaper protests . . . and that is my connexion with the Fremont movement," he protested. "But behold what a cry my few remaining friends make of it!"[75] This first foray into the formal political process certainly reinforced his desire to remain outside party machinations.

Pillsbury's opposition to Lincoln and the Republicans was not merely a sign of his "hostility to authority" and his inflexible perfectionism, as his colleagues and some historians suggest.[76] Even as he adhered to his uncompromising philosophy, he sought viable strategies. His radicalism did not prevent him from developing a shrewd approach to political change. Pillsbury understood the position of the Garrisonian radicals as one of agitation from outside the political process. By constantly pressuring politicians and the public with their extreme demands, the Garrisonians hoped to make moderate change seem more acceptable. While Pillsbury certainly sought full and immediate emancipation, he recognized that partial and slow abolition was more likely. During the war he urged Garrisonians to advocate abolition for principled reasons, no matter that they considered this impractical. "Unless we demand abolition as a moral principle," he forthrightly asserted, "we shall never obtain it as a military necessity."[77] This rare acknowledgment of the practical nature of his position shows that Pillsbury understood the complex interplay of circumstances and the political implications of perfectionist activism.

Pillsbury pragmatically employed his role as an agitator from outside the political process in other ways as well. Over the decades he had witnessed Garrison's strategy of balancing public criticism with private coaxing, and he modeled his Civil War policies on this practice. He developed a talent for conveying gratitude and sympathy in his correspondence while simultaneously criticizing the recipient's course of action and suggesting alternative strategies more in keeping with his own political tactics.[78] In his correspondence with Charles Sumner, for example, one of the leading antislavery Republicans in the Congress, Pillsbury congratulated the senator when he took a firm radical position and yet always tried to push him toward a more uncompromising stand. "I long to see the day when you . . . will proclaim, and practice too, a Harper's Ferry Rebellion against the whole despotism of political union . . . with Slaveholders."[79] Even as he publicly disparaged Sumner in speeches and articles, Pillsbury continued to privately cajole the Republican. "I am more and more impressed with the importance of your labors, and rejoice at your noble persistence in support of the principles you enacted as the guide of your political life," Pillsbury wrote. "On you I think, more than on any other member of Congress, rests the grave and solemn responsibility of determining whether we shall come back to the laws of eternal right, and so secure a great national salvation."[80] He also cleverly appealed to Sumner's sense of manliness. He hailed the senator's participation in the repeal of the Fugitive Slave Law, for example, by praising his manhood: "Let me assure you of my high and admiring appreciation of the more than noble and *manly* part you have borne in the achievement," he wrote.[81]

Pillsbury also astutely employed popular expectations about masculinity to convince his audiences that slavery in fact weakened and emasculated the nation.[82] In an article entitled "The Hour Without the Man," written at the onset of the Civil War, Pillsbury asked his fellow citizens why the nation could not produce a *man* brave and strong enough to take the necessary action—that is, declare emancipation—to guarantee the nation's future. "Throughout the North slavery is the admitted cause of all our present calamity. . . . Where is the man, in State or Church, ready to assume the responsibility of drowning it forever and ever in the billows of a now wakening and righteous indignation?"[83] Also appealing directly to the young men of the North, Pillsbury associated manhood with civil disobedience, encouraging them to renounce the war and stay home until the government guaranteed emancipation: "Die . . . by the side of your mothers. Die in the arms of your sisters, wives, sweethearts—die martyrs, and get the burial of men, rather than go down there and die and be buried like dogs, in behalf of slavery."[84] Co-opting a common war image, Pillsbury employed the open arms of female loved ones not to entice men into some far-off battle in order to protect these women, but to persuade men to remain home, and thus protect the women by refusing to fight until justice (emancipation) was guaranteed.

Although Pillsbury discouraged young men from fighting until abolition became a central goal of the war, he did not entirely forsake the use of violence. In fact, long before the first shots were fired at Fort Sumter Pillsbury had developed a flexible, if not entirely consistent, position on violence that allowed him to balance his personal commitment to nonresistance with the bloodshed of the war. Throughout the 1850s, violence in the name of antislavery had occurred repeatedly—including fugitive slave rescues, attacks against proslavery Missourians in Kansas, and, of course, John Brown's raid—and abolitionists had differed in their response to these episodes. Stephen Foster and Lydia Maria Child sympathized with the use of violence to rescue fugitive slaves, though they declined to participate themselves. Gerrit Smith and Samuel May, on the other hand, set aside their peace principles and volunteered to help liberate fugitive slave Jerry McHenry from the Syracuse police. Wendell Phillips sent money to a rifle fund in Kansas even as he publicly decried violence, and Frederick Douglass, who had discouraged slave revolts in the 1840s, now supported physical resistance to the Fugitive Slave Act.[85] Many African-American abolitionists, who were more likely to experience physical opposition than their white colleagues, had long since advocated armed revolt as a method for achieving emancipation. Henry Highland Garnet and David Ruggles pointed to the American Revolution as an example of justified violence and called on abolitionists and slaves to "complete the revolution."[86] As the 1850s progressed, more and more white abolitionists concurred with Garnet and Ruggles and abandoned their (always ambivalent) commitment to nonviolence.[87] Nearly all the Garrisonians condoned John Brown's 1859 raid and some even helped to organize it.[88]

A founding member of the New England Non-Resistance Society, Pillsbury had long eschewed violence. "I . . . would not take the life of man, under any circumstances," he declared in 1847.[89] He, like many other nonresis-

tants, even declined to vote or take an oath to defend the Constitution because it empowered the U.S. government to declare war.[90] He remained a
committed nonresistant throughout the early 1850s. Even after several abolitionists were arrested for murder in attempting to free fugitive slave Anthony Burns, Pillsbury declared, "What a pity that any lover of Liberty and
of man must ever take in his hands the instruments of death. No good can
ever come of it." But, wavering, he added as an afterthought, "Better that
blood be shed on the other side."[91] By the late 1850s, Pillsbury began sym-
pathizing with and even encouraging those who chose to resort to violence.
"If I can excite among men who believe in violence the spirit of war, that I
shall do," he declared.[92] In 1857, he advised the Massachusetts Anti-Slavery
Society, "perhaps it is time for the society to change its position, and distinctly express sympathy with every method by which slaves seek emancipation."[93] With his African-American colleagues, Pillsbury called for the true
completion of the American Revolution. "The slaves should be encouraged
to rise and assert their liberty in the spirit of 1776," he proclaimed. "I believe . . . that the time for ballots has past, and the time for bullets has
come."[94] Such public statements led to his acquiring a reputation as an advocate of physical resistance. In 1858, John Brown wrote to his friend
Theodore Parker inquiring about Pillsbury's position on violence. "I have
heard that Parker Pillsbury and some others in your quarter hold out ideas
similar to those on which I act, but I have no personal acquaintance with
them."[95] Though Pillsbury and Brown never met, Pillsbury gave dozens of
well-attended lectures after Harpers Ferry strongly supporting "Old Os-
awatomie" and depicting him as a true patriot.[96]

Pillsbury, perhaps ingenuously, claimed that his advocacy of violence was
neither in contradiction with his earlier positions nor a change of heart. And
yet his position did change, probably as a result of his growing conviction
that Southerners would never willingly give up their slaves. This recognition
forced him to consider alternative paths for achieving emancipation, including physical resistance, and he began to find justification for violence where
none had existed before. Placing antislavery violence in a religious context,
he often repeated the maxim, "resistance to tyranny is obedience to God."[97]
He considered bloodshed to be God's righteous retribution against the nation because of its long acceptance of slavery. "I do not believe that ever yet
a nation wandered so far from the true spirit of freedom, justice and humanity, as we have gone, and then returned, without passing through that
metaphorical Red Sea."[98] Although Pillsbury would remain personally committed to nonviolence, he did not demand it of others. Once the war began,
Garrison and most other abolitionists concurred with Pillsbury, supporting
the war but refusing to shed blood themselves.[99]

Even as they agreed on a morally dubious and conveniently flexible definition of nonresistance, Garrison and Pillsbury continued to clash over other aspects of the antislavery movement. While North and South each struggled to gain momentum in the bloodiest war in American history, Garrison and others began working with freedman aid societies, arguing that it was time for abolitionists to change their tactics. "Iconoclasm has had its day," declared Pennsylvania abolitionist J. Miller McKim. "For the battering-ram we must substitute the hod and trowel. . . . We have passed through the *pulling-down* stage of our movement; the building-up—the constructive part—remains to be accomplished."[100] Others concurred and actively worked to force the government to accept black troops, gain funding for the Freedman's Bureau, and help freed slaves find work. Pillsbury did not participate in these activities, preferring to continue in his role as critic and perfectionist. Moreover, he decried the decline of abolitionist agitation, arguing that such a retreat undermined the possibility of emancipation. "True and faithful men in Congress say, that, as we do not press the abolition of slavery as in time past," he warned, "the conservative Republicans in Congress are taking courage in their conservatism therefrom."[101]

This debate over the appropriate role of abolitionists during the crisis of the war came to a head in 1865, once emancipation seemed a foregone conclusion. Lincoln had finally expanded the 1863 Emancipation Proclamation with the Thirteenth Amendment, which outlawed slavery throughout the Union. By this time, the Garrisonians had already split over a number of new issues, including universal suffrage and the disbanding of antislavery societies.[102] Wendell Phillips led the contingent which argued that suffrage was a necessary tool for participation in a democratic nation and should be guaranteed to freed slaves. He also contended that antislavery societies must agitate for this right. Garrison disagreed, suggesting that suffrage was a privilege to be earned. "The elective franchise is a conventional, not a natural right," he asserted in a public letter.[103] He also opposed the participation of antislavery societies in this debate, maintaining that other new organizations should be created to address the issue. Most abolitionists favored the position of Phillips over Garrison. Even though Garrison had become a highly esteemed national figure by the end of the war, his colleagues could not agree with his contention that antislavery societies no longer served a purpose.

At first Pillsbury struggled with his position on universal suffrage. He worried that uneducated freed slaves would use their ballots unwisely. However, he quickly came to support Phillips's position and advocate full equal rights for freed slaves. In fact, he saw the campaign for suffrage as the natural offspring of the abolition movement; the opposition it received from the public was a sure sign of its importance. "What immediate, unconditional emancipation was to the popular sentiment thirty years ago, [equal suffrage] is to-day," he declared.[104] Pillsbury also opposed Garrison's assertion that antislavery societies should be immediately dissolved once slavery was abolished. "Perhaps we may never make great use of our old Societies, in the coming work," he admitted to Phillips, "but it is mysterious to me, that we are so often, by Resolution and otherwise, invited to commit *suicide* upon them when there is hardly a spot as large as the *framed sheet of our Declaration of Sentiment*, in North or South, where a colored man can stand without being outraged in some way, on account of his color."[105] When Garrison offered a resolution to disband the American Anti-Slavery Society at its annual meeting in 1865, Pillsbury spoke in opposition: "Mr. Chairman, our work is not done," he cried. "At least *my* work is not done; nor will my work be done until the blackest man has at least all the rights which I myself enjoy."[106]

After the defeat of the disbandment resolution, Garrison and a contingent of the Executive Committee, including Samuel May, Jr., Edmund Quincy, Oliver Johnson, and Anne Warren Weston, left the society. The departure of these leading figures left vacant many important positions within the organization and their replacements included field-workers like Pillsbury and the Fosters, who gained more power in the movement than they had ever had before. Pillsbury took over as editor of the leading voice of the organization, the *Standard*. The old leaders, however, continued to disparage their replacements. "If Phillips, P[arker] P[illsbury] and the F[oster]'s, and their tribe, choose to wear the 'old clothes' of the American A. S. Society after they are thrown aside, let them," grumbled Oliver Johnson to Maria Weston Chapman. "It will be the old story over again of the ass in the lion's skin."[107] Samuel May, Jr., concurred with Johnson, complaining that the Society was now left in the hands of the "soured ones." He felt that Pillsbury's appointment was especially troublesome, "Now Parker Pillsbury is the Editor of the Standard—a man who said that we could hire any Irishman in the country for two dollars a day, to do all that Abraham Lincoln ever did."[108] Undisturbed by such criticisms, Pillsbury continued to advocate uncompromising agitation in the columns of the *Standard*.

Pillsbury's decision to champion full equal rights for blacks and to support the continuation of antislavery organizations reflected his commitment to the deep-rooted transformation of American society. His perfectionism demanded constant uncompromising agitation for true justice and equality throughout the nation, and he recognized that emancipation would not achieve this. As James McPherson points out, those abolitionists who advocated the continuation of antislavery societies were the very same ones who continued to participate in social reform following the war, including labor movements, which Garrison actively opposed. Those who wanted to disband the societies tended to be "essentially moderates in their social and political ideas."[109]

Pillsbury's support for continued antislavery agitation was also rooted in his self-identity. He had devoted most of his adult life to abolition and it provided him with both personal and spiritual meaning. After he had abandoned the ministry to join the movement, social agitation became his career. He earned his livelihood from abolition lecturing, he moved up the ranks as he would in a business, and all of his friends were involved in the movement. But his Garrisonian engagement offered him much more than a career. From early on, antislavery activism had provided Pillsbury with a religious outlet, a location for his evangelical and perfectionist yearnings. As noted in the earlier discussion of the roots of Pillsbury's radicalism, the reason abolition attracted so many young ministers to its ranks was because it gave life to their activist understanding of religion. Pillsbury wanted to change the world, to pave the way for the millennium, and his participation in abolition allowed him to work toward this goal. When Garrison suggested that the work of the movement was achieved, Pillsbury and many others probably felt abandoned. While Garrison had become a national hero, an adviser to Congress, and a popular public speaker, many other abolitionists could not transform their antislavery careers into other activities quite so easily. Because Pillsbury continued to agitate against the grain, denouncing Lincoln, demanding equal rights for black men and all women, and questioning the sincerity of the sudden antislavery position of the church, he did not receive the public acclaim of Garrison. Few lyceums requested his lecturing skills and the Congregational church did not welcome him back into the fold. Antislavery continued to provide Pillsbury with both a career and a spiritual center, and he was not about to declare the movement moribund.

As editor of the *National Anti-Slavery Standard*, Pillsbury now had a national forum from which to preach his perfectionist principles. His tenure as editor, however, proved brief and controversial. Unable to modify his agitational politics to suit his Boston colleagues, Pillsbury quickly found himself back in the field, alongside his grassroots allies.

8

Imperfect Reconstruction

"**I** work like a man who is both farmer and black-smith, and an abolitionist and temperance man to boot, and whose wife keeps no maid," boasted Pillsbury to his sister-in-law in 1869. "If you know any such, or ever did know such, and if they still live, and hold fast the true faith and form of Godliness, give them the everlasting respect, esteem and love of Parker Pillsbury."[1] Four years after the end of the Civil War, the sixty-year-old Pillsbury declined to join his colleagues in retirement and instead forged ahead full steam, thundering the Garrisonian motto, "no compromise!"

The end of the Civil War and the emancipation of slaves certainly delighted abolitionists and even forced a smile from the ever somber Parker Pillsbury. The smile did not last, however, because for Pillsbury the war continued. Over the next five years he would struggle to find a reform movement to replace Garrisonian antislavery and sustain the larger and more important battle for the millennium. This struggle proved more difficult than he expected. Gradually his old associates left the reform field, making the transition to retirement or establishing a respectable position within society and no longer agitating from the outside. Exasperated by the lack of support he received from other abolitionists, Pillsbury found himself involved in a lonely and difficult quest to find personal and political fulfillment.

At first Pillsbury was hopeful. The radicals dominated the antislavery movement after Garrison and his supporters left. Wendell Phillips steered the American Anti-Slavery Society Executive Committee, advised by Pillsbury's old partners Stephen Foster and Abby Kelley Foster. Pillsbury himself voiced the concerns of the movement as the new editor of the *National Anti-Slavery Standard*. These promising developments, however, soon gave way to disappointment and conflict. From the moment Pillsbury picked up his pen trouble brewed.

As the summer finally warmed the frozen hills of New Hampshire in early June 1865, Pillsbury once again packed his valise and left his family in Concord, this time to settle into the teeming New York metropolis where the *Standard* was published. As he adjusted to his new role in the movement, he could not help but compare his current situation to the last time he had edited an antislavery newspaper, two decades earlier. There were many similarities. He reluctantly accepted both positions during crisis periods, replacing disgruntled editors. N. P. Rogers had reproached him for agreeing to edit the *Herald of Freedom*; similarly, Oliver Johnson, the resigning editor of the *Standard*, now questioned his suitability for the position.[2] One important difference, however, was that Pillsbury had his experiences from the *Herald* to guide him with the *Standard*. He recognized that he had been appointed only because of "the absence of better material" and he was shrewd enough to seek help, immediately writing to Charles Sumner to ask for advice. "I hope to hold my new position very temporarily," he admitted to the Republican senator, "but should be glad and grateful for any private hint or suggestion you might send as to the best modes of procedures, or the most important points or parts to attack, watch or defend."[3] Knowing Sumner to be a relatively reliable abolitionist and a knowledgeable political source, Pillsbury hoped that his powerful friend might provide him with useful tips and inside information.

The political turmoil that characterized the year Pillsbury served as editor certainly kept both him and Sumner very busy. As the nation recovered from the assassination of Lincoln in April 1865, political leaders attempted to develop a Reconstruction policy that would satisfy both the North and the South. Andrew Johnson's solution was to pardon leading Southern rebels and readmit the seceding states without requiring black suffrage. This infuriated abolitionists, who had expected better from the new president. Although a few continued to remain hopeful, by the fall of 1865 the increasingly anti-black comments and policies of Johnson eventually alienated even the most optimistic abolitionists. Moreover, the failure of black suffrage amendments in several northern states further disappointed reformers, who increasingly turned to leading radical Republican congressmen as the only hope for a satisfactory Reconstruction policy.[4]

Both Wendell Phillips and Pillsbury used the unsigned editorial columns of the *Standard* to voice their frustrations with Andrew Johnson's Reconstruction policies. It is a simple task, however, to identify Pillsbury's work. Certainly his convoluted writing differed from the lucid style of the Harvard-educated Phillips, but it was Pillsbury's themes and uncompromising tone that more clearly distinguished him. Wholly committed to a Reconstruction policy that guaranteed absolute civil and political equality for freed slaves as well as Northern blacks, Pillsbury rejected all plans that fell short of his perfectionist standards. He waged a full-scale attack on the political and religious institutions of the nation, sparing no one in his attempt to arouse the conscience of the North.

Pillsbury denounced anti-black sentiment across the nation. He was convinced that because emancipation had resulted from military necessity instead of moral conviction, neither the North nor the South would recognize the civil and political rights of blacks. Most of his colleagues had derided his opposition to military-forced emancipation during the war and they continued to ignore his dire predictions. Pillsbury nonetheless warned that rebellious white Southerners were determined "to make their former victims more miserable than ever" and he also pointed to the hypocrisy of the North. "The 'purer repentance' just now demanded of the South," he pointed out, "has not yet been proclaimed or practiced at the North."[5] He wrote several editorials highlighting the persistence of racial discrimination in the North. "With suffrage in Vermont, the colored man is but a 'free nigger,' " cried Pillsbury. "Taxed in Rhode Island to support the public schools, the colored man cannot send his children to them. In Connecticut and New York his condition is not better."[6] After years of witnessing discrimination throughout the North, Pillsbury astutely recognized that equality would not be achieved until prejudice was eliminated in all sections of the nation. He deemed it his duty as an abolitionist to remind the nation, especially the North, that repentance would have to precede peace.

Neither Democrats nor Republicans satisfied Pillsbury's perfectionist demands. Most other abolitionists, however, strongly supported the Republicans and worked to influence the party's Reconstruction policies. Indeed, according to Ellen C. DuBois, Garrisonians became increasingly bound to the Republicans "as a kind of loyal opposition."[7] This position reflected the moderating trend that had begun a decade earlier. In the late 1850s, the Garrisonians hesitantly cooperated with the Republicans and by the end of the war a full-fledged partnership had been established. Pillsbury had bemoaned this development from the beginning and he continued to preach against the "compromise and concession" of the Republicans after the war. In one of his final editorials for the *Standard* he even suggested that the Democrats might be an improvement over the Republicans. While he had made many incendiary statements prior to the war, such comments proved even more controversial following the rebellion. Garrisonians probably found that Pillsbury's censorious editorials irked their new Republican associates and constrained their political influence.

Unconcerned with such matters, Pillsbury openly reprimanded his co-workers for their failure to critique and challenge the Republican party. Still adhering to his understanding of reform as agitation, he deplored the complacency of abolitionists. "When does the Executive Committee propose to begin to Execute?" he demanded of Wendell Phillips in the fall of 1865. "Do you not remember when we were alive and in the fields, how we used to chafe at the slow, or the *no* movement of the Committees and Editors, and all the stationary enginery of the great enterprise?" he desperately inquired. "We must not now complain if we too are sometimes charged with a little tendency to old fogyism." Pointing to the disappointing failure of radical Republicans, including Charles Sumner, to challenge Andrew Johnson's policies, Pillsbury demanded that Phillips "shock the dead . . . into animation" and force the nation to listen to the prophetic voice of the abolitionists yet again.[8]

Many abolitionists were engaged in helping ex-slaves adjust to emancipation through freedmen's aid societies, but Pillsbury continued to reject this kind of action as inappropriate for radical reformers, whose job it was to awaken the conscience of the nation. "We may give all our old clothes to the freedmen; we may bestow all our stores of food to feed them," he explained, but "unless we do justice and execute righteousness . . . we shall be scourged and plagued until our land become a desolation."[9] These ameliorative efforts—similar to the prewar policy of aid to fugitive slaves—merely provided salve for the wound instead of a cure for the disease. Abolitionists should be stumping the nation demanding equal rights, land redistribution, and the disempowerment of the Southern planter aristocracy, he argued. Prior to the 1866 annual meeting of the American Anti-Slavery Society he pleaded with his readers to continue their tradition of uncompromising leadership, asking, "*[W]ill the Abolitionists point the way?*"[10]

One important issue on which abolitionists failed to "point the way," according to Pillsbury, was the continued culpability of the church. In one of his earliest editorials he claimed that while the church had the power to solve all the problems of Reconstruction, it chose to do nothing. "What light is the American church casting on the question of reconstruction at this moment?" he rhetorically asked. "Numerically, she could control any election in the nation. Morally, she might wield the might of omnipotence. But she asks her rebel membership to return, with no penitence for the past, no promise for the future. Her policy," he dismally concluded, "is worse than that of President Johnson."[11] When Henry Ward Beecher, one of the North's most influential ministers, offered his support to the president and his policies, Pillsbury exploded. Beecher "no longer recognizes the negro as forming any part of the people of the South," he explained. "The South which we are to conciliate and reconstruct is the *white* South." Although Beecher supported equal rights and suffrage for the freed slaves, his endorsement of Johnson's Reconstruction plan contradicted these claims. Beecher was a perfect example of the loathsome "half-way reformers" Pillsbury deplored, and he warned his readers to beware of such false prophets: "It is the men who have the reputation of being Radicals and are not Radicals, who do us the most harm."[12]

Even though he managed to promulgate his favorite themes from the editorial chair, Pillsbury remained unhappy throughout his one-year tenure with the *Standard*. He especially disliked living in New York: "The superior deities have chained me to this rock and a thousand vultures prey upon me," he complained to a friend. "I do not sleep well, and New York cooking does sharpen my appetite."[13] Uncomfortable with big-city life, Pillsbury became lonely for the companionship he had enjoyed during his years as an itinerant agitator. "I keep office all day, after dinner I am too tired to go out, were there any person to see whom I know or care to know. Such is life, my life, in New York."[14] A visit from an old acquaintance raised his spirits but also painfully reminded him of the joyous old field lecturing days: "Our good friend Joel [McMillan] has kindly hunted me up in the jungle of humanity, faith, confusion, sin and death," he wrote his Western friends, "and we have talked up old times and told how we suffered and sacrificed for the slave."[15] Frustrated with the suffocating atmosphere of New York, Pillsbury yearned for the excitement of past exploits.

Editing proved less physically demanding than field work, but he nonetheless found the labor of writing enervating. Clearly more talented as an orator than an editor, Pillsbury never managed to write easily or comfortably. Moreover, he discovered that editorial work required consensus and compromise, two qualities he lacked. His idiosyncratic personality adapted well to the unpredictable and isolated existence of field lecturing, but not to the routine of journalism. When, in December 1865, he found himself accused by the Executive Committee of the American Anti-Slavery Society of "refusing to act as a committee with the associated Editor" and "writing him a most improper letter upon our relative duties," Pillsbury responded by resigning. "Every day has but intensified my consciousness of total unfitness for the work assigned me," he humbly admitted to the Executive Committee. "I only ask to be allowed quietly to lay down the heaviest, hardest trust of my whole life thus far, that I may resume a labor for which long and varied experience has in some small degree fitted me."[16]

Pillsbury's resignation—which the Executive Committee refused to accept—resulted only in part from disagreements with his associate editor George W. Smalley (who happened to be Wendell Phillips's son-in-law).[17] The committee had also begun to question the prudence of Pillsbury's editorials and they attempted to rein in the stubborn radical. Evidence of increasing tension had first emerged at an earlier board meeting at the beginning of December. Although the committee voted to allow Pillsbury to hire a bookkeeper and "errand boy," they also began to seize more control over the newspaper. They hired someone to increase circulation (at a salary of $300) and gave Smalley the power to secure advertising, perhaps stepping on Pillsbury's toes.[18] Although he reluctantly acceded to the expansion of Smalley's duties, he vehemently protested the other appointment, explaining to Phillips, "you could not have known all the facts, when the vote was passed."[19] Less than one week later Pillsbury again wrote to Phillips, revealing that their new employee had already left his job. "If he gave us one subscriber I did not know it. He cost us many."[20]

The next executive meeting in late December was the one that resulted in Pillsbury's resignation. At this gathering, board members voted to appoint a subcommittee to "inquire whether the rates paid for publication of the Standard are economical, and whether the Office for distribution is judiciously and economically arranged."[21] Pillsbury had assured Phillips prior to the meeting that "I have pushed the printing question to the utmost and do assure you we are now at the lowest market price, and it would be cruel and unjust to change."[22] The committee's decision to question Pillsbury infuriated him. The issue of printing costs, however, was secondary in this controversy. At this meeting, Pillsbury claimed that he found himself "almost in the position of a culprit, pleading to a grave charge of malfeasance," namely, "having written an article which would have endangered the Society's reputation, organ and very existence even, had it not been snatched from the press, by more competent hands."[23] Pillsbury's sarcastic summary of the Executive Committee's accusations certainly reveal his frustrations with their tightening control over the paper. It also highlights the committee's increasing disapproval of Pillsbury's editorials. Nonetheless, the board refused to accept his resignation and voted to remind Pillsbury that he "is entitled to speak the average sentiment of the Society, and that he is requested to remember that it is an organ of the Society and not the exponent of his individual opinions."[24]

Probably feeling pressured by his conscience to fulfill his duty to the exslave, Pillsbury continued as editor of the *Standard* for the next five months, but controversy continued. During Pillsbury's brief absence from the paper in late December (when he tried to resign), Wendell Phillips printed a letter from Elizabeth Cady Stanton that raised the issue of women's suffrage. In this letter she vehemently rejected the abolitionist argument that black male suffrage take precedence over women's suffrage. Arguing that " 'Sambo' " would probably oppose women's suffrage once he got the vote, Stanton concluded, "Would it not be wiser to keep our lamps trimmed and burning, and when the Constitutional door is open, avail ourselves of the strong arm and blue uniform of the black soldier to walk in by his side?"[25] Phillips responded with an editorial reasserting the primacy of black male suffrage. "We cannot agree that the enfranchisement of women and the enfranchisement of the blacks stand on the same ground, or are entitled to equal effort at this moment," he pronounced. "Causes have their crises. That of the negro has come; that of the woman's rights movement has not come."[26] Pillsbury, who supported Stanton, immediately wrote to his feminist allies to distance himself from the Phillips editorial. "The comments on Mrs. Stanton's letter in the *Standard* were not mine," he assured Elizabeth Buffum Chace. "I had resigned my editorial post, and was in New Hampshire."[27]

Clearly uncomfortable with the official editorial policy of the paper toward women's suffrage, Pillsbury continued to criticize the Republicans and promote universal suffrage in the columns of the *Standard*, ignoring the directive of the Executive Committee that he "speak the average sentiment" of the society. In late April 1866, Pillsbury penned an editorial reprimanding Charles Sumner and denouncing the newly introduced Fourteenth Amendment, which he believed to be blatantly designed "to preserve the party in power." He concluded, "The rights of the negro, the rights of woman, are to be put in greater peril than ever to achieve that object."[28] This editorial not only castigated Republicans, it also put women's suffrage on equal ground with black male suffrage; it proved to be the last straw. Within a few weeks the Executive Committee voted to appoint Aaron M. Powell the new editor of the *Standard* and reassigned Pillsbury to the position of general agent. He learned of these changes when the secretary of the society notified him in a letter that Powell was to be the new editor. "I *infer* that I am no longer Editor," Pillsbury angrily responded.[29] In one of Powell's first editorials he clearly established the *Standard's* primary concern with black male suffrage: "The special mission of THE STANDARD . . . is . . . to promote and secure the elevation and equal enfranchisement of its four millions of colored clients." Not wanting to alienate women's suffragists, however, Powell concluded, "We recognize, however, in the Equal Rights movement a kindred purpose, and extend to it the right hand of fellowship, and hearty encouragement."[30]

Susan B. Anthony later wrote that Pillsbury resigned from the *Standard* because "he could not in conscience accept a salary . . . as editor of the Standard for another year unless it should advocate woman's claims equally with those of the negro."[31] Differences over women's suffrage certainly helped to instigate Pillsbury's departure, but there is no evidence to support Anthony's claim that this was the sole issue of contention, or that he voluntarily resigned. It is possible that Pillsbury's earlier letter to Elizabeth Buffum Chace in which he explained that he had resigned from the *Standard* and therefore was not responsible for the critical reply to Stanton's letter, was misinterpreted to mean that he had resigned because of that editorial. In any case, Pillsbury's uncompromising position on a number of issues, including suffrage, led to his conflict with the Executive Committee and his dismissal. Unable to moderate his "individual opinions" and speak with the voice of the "average" abolitionist, Pillsbury was relieved of his duties. But he was eager to escape the constrictions of the *Standard* editorship, anyway. Almost immediately upon leaving the *Standard* he began working with the American Equal Rights Association, lecturing in support of equal suffrage irrespective of sex or race.

Before returning to the "field of moral conflict," Pillsbury retreated to the familiar and hospitable landscape of the West. Hoping to visit his old friends and "rest a little," he traveled to Ohio, Michigan, Illinois, and Iowa.[32] Unable to avoid the podium when the opportunity arose, however, he found himself lecturing as well as working with local radicals throughout his journey. Writing to Gerrit Smith from Freeport, Illinois, Pillsbury asked his old friend to send a pamphlet to a local woman who "dares to stand alone in her opinions, confronting the Sectarian hydra of this large prairie town."[33] Stirring up like-minded people wherever he went, Pillsbury managed to maintain a strong presence in the reform movement. During his return trip to the East he arranged to speak in communities all the way to New York, with "more calls by far to lecture than could be accepted."[34] Back in the field, Pillsbury felt the excitement of the old days for the first time since the war.

His enthusiasm for women's rights was certainly nothing new. Since the beginning of his tenure in the abolition movement Pillsbury had vocally championed women's equal access to education, employment, and suffrage. He attended women's rights conventions and worked with the movement's leaders, including Lucy Stone, Lucretia Mott, Anthony, and Stanton. He demanded that black women be admitted to feminist organizations and he openly confronted racism in the movement. He even advocated women's empowerment in the home, an area that many abolitionists preferred to ignore. Calling for liberal divorce laws and more egalitarian child custody rules, Pillsbury developed a well-rounded and uncompromising women's rights agenda. His decision to transfer his energy to the newly developed

American Equal Rights Association, therefore, was a natural and comfortable one.

Created in May 1866, the same month Pillsbury left the *Standard*, the Equal Rights Association was designed to bring together abolitionists and women's rights activists through the common goal of universal suffrage. Many women's suffragists had become frustrated in the year following the end of the war as they saw black male suffrage claim the national political limelight. Hoping to reestablish the old Garrisonian commitment to all radical reform causes, women's rights leaders Lucy Stone and Susan B. Anthony pleaded with the American Anti-Slavery Society in January 1866 to unite with the women's movement. Wendell Phillips, however, was convinced that women's suffrage would discredit black male suffrage and he used his formidable influence to prevent the merger. Unwavering, the women decided to initiate the unification on their own, establishing the American Equal Rights Association.[35] Pillsbury fully supported this effort because it seemed to embody the uncompromising spirit of the early Garrisonians. Comparing the anniversary of the Equal Rights Association to the antislavery gatherings of twenty years past, Pillsbury confidently declared, "The Equal Rights Association stands where then stood the anti-slavery host."[36]

In the summer of 1866, Pillsbury buoyantly resumed his position in the field, hoping he would be able to rely on the old abolition networks to attract support for the new organization. "What would you think of a meeting in Portsmouth on the question of Equal Suffrage and citizenship without distinction of sex or complexion?" he inquired of former abolitionist Benjamin Cheever in June 1867. "I am holding such at present in this state on Sundays . . . and generally all our friends and some others are interested."[37] Emphasizing what he considered widespread support for universal suffrage among abolitionists, Pillsbury attempted to entice his former colleagues by connecting their antislavery background to the movement for universal suffrage. "To the colored man's claim for suffrage, I now add also the claim of woman; since everywhere one helps the other," he explained to Elizabeth Buffum Chace. "Perhaps I should not trouble you, and I would not, only that I trust in this subject we have a common interest."[38]

Not all abolitionists agreed, however, that "one helps the other." More than a year after the inauguration of the Equal Rights Association, leading abolitionists still refused to merge the two causes, and the universal suffrage campaign weakened. In late 1866 and early 1867, the Equal Rights Association waged a campaign in New York to remove the word "male" from the state constitution and to eliminate the property qualification for black male voters. Pillsbury, Anthony, and many other Equal Rights workers traversed New York gathering signatures for petitions and lobbying voters before the

June 1867 constitutional convention. Although the *Standard* published notices about Equal Rights meetings and even a few sympathetic editorials, support from abolitionists was inadequate.[39] Wholly concerned with black male suffrage, abolitionists devoted little time to women's suffrage.[40] Predictably, the Equal Rights Association failed to influence the New York constitutional convention and they lost both battles.

Angered by abolitionists' neglect of women's suffrage, Pillsbury and his longtime radical partner Stephen Foster forced their former allies to confront the issue of universal suffrage during the May 1867 anniversary of the New England Anti-Slavery Society. Pillsbury urged his fellow reformers to pass a resolution that recognized the equal natural right of all women and black men to enfranchisement. "It is time we had done with this trifling," he cried. "The right of suffrage, if it came from God, came for woman as well as man."[41] Phillips, skillfully avoiding the conflict, argued that the antislavery platform was not the appropriate place to call for women's suffrage. "All we have to do with reconstruction has reference to the negro's interest in it, nothing else," he maintained.[42] The moderate call of Phillips for "common sense and conciliation" was heeded and the radicals were defeated by a "large majority."[43]

Undaunted by this setback, the Equal Rights Association headed west, to Kansas, where both women's and black male suffrage would be voted on in the November election. While Pillsbury stayed behind to nurse a sick brother-in-law and run the Equal Rights office in New York, Lucy Stone, Henry Blackwell, Anthony, and Stanton all spent several months holding meetings and giving speeches throughout Kansas.[44] Despite the pleas of the suffragists, prominent male abolitionists, including Wendell Phillips and Frederick Douglass, refused to join the Western campaign. Probably realizing that Kansas Republicans would endorse only the black male suffrage referendum, they avoided the inevitable conflict with feminists. When the Republicans not only failed to support women's suffrage but began openly attacking it, Stanton and Anthony desperately appealed to the Democrats for support, a move that infuriated abolitionists and many of their own colleagues. Officially opposed to equal rights for blacks, the Democratic Party was clearly using women's suffrage as a wedge to divide and defeat Republicans. Democratic support for the cause proved predictably ephemeral. Stanton and Anthony further alienated abolitionists when they began collaborating with George Francis Train, an openly racist Democrat who supported women's rights. Train's exuberance, combined with his generous financial and political patronage, made him impossible to resist. Despite his tendency to denigrate blacks as he lauded white women, Stanton and Anthony engaged in a well-publicized lecture tour with Train across Kansas. Driven to drastic measures as a result of the indifference of abolitionists and the opposition of Republicans, Stanton and Anthony found allies wherever they could, even if these new supporters meant abandoning their commitment to racial equality.[45]

Abolitionists accused Train of causing the defeat of both referenda in Kansas, but Stanton and Anthony blamed the apathy of abolitionists and the opposition of Republicans.[46] While everyone was busy pointing fingers, the Equal Rights Association experienced a mortal wound. Lucy Stone and Henry Blackwell, important leaders of the association, attacked Stanton and Anthony for their association with Train. Branding him a "lunatic," Stone complained, "his presence as an advocate of woman suffrage [is] enough to condemn it in the minds of all persons not already convinced."[47] This divide in leadership caused the Equal Rights Association to quickly lose its already limited support. Moreover, the death of the organization marked the decline of efforts to combine black men's suffrage with women's suffrage. The final nail in the coffin came when Stanton and Anthony accepted George Train's offer to fund a new women's rights paper.

Pillsbury remained on the east coast throughout the costly Kansas campaign, safely protected from this vituperative battle. He did not maintain his neutrality for long, however. By January 1868, he found himself back in New York editing another newspaper, this time working with Stanton and Anthony on *The Revolution*.

In the few months before he returned to New York, Pillsbury had become frustrated. The Equal Rights Association was unable to pay him for his services as either lecturer or secretary.[48] Moreover, the continued refusal of abolitionists to support women's rights confused and angered him. Even his trusted friend Wendell Phillips seemed more interested in victory at any cost than in moral integrity. In November 1867, he returned home to Concord feeling lonely, but determined to continue following his convictions. He immediately began working independently for universal suffrage, relying on his meager investments and small contributions from wealthy friends for support.[49] "I am alone, and can only *work*," he wrote Gerrit Smith. "Were there more men like yourself ready to toss me the few needed Greenbacks, now and then, I could do something at least for a beginning."[50] A one-man reforming tornado, Pillsbury scattered radical pamphlets and private correspondence across the North. This "sharp shooting," as he called it, was exhausting work that yielded limited rewards. "I write with extreme labor, and slowness too. But work I must."[51] Convinced that "never more than now were the true prophets and evangelists needed," Pillsbury determinedly penned instructive dispatches to friends, politicians, and newspapers, hoping to attract more support for the cause.[52]

This desire for meaningful work, combined with his growing alienation from other abolitionists, certainly influenced Pillsbury to accept Susan Anthony's offer to co-edit *The Revolution*. His home life, however, also pushed him toward New York. By the late 1860s, Pillsbury had become uncomfortable remaining in Concord for more than a few months at a time. His desire for the nomadic lifestyle would quickly overwhelm him, and his family seemed to function quite well without him. Sarah Pillsbury had learned to accept her husband's absence and had created a life of her own. Always busy with friends, family, and boarders, she singlehandedly maintained a thriving household. Although their marriage remained cordial, Sarah and Parker seemed more comfortable exchanging brief letters than living together. "The harmonies of a divine home, are held in reserve to me," he admitted to his western friends. "So I board. Have in a sense always boarded. It is desolation, it is orphanage . . . but I am now used to it."[53] Pillsbury tried to remain linked to his family through regular correspondence as well as occasional visits from his daughter, Helen. During one of Helen's extended stays with Parker in New York she wrote to Sarah describing her adventures as she explored the city and met her father's famous friends, including Henry Ward Beecher and Theodore Tilton. Perhaps Sarah was pleasantly reminded of her own early travels with Parker as she read her daughter's boisterous correspondence. She missed Helen, however, and must have felt disappointed when her daughter concluded by explaining that she did not know when she would return home: "Father is really quite desirous to keep me as long as possible."[54]

In addition to offering an avenue of escape from Concord, *The Revolution* also enticed Pillsbury because it provided him with a platform to promulgate his perfectionist creed. One of the most innovative women's rights journals ever published in the United States, *The Revolution* did more than advocate women's suffrage, it offered an unsparing critique of women's oppression.[55] The editors addressed everything from woman's political disempowerment to her subordination within marriage. They highlighted and denounced the exploitation of working women and the exclusion of women from the professions. They told the long-lost stories of courageous women in history and they published the writings of feminist authors like Mary Wollstonecraft. Pillsbury thus found himself working with two colleagues whose ideas and strategies proved as uncompromising as his own. Even when the editors disagreed, they publicly aired their differences and allowed the readers to decide for themselves.[56] Unlike the *Standard*, where editorials were subject to the approval of the American Anti-Slavery Society's Executive Committee, *The Revolution* allowed its editors free rein.

Pillsbury immediately took advantage of this open-minded environment and blasted political and religious institutions, locating in them the source of all the nation's problems, including women's oppression. Pointing to the general lack of ethics among politicians, he argued that both Democrats and Republicans sought personal gain from office. "Birds of prey, they snuff the carcass from afar."[57] Neither party would consider expanding suffrage until this suited its purposes. "Both political parties sue for the votes of the males wherever they can be turned to party account," he cynically recounted, "but the women still drink the sorrowful sacraments of cruel proscription."[58] The church, with its long tradition of persecuting outspoken women, was equally guilty, according to Pillsbury. "Woman's first mishap in Eden has always been against her," he explained in an editorial denouncing the history of witchcraft accusations in the church. "Many thousands of poor, old innocents, mostly women, suffered violent and terrible deaths through this grim and bloody superstition."[59] With this history, it should be no surprise, he reasoned, that denominations like the Presbyterians refused to allow women to vote on church matters, despite the fact that they outnumbered men in the church. "Presbyterian priesthood virtually hold all the women of their charge in absolute spiritual despotism."[60] Just as religion and politics had opposed emancipation until it became expedient, these institutions remained ignorant of the need for women's enfranchisement because it did not benefit them.

Despite the perfectionist opportunities his work with Stanton and Anthony afforded him, Pillsbury's decision to work for a paper financed by George Train cost him dearly. During his two years working for *The Revolution* he scarcely spoke with any of his old abolitionist comrades.[61] Samuel May, Jr., could barely believe that Pillsbury had decided to "take up that disgusting blackguard Geo[rge] F. Train as a representative and leader in Woman's Rights and the 'New Revolution'! What a fall! What a prostitution of a noble idea and cause!"[62] Oliver Johnson sneered at Pillsbury's women's rights activism, concluding, "The mock heroism of these doughty knights of reform is to me simply ludicrous."[63] Although he felt deeply the disapproval of his colleagues, Pillsbury did not regret his decision. "It is more than kind and friendly in you still to remember me in my exile and low estate," he sullenly wrote Ellen Wright Garrison in 1869. "My Boston correspondence has long since ceased. It may be fault of my own, but I could not help it. I saw an opportunity to strike a blow for woman, and to resist the conviction I felt, was not possible."[64]

Pillsbury's involvement with Train, though limited and reluctant, offended his old friends for several reasons. For those working closely with the Republicans it was an embarrassing disruption that endangered their influence within the party. Although most abolitionists remained willing to criticize the Republicans, they never considered working with the Democrats. Pillsbury's open association with Train offered powerful ammunition for the Democrats, who could argue that leading abolitionists had abandoned the Republicans. By the late 1860s, abolitionists had established an esteemed position in Northern society and their opinion carried some weight.[65] As they attempted to push the Republicans to enfranchise black men, abolitionists probably feared that Pillsbury's involvement with Train would distract the Republicans and derail their efforts.

Train's anti-black sentiments also fueled the radicals' anger with Pillsbury. How could a veteran Garrisonian abolitionist write for a paper funded by an open bigot? Train persistently ridiculed and stereotyped black men in his speeches supporting women's suffrage. Certainly this represented a betrayal of the egalitarian spirit of the abolition movement. "I would as soon have looked to see the leopard change its spots, as to see . . . *Parker Pillsbury* hand in glove with George Francis Train and the old pro-slavery leagues," cried abolitionist Aurora C. Phelps.[66]

Pillsbury's critics had other reasons, on the surface, to question his continuing commitment to the spirit of the abolition movement. By 1868, he had reversed his position on educational requirements for suffrage, now vocally endorsing literacy tests for all potential voters.[67] Pillsbury must have been aware that most abolitionists believed educational qualifications would be used by white Southerners as a tool to disenfranchise freed slaves. And yet in an early editorial for *The Revolution* he asserted that the increase in uneducated voters resulting from "emancipation and emigration" would lead to further decline in "national decency."[68] The only way to avoid this catastrophe, he argued, was an educational qualification for suffrage, to be initiated in 1872, thus allowing freed slaves time to learn to read.[69] Other abolitionists, however, revealed the practical costs of educational qualifications. In a letter to the New York *Tribune*, abolitionist Thomas Wentworth Higginson ridiculed the "soap and sanctity" of Pillsbury's call for educated suffrage, arguing that the practical need of freed slaves for a political voice outweighed all other concerns.[70]

Abolitionists also objected to some of the arguments Pillsbury used to promote women's suffrage in the columns of *The Revolution*. When feminists in the antebellum period had sometimes succumbed to racism, Pillsbury had spoken out against this tendency.[71] After the war, however, he occasionally employed racist and nativist stereotypes to advance women's rights, depicting blacks and immigrants as shiftless and unpredictable.[72] "I would rather see suffrage in the hands of the Lydia Maria Childs of the North, for the salvation of the country, than in the hands of those poor men at the South."[73] Convinced that slavery had demoralized blacks, Pillsbury trusted middle-class white women, rather than irresponsible black men, with the vote. Immigrant men, whom Pillsbury stereotyped as poor and servile, were also less deserving than middle-class women. Women's suffrage, he mockingly pointed out, "will make educated, cultivated, refined, loyal, tax-paying, government-obeying woman equal to the servants who groom her horses, and scour the pots and pans of her kitchen."[74] Following the lead of Anthony and Stanton, Pillsbury constructed a vision of the suffrage debate that pitted respectable middle-class white women against ignorant immigrant and black men.[75]

Already dismayed by Pillsbury's seeming betrayal of principles, his former colleagues were further infuriated by a few controversial editorials he published in 1869. During a brief trip to South Carolina, where he visited with his brother Gilbert, the federally appointed mayor of Charleston, Pillsbury wrote a letter to *The Revolution* describing his sense of the problems facing freed slaves. "The present is not the time to agitate [suffrage] here in the South," he advised.[76] Freed slaves needed the benefit of "moral culture and domestic and social" training, as well as food and decent housing, much more than the vote. This letter, which also suggested that intemperance, immorality, and infanticide predominated among freed slaves, outraged abolitionists and thrilled Democrats, and both groups immediately responded to Pillsbury's depiction of ex-slaves. While some Democrats employed Pillsbury's letter as evidence of black inferiority, abolitionists condemned it as "wantonly false" and based on a "hasty glance" at the South.[77] Even Gilbert, who had lived in the South for five years, refuted him in a public letter, arguing that freed slaves had made great progress.[78]

Surprised by the amount of attention his letter received, Pillsbury tried to clarify his position by emphasizing that slavery was the source of the degeneracy he found among free blacks. "The Democratic journals . . . profess to regard me as . . . regretting my life-long labors in [slaves'] behalf," he wrote. Emphatically denying these accusations, Pillsbury made clear that witnessing the results of slavery had in fact deeply reinforced his commitment to abolition and his opposition to political parties and religion, the institutions that had supported slavery. "New language must be invented before my loathing of the democracy and religion that have thus enslaved, degraded, brutalized them, yea, *beastialized* [*sic*] myriads of them, can be half expressed."[79]

Despite the angry opposition of his former friends, Pillsbury was convinced that his decision to work for *The Revolution*, his support for educated

suffrage, and his solutions to the problems facing freed slaves were all principled and pragmatic. A close look at Pillsbury's understanding of reform
helps to make sense of this conviction. Since his first antislavery lecturing
tours in the early 1840s, Pillsbury was convinced that "halfway reformers"
who claimed to be abolitionists but failed to fully embrace the uncompromising positions of the Garrisonians were in fact destroying the movement
from within, poisoning the perfectionist environment created by the radicals. He often expressed his preference for the open sinfulness of slaveholders over the deceptive and slippery righteousness of halfway reformers. At
least slaveholders, he insisted, honestly admitted their true position, no matter how reprehensible it might be. Pillsbury's willingness to work with the
openly prejudiced George Train makes sense within this context. Although
he opposed Train's position toward blacks, he could at least respect the
Democrat's forthrightness. This made it easier for Pillsbury to ignore Train's
racism and focus on his wholehearted support for (white) women's suffrage.
His conviction that abolitionists themselves had become halfway reformers
also helped him to tolerate Train. With no "true" reformers remaining, to
whom could he turn? Better the enemy you know than the friend you distrust.

Pillsbury's endorsement of educated suffrage also reflects his vision of reform, particularly the moral values he considered so central to the millennium. He believed that voting was a sacred responsibility— "a power whose
end may be death on the battlefield, in prison, or by the halter."[80] This important responsibility for governing others was based on certain essential requirements, including the "capacity for self-government."[81] He assumed that
education would inculcate this self-governing ability in new voters, as well as
the principles of temperance and honesty—values he believed to be lacking
in freed slaves and immigrants through no fault of their own. Educational requirements, therefore, would produce an "enlightened citizenship" and a
civilized government. Genuinely convinced that the ability to read and write
would result in improved morals and a more perfect society, Pillsbury had no
desire to see blacks disenfranchised.

This concern with such issues as temperance and cleanliness also influenced Pillsbury's depiction of freed slaves in the South. Predisposed as he
was to find that slavery had degraded blacks, this was exactly what he did
find. And because he considered the moral state of ex-slaves so much more
important than their political rights, he called for moral education instead of
suffrage. Freedmen and freedwomen needed training in housekeeping,
cleanliness, diet, temperance, and especially self-control. As they learned
these important values, Pillsbury argued, then they would be prepared for
political representation.

Pillsbury's colleagues were quick to point out the flaws in his arguments. While they could sympathize with his good intentions, reformers recognized their devastating practical implications. Agreeing to work with Train was the epitomy of compromise, they protested, not a valiant effort to avoid halfway reform. Educated suffrage might produce an "enlightened citizenship," but it would also likely disfranchise freed slaves as well as new immigrants. And what good were housekeeping skills and dietary knowledge without a home to live in nor food to eat?—a scenario guaranteed if ex-slaves were politically disempowered.

Throughout Pillsbury's first year editing *The Revolution* he certainly attracted the ire of most abolitionists. In 1869, however, Congress passed the Fifteenth Amendment and tensions between Pillsbury and his old friends intensified. With each side claiming to be carrying on the traditions of the abolition movement, the stakes in this conflict became—personally and politically—very high.

Abolitionists played an important role in pressuring the Republicans to pass the Fifteenth Amendment, which barred states from denying the vote to citizens on the basis of race, color, or previous condition. Although the amendment failed to include provisions to prevent white Southerners from developing educational and property qualifications, abolitionists considered it a great achievement. Pillsbury, Stanton, and Anthony, on the other hand, decried the amendment because it failed to include women, and *The Revolution* quickly became dedicated to its defeat.

Not all women's suffragists concurred with Stanton, Anthony, and Pillsbury. A strong contingent of women's rights advocates, in fact, supported the Fifteenth Amendment in the hope that Republicans would eventually reward them with a women's suffrage amendment. Led by Lucy Stone and her husband, Henry Blackwell, these reformers expressed disappointment with some of the policies of Republicans, but they also believed that the party was their only hope for eventual success. In order to counter the anti-Republican message of *The Revolution*, Stone and Blackwell created the New England Woman Suffrage Association in November 1868. Working at the state level to avoid competing with black male suffrage, which dominated the federal level, this group attracted the support of leading Republicans and abolitionists.[82]

Delighted with the cooperative attitude of the New England group, abolitionists expressed dismay at the stubborn opposition of *The Revolution*. Holding that the Fifteenth Amendment represented the final achievement of the antislavery movement, Wendell Phillips and the American Anti-Slavery Society insisted that woman's suffragists wait patiently for their turn. The

Fig. 9. Wendell Phillips. From Wendell Phillips Garrison and Francis Jackson Garrison, *William Lloyd Garrison, 1805–1879: The Story of His Life Told by His Children* (Boston, 1894).

editors of *The Revolution* doggedly refused to accommodate their opponents and found themselves accused of irresponsible greediness. "The Women's Rights movement is essentially a selfish one," declared Phillips, "not disinterested as the Anti-Slavery cause was. It is women contending for their own rights; the Abolitionists toiled for the rights of others." Ignoring the contingent of male advocates for women's suffrage, including Pillsbury, Phillips continued, "Their lack of breadth does not surprise us. . . . A little experience and a more profound consideration will, we believe, lift them to the level of a full faith in principles."[83] Phillips himself knew this attack was un-

founded. Anthony, Stanton, and Pillsbury could all point to decades of reform experience, including lecturing, writing, and fund-raising. The commitment and self-sacrifice of Pillsbury and Anthony were unquestionable;
both scraped together a living from the meager earnings they gathered at
public lectures and from antislavery agencies. Phillips's unjust denunciation
of the opponents of the Fifteenth Amendment reflected his frustration with
the unrelenting attacks of Pillsbury, Stanton, and Anthony and his own understanding of the momentousness of black male suffrage. He recognized
the potentially devastating effect of opposing the radical Republicans during
this time of political change and realignment. The enfranchisement of black
men represented the staggering possibility of achieving the objectives of a
movement that for thirty years had been ridiculed and violently attacked by
the general public as well as the political and religious leadership of the nation. Abolitionists, he believed, had to guarantee this victory before concerning themselves with secondary issues.

Phillips's unusually personal assault on the character of women's rights activists suggests also a conservative understanding of gender. In accusing feminists of "selfishness" he relied on traditional ideas about women's character,
including sacrifice, domesticity, and virtue. Stanton and Anthony abandoned
all pretext of such "feminine" characteristics when they vigorously demanded their own rights and dared to question Phillips. Moreover, as his biographer James Stewart argues, Phillips believed that "women already possessed enormous social influence . . . through the home, the church, and the
benevolent association."[84] Although he recognized that society "curtailed
their political activities and economic self-determination," Phillips downplayed women's subjugation.[85] In fact, Phillips and many other radical abolitionists advocated a traditional division of labor between men and women,
reflecting the "natural" talents and inclinations of each. Women's participation in the abolitionist movement had proved acceptable because they virtu-
ously fought on behalf of a downtrodden group, including their "sisters"
who were deprived of their "femininity" in slavery.[86] The women's rights
movement, on the other hand, directly challenged these "natural" gender
roles by calling for women's economic independence, political participation,
and legal empowerment within marriage.

While assumptions about gender certainly mingled in the debate over the
Fifteenth Amendment, so too did ideas about the meaning of reform. All of
the Garrisonians who remained active in the postwar period were certain of
their faithfulness to the spirit of the antislavery movement. But times had
changed and many developed different strategies for achieving their goals.
As abolitionists began to work more within the political system and their
voices were legitimized, the uncompromising tactics of the past seemed un-

productive. Phillips, for example, helped to end the stalemate in Congress over the Fifteenth Amendment by accusing the Senate of being too radical! The version of the Fifteenth Amendment passed by the Senate had included prohibitions of educational, property, and nativity qualifications. Phillips deplored the Senate's "total forgetfulness of the commonest political prudence" and urged them to pass the more conservative House version.[87] His timely intervention proved critical in breaking the deadlock.

Pillsbury did not see any need for such compromises. Still guided by perfectionism, he deplored the changing tactics he witnessed among his coworkers. Deeply influenced by what he considered to be the failures of the Civil War, Pillsbury continued to value the principles that guided reform as much as its goals. Throughout the war he had pressed for nationwide recognition of slavery as sin, arguing that the war represented God's punishment for this immoral institution. Absolution could come only through repentance and emancipation. He had beseeched his fellow citizens to embrace abolition as a moral requirement and not a military necessity. The principle behind emancipation, therefore, remained as important as the objective itself. Because the nation had accepted an unprincipled reason for guaranteeing emancipation, he contended, freedom for blacks was false and shallow.

Most abolitionists had rejected this argument during the war, and they maintained their objections throughout Reconstruction. As they worked through the political system to guarantee political and civil equality for freedmen, they relied even more on pragmatism and focused increasingly on results. This was certainly the case when Phillips opposed the American Equal Rights Association, insisting that the movements for women's and black male suffrage "were not equally ripe." He emphasized the state of public opinion: "Thirty or forty years of agitation, followed by five years of war, had made the Nation fully ready to grant all the negro needed and asked. It was not ready to concede the woman's rights."[88]

The rejection of women's suffrage because of its inexpediency contradicted twenty-five years of Garrisonian policies, according to Pillsbury. When William Lloyd Garrison attended the 1840 World Antislavery Convention in London he had refused to participate in the proceedings because women were excluded: "After battling many long years for the liberty of African slaves," Garrison said, "I can take no part in a convention that strikes down the most sacred rights of all women."[89] Wendell Phillips had also supported women's participation, flatly stating, "We cannot yield this question if we would; for it is a matter of conscience."[90] Pillsbury considered these acts of defiance symbols of abolitionist commitment to justice above all else. In spite of the powerful lure of expediency, he insisted, Garrisonians had always adhered to their battle cry, "no compromise."

Convinced that his support for women's suffrage represented this spirit of no compromise, Pillsbury expressed outrage when abolitionist supporters of the Fifteenth Amendment accused himself and his colleagues of abandoning the antislavery philosophy. "Most ludicrous of all," exclaimed an astonished Pillsbury, "is to hear old antislavery leaders and teachers referring to the past for defense of their present hostility, and challenging us to re-read that history and be ashamed of our present course."[91] Those who supported the Fifteenth Amendment were the ones who were guilty of betraying the spirit of antislavery, he insisted, motivated by their newfound celebrity. "The people have paid Mr. Garrison a tribute of fifty thousand dollars (well earned too in their behalf)," he explained. "They have also taken Mr. Phillips into their confidence, esteem and admiration. . . . But the tests of virtue in one period are never those of another. It is no less an outrage now to rob woman of her just rights, than it was forty years ago to plunder the slave of his."[92] Garrison and Phillips, he concluded, "are both blind as the church and pulpit were before."[93] Not fettered with the burden of celebrity, Pillsbury believed himself better able to perceive the period of Reconstruction as a continuation of the battle abolitionists had begun forty years prior.

Phillips interpreted the lessons of the abolitionist movement quite differently. The Garrisonian experience, he argued, dictated that extraneous issues must not take precedence on the antislavery platform. Although Garrisonians had been in the forefront of the women's rights movement during the antebellum period, the official societies had always primarily focused on the abolition of slavery and equal rights for blacks, he explained. It was inappropriate to confuse the issue by promoting women's rights, temperance, or any other equally deserving cause on the antislavery platform. "The [antislavery] movement has never undertaken to settle whether suffrage is a natural right, or whether woman has the right to the suffrage," explained Phillips. "We had a definite, distinct and limited purpose, announced in our original Declaration of Sentiments and in the constitution of our Society, which was to put the black race where the white race were."[94]

Phillips's position on the Fifteenth Amendment was more consistent with the later trends in Garrisonian antislavery. Beginning with the rise of the Republican Party in the mid-1850s, the radicals softened their uncompromising philosophy. As their movement became increasingly viable, they considered more seriously the practical implications of their policies. Pillsbury's position, on the other hand, exemplified the early days of the movement, when nonresistance, disunionism, and come-outerism guided the radicals and compromise was a dirty word. He simply could not follow the lead of his mentors and moderate his position. Perhaps his years in the field, dodging rocks and facing down mobs, had created in him a different understanding of the enemy, one that demanded constant vigilance. His postwar correspondence overflowed with urgent reminders to his colleagues of the need for continued agitation. Fighting had become a way of life—a religion even. He could not give it up.

Pillsbury nonetheless regretted the division that had developed among abolitionists and women's rights activists, and he struggled to reunite the two groups. "Do you not think the integrity of the cause of human progress and reform demands that an effort be made to reconcile differences among some of our noblest leading men and women?" he asked Martha Coffin Wright, a women's rights activist.[95] "[I]t seems to me no concession, no confession can be so humiliating that I, for one, would not make it, for the sake of complete reconciliation, the moment my error had been made to appear." Neither Pillsbury nor any of the other leading reformers, however, were ever made conscious of their "error." In late 1869, women's rights supporters formed two rival organizations, the American Woman Suffrage Association, headed by Lucy Stone, and the National Woman Suffrage Association, led by Stanton and Anthony. Still hoping to find an honorable compromise, Pillsbury attended a unification meeting organized by Theodore Tilton in April 1870. Although by this time Pillsbury had already left *The Revolution* because it could no longer afford to pay him, he remained committed to the movement.[96] Representing the National group along with Charlotte Wilbur and his old friend Josephine Griffing, he met with the American delegates, Stone, Higginson, and George Wentworth Curtis, for many hours. Unable to find common ground, however, the disappointed activists returned to their separate groups and the divide continued for another twenty years.

Between 1865 and 1870, Pillsbury and most abolitionists struggled to adapt to the decline of antislavery. For some, the transition proved uncomplicated. Maria Weston Chapman called for a dissolution of antislavery societies as early as 1861. She immediately began pouring her considerable financial resources into freedman aid societies, convinced that this was now the appropriate focus for abolitionists.[97] Former Executive Committee members William Lloyd Garrison, Samuel May, Jr., Edmund Quincy, and Oliver Johnson all comfortably left the movement and even derided those who continued to work with existing organizations. For some of these abolitionists the decline of the movement corresponded comfortably with old age, making the transition seem natural. For others, newfound fame and fortune enabled them to adapt to postwar life smoothly. But for Parker Pillsbury, neither old age (he turned sixty in 1869) nor fame and fortune (which he did not have) could rationalize a life of ease. Garrisonian field lecturers like Pillsbury and the Fosters continued to agitate for uncompromising justice throughout

Reconstruction.[98] Unwilling to abandon their perfectionism and unable to embrace a sedentary life, they continued their radical activism.

When Pillsbury left *The Revolution* in 1870, he was unemployed but still chomping at the bit. His hair had grayed and his body frequently betrayed his age, but his determination to reconstruct society had not faltered. He immediately immersed himself in another radical reform movement that had emerged amidst the conflict over women's suffrage. The Free Religion movement offered Pillsbury a chance to return to the field, continue his uncompromising agitation, and, best of all, focus all his fury on the church.

9

The Postbellum Quest for the Millennium

In 1870, the same year Pillsbury left his unpaid position with *The Revolution*, the American Anti-Slavery Society voted to disband. Although he had not participated in the society for several years, Pillsbury was saddened by the formal termination of the organization to which he had dedicated most of his adult life. He still treasured the relationships forged in the cause. "I have traveled long and far and made many fast and firm friends, but none to be measured with those made at the very cannon's mouth in the old Anti Slavery strife," he reminisced to his wife in 1874.[1]

For the next twenty-five years, Pillsbury searched for the movement that would replace Garrisonian abolition. Although he found support and kinship among the old grassroots radical community, especially in the West, only a few of the leading abolitionists joined him in his search, including Wendell Phillips, Thomas Wentworth Higginson, and Elizur Wright. Pillsbury outlasted all of these men, however, lecturing until the 1890s, when paralysis forced him to remain at home.[2] "As to my old coadjutors in the lecturing field, where are they?" he sadly wondered. "Alas, where? Not one of them at my side; not one!"[3] This perceived desertion disappointed Pillsbury, but also intensified his resolution to remain a "soldier" in the field of moral reform. "I seem alone, and a great way off," he confessed to his family in a missive written from Michigan. "But having voice and some audience yet, I keep the ground with more to say than time or breath will allow. For the slaveries are not all abolished yet. And so I am an abolitionist and glory in the name."[4]

Pillsbury was disappointed with the new generation of social activists he encountered in his postwar agitation efforts. "Reform and Reformers now

157

do not seem much as in those dear old days."[5] The younger activists of the postbellum period were influenced by different issues from those that influenced the antebellum Garrisonians. The religious fervor of the Second Great Awakening had motivated most earlier reformers like Pillsbury, while the Civil War, with its new focus on efficiency, order, and "scientific" principles, was the central defining experience for the new activists. This younger generation often boasted impressive educational backgrounds and more extensive training in the new social science fields, including sociology, economics, and political science.[6] Although Pillsbury was at first frustrated by the growing importance of science for reformers, he quickly adapted. As he lectured in support of a variety of causes, including Free Religion, health reform, women's rights, and labor issues, he attempted to combine the perfectionism of his antebellum years with the science of the postwar generation.

Racial inequality was among the "slaveries" Pillsbury battled in the postwar period, but it remained a secondary issue for him. He did often express concern about the increase in racial violence and discrimination in the North and South in his speeches and writings. At a Cincinnati meeting in 1875, for example, he protested, "We have given the slave political freedom. But he has no social freedom. . . . We have shut him out of our schools, and driven him from our factories and workshops, and what chance has a black man today?"[7] Two decades later, he anxiously wrote a friend, "Since slavery was abolished by 'Presidential Proclamation,' it has returned almost with redoubled horrors to torment us with Lynch law."[8] Pillsbury did not, however, join other former abolitionists who devoted their lives to the fight for the rights of African Americans. These reformers organized to eliminate segregation, disfranchisement, and lynchings—all of which were on the rise, especially in the South, in the last few decades of the century.[9] Even Pillsbury's daughter eventually became active in supporting black education through Booker T. Washington's Tuskegee Institute.[10] Some abolitionists criticized Pillsbury for his seeming lack of concern for freed slaves, especially when he spoke in favor of President Hayes's efforts in the late 1870s to end Reconstruction. "For the last half a dozen years," William Lloyd Garrison wrote Stephen and Abby Kelley Foster in 1877, "our friend P[illsbury] has expressed no interest in the efforts made to give protection to the colored citizens of the South, and has evinced no sympathy with them when hunted and slaughtered to make the elective franchise in their hands null and void."[11] Although Garrison exaggerated Pillsbury's disregard for racial equality, the old New Hampshire radical certainly preferred to focus on other "slaveries" which he considered more important, especially the continued "tyranny" of the church.

The first reform organization that raised Pillsbury's hopes after he left *The Revolution* was the Free Religious Association. This movement, which attracted many religious radicals like Pillsbury, was spearheaded by frustrated Unitarians Francis Abbot and William Potter in the late 1860s. Although the Unitarian church had emerged in the antebellum period as an unorthodox splinter group that rejected the authoritarianism of traditional Protestantism, the church quickly established its own orthodoxy. Divisions erupted when influential Unitarians Ralph Waldo Emerson and Theodore Parker questioned certain traditions within the church and also embraced Transcendentalism. Fearing the growing popularity of these religious radicals, leading Unitarians pushed the denomination to a "tightening of theological lines" intended to force the Transcendentalists to either conform or leave the fold.[12] But the radical Unitarians had learned the lessons of their movement's history well and they refused to be bullied, citing the precedent of the early Unitarians who had stood their ground against orthodoxy and tradition. Despite their determination, the radicals were defeated, and many decided to form "free" churches unbridled by the regulations of the new Unitarian orthodoxy.

The Free Religious Association emerged out of these new independent churches, but it was more than simply a continuation of Transcendentalism. In fact, Free Religion rejected the mysticism of Transcendentalism, focusing instead on rationalism and science as the key to all religious truths. Free Religionists looked to systematic study and organized knowledge to understand their world and sustain their faith, eschewing intuition and instinct. Science became the foundation of Free Religion. Transcendentalists did, however, influence Free Religionists in other ways, especially through their writings on non-Christian religions. Religious radicals learned through these studies that there existed fundamental principles common to most religions around the world, including "faith in God, a future life, and obligations to one's fellow men."[13] This sense of religious interconnectedness inspired Free Religionists to develop a scientific non-Christian theism which they hoped would attract a worldwide following.[14]

In addition to these essential principles, the Free Religious Association emphasized a rejection of authoritarianism. William Potter, a former Unitarian minister and founder of the Free Religious Association, referred to the new religious organization as a "spiritual anti-slavery society."[15] He expressed particular interest in "freeing" people from the "thraldom" of religion imposed by a tyrannous clergy. Clearly influenced by the deists of the eighteenth century, especially Thomas Paine, Free Religionists rejected the Bible as the inspired word of God and instead emphasized reason and nature as guides to spiritual life.[16] The Free Religious Association committed itself to absolute individual freedom, requiring very little either theologically or organizationally of its followers. A faith in "man as a progressive being" and a commitment to individual moral development was all this new faith demanded.[17] Despite this celebration of individual freedom, Free Religion also emphasized the importance of cooperation and mutual dependence, rejecting the idea that any one person could "function without social help."[18] The awkward tension created by this emphasis on both individualism and cooperation would eventually cause problems for the Free Religious Association.

Parker Pillsbury did not immediately embrace the Free Religious Association when it emerged in the late 1860s. Still engaged in a heated battle with his former abolitionist colleagues over the relationship between black male and women's suffrage, he had little time to participate in other radical movements. His first public reaction to the new religious organization came in the spring of 1868, when he reviewed their annual convention in Boston for *The Revolution*. Pillsbury praised Free Religion for its ability to attract many former abolitionists, declaring, "It was really the legitimate substitute for and successor to the old Anti-Slavery Convention."[19] He also reprimanded the new organization, however, and offered the religious radicals some critical advice. Displaying his familiar irascibility, he criticized the meeting for what he perceived to be too much harmony among the obviously divergent speakers. Leaning "towards points of agreement rather than of difference," the participants, he explained, simply ignored real and important issues of contention. This was, he argued, "too serious a subject . . . to be treated with courtesies, amenities and mutual admirations."[20] What Pillsbury did not realize was that this harmony had been prearranged by the convention's organizers because the previous year's meeting had been rife with unproductive arguments and accusations. The speakers at this meeting were encouraged by Free Religion leaders to "bring out underlying agreements" and avoid conflict.[21]

While the scripted conciliatory environment of the convention disappointed him, Pillsbury was even more disturbed by the elitism and clerical authoritarianism he perceived throughout the meeting. As ministers monopolized the rostrum with "dull" sentiments dully delivered, a "great impassable gulf betwixt platform and people" further widened.[22] The true leaders of Free Religion, "humble men and women who write no poems, preach no sermons, make no orations, hold no offices and claim no distinctions, whose daily lives and work are sermons shaming all pulpits," remained unrecognized throughout the convention.[23] Perhaps feeling a bit forgotten himself, Pillsbury chastised the radicals for engaging in the very same exclusionary behavior of which they accused other churches. His complaint was well founded. The 1868 meeting had been specifically designed to attract participants from outside Unitarianism, with leading ministers from several different denominations invited to give speeches. The result was a series of long-winded and unsatisfactory testimonies that disappointed many radicals besides Pillsbury.[24]

Despite his disparagement of its annual convention, Pillsbury joined the Free Religious Association not long after he left his position at *The Revolution* in May 1870. "The new enterprise of spiritual emancipation appears to me the most sublimely important of all committed to man in at least eighteen hundred years," he solemnly proclaimed.[25] The Free Religion movement appealed to Pillsbury because of its focus on anticlericalism and science. These two issues, one old and the other new, helped him to create a viable postwar perfectionist philosophy. Through anticlericalism he hoped to continue tearing down the corrupt and authoritarian church, and through science he sought to create a rational, egalitarian religion that would usher in the millennium. He earnestly believed he had found a satisfying substitute for Garrisonian abolition.

Anticlericalism pervaded the Free Religion movement and made him feel at home. One of the most relentless "come-outers" in the antebellum period, Pillsbury had encouraged his audiences to abandon their traditional churches since 1840. Free Religion offered the perfect avenue through which to further his attack on the church and provide his converts with a hopeful alternative. Because the radicals who formed the Free Religious Association had withdrawn from their restrictive and traditional churches, Pillsbury considered them the legitimate heirs to abolitionist come outerism.

Both Pillsbury and Abbot agreed that the church sought to enslave the American public through superstition and fear, using the authority of the clergy to keep their congregations pliant and subservient. Abbot argued that the Bible was employed to create a rigid and backward religious environment that stultified the American people. The predominant image of Jesus Christ as "lord and master," he contended, was anathema to the idea of democracy and undermined the development of an independent and thoughtful citizenry. Until people "recognized the supremacy of their own consciences" and rejected superstition, true democracy would remain a dream.[26] Only Free Religion, he concluded, offered a virtuous spiritual foundation for a democratic nation. Pillsbury enthusiastically concurred with Abbott and often compared the abolitionist goal of ending chattel slavery to the Free Religion objective of eliminating spiritual slavery. Those enslaved by the church, however, did not recognize their bondage as did chattel slaves. Most spiritual vassals, he complained to his daughter, "say they have all the rights they want and spurn us from their presence and will hug their chains, their churches and their priesthoods, till they die."[27] Spiritual slavery also proved more pervasive and powerful than chattel slavery. "Priestly power and domination," he warned, was aligned "against the equal rights of every man and of every woman."[28] The clergy, which Pillsbury characterized as "the deadliest enemy to all human liberty, growth, and progress," would not be satisfied until they were "sovereign, supreme in power."[29]

While Pillsbury was attracted to Free Religion because of its unswerving anticlericalism, he was also intrigued by the movement's scientific foundation. In the 1870s and 1880s, science developed a cult-like following among American reformers. Beginning with Darwin's theory of evolution and ever more enthusiastically with every new discovery that followed, devotees promoted science as the answer to all of humanity's problems. Evolution popularizers Lester Ward Frank and E. L. Youmans convinced their fellow reformers that any effective social movement had to be grounded in the rationalism and progressivism of science.[30] For Abbot and Free Religionists, the new scientific discoveries offered further evidence of their perfectionist creed. They interpreted evolution as proof of the coming millennium, as well as corroboration of man's progressive nature. Through the rational study of biology and other sciences and adherence to the laws of nature, reformers hoped to accelerate society's inevitable progress toward the millennium. Pillsbury quickly became a devoted partisan, cheering the "sunlight of scientific research and investigation."[31] He persistently advised his audiences that no matter what their religion, all should worship at the altar of science and nature. "Let us welcome the reign of law and order in its infinite unfoldments, till spirit and matter are reconciled, harmonized, if not indeed one and the same forever."[32] By the 1880s, Pillsbury even briefly joined Loring Moody's Institute of Heredity, a scientific organization committed to rational social and sexual reform, especially through women's control over reproduction. Combining his commitment to women's rights and science, Pillsbury hoped that the study of heredity would empower women to refuse sexual relations with abusive or alcoholic partners, since these deplorable traits were sure to be inherited by the children. The result, he argued, would be an improved, even perfected, humanity.[33]

Science was also useful for Pillsbury and Free Religionists because it sustained their anticlericalism. While Darwin's conclusions about evolution confirmed their vision of a progressive humanity, it contradicted the teachings of the orthodox clergy, who still advocated a literal interpretation of the Bible.[34] Recognizing the increasing influence of the scientific revolution, the church worked diligently to discredit its leaders. Science, however, was a powerful new weapon that worked effectively against the strong armor of the traditional church.[35] Popular and radical religious leaders like Minot J. Savage skillfully employed Darwin to condemn orthodoxy, emphasizing the need to "free the human spirit" from the unscientific dogmas of the church.[36] Moreover, several alternative sects in addition to Free Religion protested religious obstruction of scientific advances. Spiritualists certainly disdained the anti-intellectual trend they perceived among the clergy and berated the church for their failure to accept and encourage scientific developments.[37] Mary Baker Eddy and her newly organized Christian Science church embraced the method and order that science could bring to religion and offered a practical alternative to the antiscientific traditional church.[38]

For Pillsbury, science became almost an obsession, probably because it could be used so effectively against his enemy, the church. "In these piping times of religious action," he explained in a pamphlet eulogizing scientific advances, "no word is more dreadful to the priesthoods . . . than this word *Reason*."[39] As soon as clerical tyranny was destroyed, he argued, science would provide the foundation for a new, more perfect world. "No miracle, no mystery, nothing supernatural, nothing *unscientific*" would be tolerated in this new Eden, toward which society inevitably marched.[40] Having waged an unpopular and unsuccessful four-decade-long battle against the clergy, Pillsbury recognized the significance of gaining such a powerful confederate as science. Even such an outspoken agnostic and infidel as his friend Robert G. Ingersoll, wielding the logic of science as a weapon of both offense and defense, could gain nationwide attention in his bombardment of the Christian church.[41] By the 1880s, many clerical leaders, sensing defeat, began to accept evolution. Finally, Pillsbury could claim at least a partial victory.

Although he certainly found the basic principles of the Free Religious Association appealing, Pillsbury was also attracted by the opportunity to work in the field as a lecturer again. Confined to a small office in New York for over two years, writing editorials for *The Revolution*, he yearned for his old nomadic lifestyle. Not long after Francis Abbot moved to Toledo, Ohio, in 1870, to take the reins of an independent church and edit the new Free Religion journal, *The Index*, Pillsbury took to the road as an independent lecturer connected with the Free Religious Association.[42] He spent the winter of 1870–71 in the states of Ohio, Michigan, Indiana, and Illinois, continuing his abolitionist tradition of devoting part of every year to the Western states.[43] Pillsbury's lectures focused primarily on "the degrading practice of Bible-worship and Christ-worship," but also included discussions of women's rights and labor issues.

After twenty-five years of field work, Pillsbury proved unable to adapt to any other lifestyle. Even at the age of seventy, he continued his hectic lecturing schedule. As he explained to his daughter, "Labor agrees with me better than leisure."[44] He devoted almost every winter between 1870 and 1890 to lecturing in the West and continued his field work in the East during the spring and summer. Even as his voice failed him and his body refused to uphold the old Garrisonian pace, he continued lecturing, simply working with smaller, more intimate groups. "My work is mostly in Parlors to select circles," he admitted to an old friend in 1882, "and includes lectures, readings and conversations on various themes."[45]

Certainly the financial rewards of field work in the 1870s and 1880s reminded Pillsbury of his meager abolition earnings. "My time is worth nothing in any place," he complained to his daughter in 1879.[46] This lack of adequate salary proved especially irritating to Pillsbury because other, more fashionable lecturers received handsome compensation for their work. Even the Reverend Henry Ward Beecher, who had survived a public trial for adultery with his best friend's wife, attracted large audiences: "Beecher has 500 dollars a lecture," groused Pillsbury, "I have that for *100 lectures*. So much for notoriety."[47] And yet such inequality also reinforced Pillsbury's belief in the importance of his lectures. Abolition meetings had attracted small audiences and little compensation but, he believed, the ideas they had spread had been borne out by events. Moreover, by the late 1870s, Pillsbury and his wife had become financially comfortable. The benevolent Charles Hovey, who died in 1859, left a generous bequest to the Pillsburys in his will, as did Charles Sargent, Sarah Pillsbury's brother, who died in 1875.[48] This allowed Pillsbury to continue field lecturing even though he did not receive a salary from the Free Religious Association or any other organization. He usually collected some recompense from his audiences, but these voluntary donations barely covered his outlay. "I endeavor to be true to my divine trust," he explained, "whether my audiences will *pay*, or whether they will forbear."[49]

Field work also allowed Pillsbury to reconnect with old friends and contacts. While many of the leaders in the abolition movement retired soon after the Civil War, antislavery activists at the local level often continued to participate in community radicalism, agitating on behalf of such causes as Free Religion, women's rights, labor, spiritualism, or racial equality. "Most of the free religionists everywhere," reported Pillsbury after six months in the field, "were ten or twenty years ago living, working abolitionists."[50] When Pillsbury first returned to the field he mapped out a lecturing tour that brought him to many of the old familiar Garrisonian homes and communities. This allowed him to reminisce with former colleagues, but more important, he recognized that ex-abolitionists would probably find his radical message more palatable than the general public. Indeed, many of the most active abolition towns welcomed Free Religion and other reform movements. "Abington was formerly one of the strongholds of Anti-Slavery," explained Pillsbury in a missive to *The Index*. "Now some of the

best of them are continuing their labors in the cause of human emancipation. . . . And an excellent work and warfare they are carrying on in behalf of
Temperance, Rights of Woman, of Labor, and of religious emancipation and
toleration."[51] Pillsbury also devoted several months every year to Salem,
Ohio, and Battle Creek, Michigan, where abolitionists had formed independent churches. Long since frustrated with clerical authoritarianism and orthodoxy, abolitionists led the way in encouraging churchgoers to abandon
orthodoxy for independence, as they had in the 1840s and 1850s.[52]

By the late 1870s, even the most indomitable Garrisonians began to suc-
cumb to old age and illness. Pillsbury, who turned seventy in 1879, occasionally battled attacks of painful boils, but retained his sense of humor and
good overall health. For example, he commiserated to a friend in 1872 that
he "boarded ten to fifteen [boils]" which were "hungry as hyenas" and stubborn, too, "laughing all diets and doctors to scorn."[53] Pillsbury continued
lecturing into the 1880s, although he felt increasingly desolate and unappreciated. Frederick Douglass sympathized with his loneliness: "You are looking over a field where the workers were once numerous, but now few, and
from which in the order of nature, the few that remain will soon be gone."[54]
But Pillsbury refused to submit to "the order of nature." He took pride in his
ability to outlast his old colleagues and in letter after letter he depicted himself as the last soldier in the field. "I stand, as you must know, almost alone
of the old anti slavery cohorts," he reminded William Lloyd Garrison, Jr., in
1878, "all the rest of the field soldiery, dead, disabled, or retired."[55] In describing himself as a soldier, Pillsbury adhered to the familiar abolitionist
images of the "war" on slavery and thereby revealed his lingering identifica-
tion with that expired movement. He clung to field lecturing because it allowed him to revive his old feelings of usefulness and fearlessness.

Although many of his former co-workers may have felt the same yearnings, several factors kept them out of the field. By the 1870s, it was no longer
as feasible for radicals like Pillsbury to make a living as full-time agitators.
More people lived in large urban areas where only the most well-known
public figures attracted sizable audiences. With the appearance of such glit-
tering entertainers as P. T. Barnum, social reform lecturers found it difficult
to compete. Even the Spiritualists capitulated to sensationalism, with a more
carnival-like atmosphere pervading their camp meetings in the 1870s. Mediums such as Lucie Marie Curtis Blair, whose only talent consisted of painting flowers while blindfolded, supplanted women's rights speakers like Lucy
Stone and Amy Post.[56] Pillsbury's sense of dislocation stemmed in part from
his inability to accommodate himself to this new environment.

While Free Religion allowed Pillsbury to remain in the field—promoting
science and denouncing the church—certain other aspects of the movement

disappointed him. Despite his initial criticism of the Free Religious Association for displaying "too much harmony," he quickly reversed himself and censured his colleagues for wasting too much time bickering amongst themselves, instead of working with like-minded reformers to construct a powerful and united movement. The lack of cooperation between Free Religionists and Spiritualists proved especially irksome for Pillsbury, who had worked cordially with Spiritualists in the abolition movement. Spiritualism had emerged as an alternative religion in the 1850s, attracting a diverse assortment of followers who found comfort in the idea of communicating with the spirits of the deceased. Some popular Spiritualists were eventually discredited, such as the Fox sisters, who were discovered to be using their loose joints to create the knocking sounds supposedly made by spirits. Many thousands, however, took Spiritualism very seriously and held regular seances to communicate with long-gone loved ones. Claiming that the science of electricity was the key to speaking with the dead, Spiritualist "mediums" used the electric current between themselves and the spirit world to give voice to departed souls. The traditional church considered these claims to be evidence of infidelity of the worst kind and condemned the movement. Most Spiritualists had already abandoned the church and so disregarded such criticism.[57]

On the surface, Spiritualism, with its emphasis on the otherworldly, and Free Religion, with its focus on earthly existence, seemed to be at opposite ends of the spectrum. And yet by the 1870s, they had much in common. Both groups enthusiastically embraced science; in fact, Spiritualists even referred to their mediums as "spiritual telegraphs." Both groups also emphasized religious universals through the study of comparative religion and supported many of the same progressive movements, including women's rights and labor reform. Finally, both groups opposed clerical "tyranny" and separated themselves from orthodox sects.[58] Many reformers considered themselves both Spiritualists and Free Religionists, including Thomas Wentworth Higginson, Abigail Scott Duniway, and Lucy Colman.[59] Spiritualist author Robert Dale Owen served as a vice president of the Free Religious Association. And yet, despite this overlap, Pillsbury discovered that Free Religionists and Spiritualists usually misapprehended one other, to the detriment of both causes. "When the two organizations shall sufficiently understand each other, I think they will co-operate without an uncomfortable friction," predicted Pillsbury, "and certainly with immense augmentation of power."[60]

One of the reasons for this lack of camaraderie had to do with each group's attitude toward social activism. During the antebellum period, Spiritualists had participated in a number of social reform movements, including women's rights, antislavery, and nonresistance.[61] Reform activism, therefore, became an integral part of their philosophy. Free Religionists, on the other hand, found it difficult to develop a strong, clear activist agenda. Their commitment to a "universal, non-sectarian character" and complete individual freedom made them reluctant to commit to any one particular goal or social issue.[62] A division quickly developed between those who wanted active participation in social reform and those who preferred a more detached focus on intellectual issues.[63] Siding with those who advocated action, Pillsbury rebuked the intellectuals for neglecting their duty to uplift humankind. "Probably in scholarship . . . the leaders of the Free Religious movement are second to no men," he admitted. "But intellectual bread alone will not save the world—will not even save those who bake, break, and dispense it."[64] Pillsbury often pointed to the social activism of one of the acknowledged forefathers of Free Religion, Theodore Parker, to spark his more cerebral colleagues. Theodore Parker's pronouncements on issues like poverty and capital punishment, women's rights and antislavery, argued Pillsbury, "stand forth . . . as his ever-living memorial . . . to the intensely practical, vital, spiritual character of the religion he taught."[65] Pillsbury also suggested that it was the Spiritualists, not the Free Religionists, who best honored the memory of Parker through their work. "Wherever I go, the Spiritualists are doing more than all other influences combined to arrest the tide of religious bigotry and superstition," he reported to his colleagues, "and to uphold the rights of free speech and discussion on every important question."[66] He implored the Free Religious Association to follow the example of the Spiritualists and the abolitionists and employ more field lecturers. "The Free Religious movement . . . needs a class of devoted, brave, cultivated men and women like the first Christian apostles: or like the early Abolitionists, who used to go on foot and sometimes on bare feet, but with head and heart so on fire with the divinity of their mission as to defy the elements . . . as well as dare every other opposition."[67]

Pillsbury was disappointed not only by Free Religion's failure to agitate the people, but also by the movement's lukewarm radicalism. While his Free Religion colleagues hoped to create a religion broad enough to encompass people from all backgrounds and political positions, Pillsbury sought to construct a truly radical organization, much like the Garrisonian abolitionists. Willing to sacrifice numerical support for purity of purpose, he opposed any efforts to attract members who seemed less than wholly radical. When one associate argued that anyone who did not attend church qualified as a Free Religionist, Pillsbury responded passionately, "What do we mean by Radical, Liberal, Spiritualist or Progressive? Do we mean the mere driftwood on the tide of human society?"[68] Even when many of the traditional churches seemed to be moving toward a more liberal position in the late 1870s, Pillsbury demanded that Free Religionists continue to keep themselves separate.

"Many ask me whether the general increase of liberal religious sentiment among all the sects is favorable or otherwise to the spread of Free Religion," he explained to the readers of *The Index*. "To me, the Free Religious statement is something positive and distinct, as well from liberal Christianity as conservative."[69] Citing the example of supposedly liberal churches that continued to indoctrinate children with superstitions and catechisms, Pillsbury concluded, "And so I am not sure that increase of what often passes for 'liberalism,' is any advantage to the cause of Truth and of Free Religion."[70] Just as he had feared the conservative influence of such "halfway reformers" as Henry Ward Beecher and Charles Sumner during the 1850s, Pillsbury cautioned his Free Religion colleagues about the detrimental effect of liberal religion. "There are some *Liberal* Congregational preachers now, as well as Unitarian, deceiving almost the very elect," he anxiously wrote in 1877. "Many Spiritualists and Free Religionists run after them, leaving their own meetings to languish and die."[71] He hoped to make Free Religion as uncompromising as Garrisonian abolition, untouched by political or religious pollution and unwilling to sacrifice any aspect of its perfectionist philosophy.

Free Religion satisfied Pillsbury's perfectionist standards just often enough to keep him committed to the movement. In the mid-1870s, for example, when orthodox religious leaders attempted to blur the line between church and state, Free Religionists reacted with angry passion. As many popular denominations experienced a decline in membership in the postwar decades, religious leaders expressed concern over what seemed to be a spiritual "crisis" pervading the nation.[72] This anxiety led to the formation of the National Reform Association, a group dedicated to "Christianizing" the federal Constitution.[73] Established during the Civil War, this organization expanded its activities in the 1870s to include lobbying for required Bible instruction in public schools and more strict enforcement of existing Sabbath laws, which restricted certain kinds of activity on Sundays. Radicals of the Free Religious Association reacted by forming a new organization of their own, the Liberal League, dedicated solely to the enforcement of the church-state separation.[74] Throughout the 1870s and into the 1880s, Pillsbury scolded the National Reform Association and demanded the elimination of all laws upholding religion, particularly Sabbath edicts. When authorities in Worcester, Massachusetts, the home of his old abolitionist friends Abby Kelley Foster and Stephen S. Foster, prosecuted a young man for selling newspapers on Sunday morning, Pillsbury helped to lead a campaign against the local Sabbath law. "The pursuit of the newsman with so much zeal amounted to a real *persecution*, and has awakened much interest, as well as apprehension, on the part of the friends of true religious and civil liberty," Pillsbury informed the readers of *The Index*.[75] While he found some support for religious radicalism in Worcester, Pillsbury ominously reported that very few people understood the threat posed by such groups as the National Reform Association. "Were you abroad among the people as I am," he instructed Abbot, "your heart would sink in absolute despair, when you see how the apathy, the indifference of the people prevent them from knowing or even seeing how fast their liberties are sliding from under their feet."[76] Pillsbury was familiar with the costs of such ignorance: "The people wouldn't hear Garrison, nor Phillips," he recalled, and yet "they heard Fort Sumter."[77] Even in the face of failure he admonished the Free Religionists to maintain their struggle against "the daring conspiracy, led largely by clergymen, to subvert the Republic to a Theocracy more fearful than the world ever saw."[78]

This "daring conspiracy" manifested itself in another form during the late 1870s, only this time the Free Religionists divided over how to respond. When Anthony Comstock, a former agent of the orthodox Young Men's Christian Association, successfully guided through Congress vaguely worded anti-obscenity legislation, some religious radicals expressed concern about how obscenity would be defined. Comstock proved their concern justified when he began using entrapment techniques to prosecute sexual reformers, political radicals, and religious infidels. With Comstock's loose definition of "obscenity," anyone who questioned the status quo became vulnerable to imprisonment. And yet, Comstock's obscenity laws attracted a great deal of support among the general population. As anxiety about vice and prostitution, women's rights and rising immigration began to increase, obscenity laws offered a simple answer to complex social, sexual, and economic problems. Echoing the arguments of the National Reform Association, Comstock cited the need to infuse politics and laws with Christian values. "Religion and morality," he propounded, "are the only safe foundations for a nation's future prosperity and security."[79]

Radicals of all stripes, including Free Religionists, soon found themselves the targets of Comstock's campaign. In November 1877, sexual reformer Ezra Heywood was arrested for the publication of *Cupid's Yokes*, a provocative pamphlet that compared marriage to prostitution and advocated free love.[80] Ten days later D. M. Bennett, a vice president of the Liberal League and editor of the radical paper *Truth Seeker*, was also incarcerated, for publishing a pamphlet entitled *An Open Letter to Jesus Christ*. A group of Free Religionists immediately petitioned the Congress for repeal of the Comstock laws, arguing that these measures violated the constitutional right to freedom of speech and religion. Not all Free Religionists concurred with this argument, however, and a lively debate ensued at the 1878 annual convention of the Liberal League. While the majority of attendees voted for a repeal of the laws, a few outspoken leaders, including Abbot, favored a reform of the laws. Concerned that any connection with radical sexual politics would forever doom their movement, Abbot and his supporters advocated a compromise that called for a more clearly defined law. The repealers eventually won the debate, but their victory led to a permanent division among Free Religionists.[81]

For Pillsbury, the Comstock controversy raised a number of important issues. First and foremost, it involved his commitment to perfectionism and his unwillingness to compromise. Pillsbury recognized that Abbot's attempt to reform the Comstock laws offered an expedient solution to the conflict, but he maintained that adherence to principle was more important. Heywood's arrest represented a terrible injustice, he believed, which needed to be vocally opposed, not quietly resolved. Pillsbury delivered dozens of lectures in support of Heywood throughout the unusually warm summer of 1878. When he was tempted to return home to rest, he reminded himself, "my old friend and coworker in Anti Slavery is in Dedham Jail, heat or no heat."[82] Pillsbury's call for the repeal of the Comstock laws also involved his sympathy for Heywood's free love philosophy. Long a supporter of increased sexual freedom as well as liberal divorce laws, Pillsbury hoped that Heywood's book would receive a wide reading. "Heywood goes to prison with felons for a work which will one day be seen to be of more worth to the human race, than all the statute books produced in the nineteenth century!" he enthusiastically predicted.[83]

Most important, however, Pillsbury's anticlericalism influenced his opposition to the Comstock laws. Contending that Comstock and the religious establishment that he represented would always define the unorthodox and untraditional as obscene, Pillsbury demanded a full repeal. "I have many times said . . . that it is '*blasphemy*,' as the Church understands or defines it, which is to be suppressed, much more than obscenity."[84] For Pillsbury, this controversy was merely another example of clerical hypocrisy and tyranny. After all, he argued, there were many more examples of outright obscenity in the Bible than in any pamphlet religious radicals published. He even wrote a public letter to prove this point, with the inflammatory title, "*Cupid's Yokes*" *and the Holy Scriptures Contrasted in a Letter from Parker Pillsbury to Ezra H. Heywood.*[85] Panicked at its loss of power and prestige, he contended, the church was attempting to stamp out its opponents in this illegal prosecution of men solely because of their religious views.

While Free Religion offered Pillsbury a reform movement sympathetic to his anticlerical and perfectionist ideas, it lacked the activist and uncompromising elements of Garrisonian abolition. After several years of unsatisfactory full-time lecturing for the Free Religious Association, Pillsbury began supplementing this work with other social causes, including health reform, labor, and women's rights. His participation in these other activities blended smoothly with his commitment to Free Religion. Each emphasized science, maintained a critical attitude toward the church, and espoused, in varying degrees, perfectionism. Employing these common themes, Pillsbury often deftly integrated all of them in a single radical lecture.[86]

Unlike Free Religion, which emerged as a coherent movement after the Civil War, health reform, labor activism, and women's rights originated earlier, in the antebellum period. Each had a devoted following in these early years, including a strong contingent of abolitionists. Health reform especially intrigued Pillsbury during his years as an antislavery lecturing agent. Constantly exposed to the harsh conditions of field work, Pillsbury often found himself in need of medical advice and aid. Because his ailments usually included only minor infections and exhaustion, health reform practices, which were less invasive than orthodox medicines, offered satisfying and even enjoyable relief. His well-developed distrust of tradition and authority also made the alternative hygiene movement much more appealing than the medical techniques of elite doctors. Health reform specialists encouraged Americans to reject expensive physicians and take control of their own bodies through diet, physical exercise, water therapy, and other self-regulated practices. Finally, Pillsbury's understanding of masculinity, which necessitated a strong healthy body maintained through discipline and self-control, corresponded perfectly with the dictates of the health reform movement. By the end of the Civil War, Pillsbury had become a zealous advocate of the movement, earnestly proselytizing the latest fitness craze or medical miracle.

Much like other social movements born in the antebellum period, health reform experienced some change as a result of the Civil War and its aftermath. The overwhelming problem of disease throughout the war significantly influenced the development of medicine in the period that followed. Women nurses and administrators, for example, developed new efficient hygiene practices as well as other medical techniques. The dispiriting and demoralizing aspects of the war also affected health reform, diminishing the hopeful perfectionist trend that had dominated the field in the antebellum years. In the postwar period a blend of subdued perfectionism and faith in science offered health reformers a new foundation for their medical movement.[87] Dissatisfied by what they perceived to be a general decline in the nation's health, hygienicists hoped to improve both the spiritual and physical health of Americans and thereby cleanse the nation of all decay and disease.

"To Faith, Hope and Charity, as the three Graces of religion, should be added Cleanliness," suggested Pillsbury in 1869.[88] Writing about the new "Turkish Bath" establishment that had opened on Lexington Avenue in New

York, Pillsbury took the opportunity to extol hydropathy as the answer to society's ills. Regretting that "bathing of every kind is most shamefully neglected by our American christendom," he suggested that when everyone had access to regular bathing, the nation would be "cleansed of impurity, healed of disease, and ravished with its delights."[89] First introduced as an element of Sylvester Graham's morally imbued health reform system in the 1830s, hydropathy became increasingly popular both in the antebellum and postwar periods.[90] Hydropathic experts argued that internal and external application of cold water would cleanse the body of disease and debility. Many health reformers in this period rejected the popular notion that God punished sinners with physical pain, arguing instead that illness was the body's natural response to the abnormal physical and moral practices of the day. Excessive eating, intemperance, lack of exercise, and unregulated sex all combined to create an unhealthy America. The "water-cure," as it came to be known, offered Americans a simple, inexpensive, accessible, and most important, natural solution to these health problems. Regular bathing and increased consumption of water, hydropaths asserted, offered people improved spiritual as well as physical health.

Long before Pillsbury's enthusiastic support for the Turkish Bath, he had employed the water-cure as a medical therapy for the innumerable aches, pains, and illnesses he experienced as a field-worker.[91] Even as early as 1844, one of his colleagues encouraged him to use "simple waters" as an invigorating medicine: "Drink it and pour it on to you and rub yourself . . . so as to restore some nerve to your system."[92] By the late 1860s, Pillsbury embraced hydropathy as a scientifically sound and effective medical cure. In discussing the New York Turkish Bath, for example, he specifically noted that the owner of the institution was a "well known . . . medical practitioner" who enjoyed great respect as a scientist. While Pillsbury's interest in science certainly influenced his increased support for hydropathy, his perfectionist tendencies also guided him toward water therapy. "In the 'good time coming' and coming fast, every well-arranged house will have its own bath," predicted Pillsbury, "and a kind and degree of health and happiness to-day unknown, shall bless the whole family of mankind."[93] The water-cure, with its foundation in nature, its widespread availability, and its physical and spiritual cleansing effect, would surely help to bring about the millennium, he argued. Pillsbury and other reformers found this simple solution to the nation's difficulties very appealing in the late 1860s, when the effects of the Civil War still plagued both North and South. Convinced that the war represented the horrible result of the nation's mistaken inclination toward unnatural practices, ranging from slavery to intemperance, some health reformers embraced hydropathy as the most natural and virtuous response to past errors.

What better to accompany a fresh clean glass of water than a virtuous repast of wholesome vegetables? Unlike Pillsbury's advocacy of hydropathy, a vegetarian diet did not become a part of his health reform regime until the 1880s. Vegetarianism itself had a long history dating back to Pythagoras, who argued that a vegetable diet distinguished men from beasts and brought them closer to the divine. While a number of people had developed theories promoting vegetarianism since then, it was the English poet Percy Bysshe Shelley's writings on the subject in the 1820s that caught the interest of Americans like Sylvester Graham. Associating meat-eating with the onset of the debilitating influence of "civilization," Shelley linked vegetarianism to good health and traditional social values.[94] The act of killing animals and eating their flesh symbolized to both Shelley and Graham the immoral and unhealthy tendencies of modern civilization. People suffered both spiritually and physically as a result of meat-eating.

Pillsbury found these assertions very appealing, especially later in his life, when he began to suffer from the natural physical ailments that accompanied old age. After a long lecture tour in the West in 1890, for example, Pillsbury returned home only to find himself in the "very fangs of Pneumonia." During the course of his recovery, he wrote to a friend, "no beast, bird, nor fish of the waters, not even the poor oyster had to bleed or die that I might live."[95] His vegetable diet represented not only the solution to his poor health, but also the virtuous choice. Indeed, the suffering of animals became for Pillsbury an issue of great concern: "O the shrieks of the slain victims, beasts and birds, and the innocent blood we compel the poor Earth to drink in horrid sacraments, every year!"[96] In almost all of his many reform lectures in the 1880s and 1890s, Pillsbury earnestly advocated vegetarianism as a healthy and moral practice that would help to create a perfect society. "For myself, the Fruits and Grains shall be for meat," he averred in 1893. "One day the world will go and do likewise. Then wars will cease forever under the heaven."[97] His growing concern at the worldwide increase in hostility between nations in the 1890s, and especially the escalation of U.S. imperialism, convinced him that meat-eating actually caused violence and war. "While we kill and eat animals, we shall as remorselessly devour one another in war," he warned in 1891. "None of us can help to restore the Golden Age of Peace and Love to the world till we first restore it in ourselves."[98] Much like the water-cure, vegetarianism offered health reformers a simple and natural solution to the complicated problems of physical and social disease.

Both hydropathy and vegetarianism also allowed people to practice health reform individually, without expertise or training, emphasizing personal responsibility and self-control. After all, reformers felt strongly the need to exert some control over their lives, even as their hope for witnessing the millennium grew dim with the decline of perfectionist social movements following the war years.[99] Embracing a strict dietetic regime, Pillsbury and others hoped to at least perfect their bodies, over which they had complete supremacy—unlike their society. Physical exercise emerged in this period as another element in the overall effort toward perfecting individual physiques. Though exercise was important to prewar reformers, Graham and other health experts were more concerned with diet and sexuality than muscle-building.[100] Not until the 1860s did exercise become an independent force in the health reform movement. Several issues influenced the growth of physical education, including the popularity of "muscular Christianity" as promoted by celebrated author Tom Hughes and the increased immigration of Germans who brought with them the sport of gymnastics.[101] Health reformer Dioclesian Lewis, who dominated the early movement for physical education, argued that disciplined exercise helped to strengthen intellectual and moral characteristics as well as the physical body. He popularized a "New Gymnastics" program that included both men and women and focused on building mental focus as much as muscles.[102]

Predictably, Pillsbury found this blend of moral and physical elements in the new exercise movement very appealing. Writing about the "lifting cure," the latest fad in physical exercise, Pillsbury opined, "health and vigor of body, purification of soul and spirit are promised and inculcated at the Lifting Cure."[103] Not only strengthened muscles, but also invigorated virtue, resulted from exercise. Long since convinced that strength of body was necessary for true manliness, Pillsbury hoped that weight lifting would purify the nation's troubled manhood. Discussing a newly opened New York exercise institute, Pillsbury announced, "This effeminate and diseased population has at hand an institution for both cure and prevention of disease." Certainly New York, the hub of civilization and therefore the center of physical and moral decay, was especially in need of a health reform organization. Exercise trends like weight lifting appealed to Pillsbury also because they employed nature and science to construct a stronger and more healthy society. Arguing that the "lifting cure" was grounded in "the laws of human nature itself," Pillsbury professed that "a systematized, scientific application" of exercise to every faculty, "bodily, mental and spiritual," would result in a perfected individual and "Eden" on earth.[104] Science, individual responsibility, and self-control combined in Pillsbury's vision of physical exercise to bring about the millennium he so desired.

Pillsbury's advocacy of the "lifting cure" was not limited to men alone. In fact, he encouraged women to throw aside the feminine stereotype of fragility and build strong bodies. "Woman," he counseled, "should be ashamed, not proud, of her physical weakness and helplessness."[105] He extolled the robust woman who directed the "ladies department" at the Boston-based Lifting Cure Institute, claiming, "she can raise, easily, six or seven hundred pounds, and can endure other fatigue and exposure in similar proportion." These physical abilities, he assured his readers, did not affect her femininity: "none who know her complain that she has lost any refinement."[106] Women benefited from physical exercise just as did men, but they had even more reason to build their strength, according to Pillsbury: to defend their rights against men. In most areas of society women faced inequality, he argued, and they required great physical and moral endurance to fight this oppression.

Like many other reformers, Pillsbury comfortably advocated both women's rights and health reform, understanding their connections. Indeed, health reform offered women an "empowering medical and social ideology" that disdained traditional notions of the weak female body and encouraged them to take control of their own health care and, ultimately, their own lives.[107] The postwar period witnessed a great deal of diverse women's activism in addition to health reform. Organizations were created that focused on issues like temperance and education and resulted in the politicization and radicalization of thousands of women across the nation.[108] Frances Willard, the leader of the Woman's Christian Temperance Union, for example, developed a powerful anti-alcohol campaign and then gradually expanded the activities of her organization to include suffrage agitation. Moral educationists emboldened women to demand supremacy over their sexuality, and social reformers like Jane Addams and Vida Scudder embraced social science and used it to advocate cooperation and harmony in place of laissez-faire.[109]

With so many women's issues to choose from, Pillsbury could not resist participating in the movement even after he left his editorial position with *The Revolution*. "I should regard any Lecture of mine, that left woman unremembered," he proclaimed in 1873, "as a church might their sacrament, should the name of him commemorated not once be mentioned over the bread nor the wine."[110] Even in the 1890s, after experiencing debilitating paralysis, he insisted on helping Susan Anthony distribute copies of her *History of Woman Suffrage*.[111]

One of the most exciting new aspects of women's rights in the postwar period was the scientific bent that seemed to permeate all radical groups.[112] Feminists found theories of heredity useful, for example, claiming that children inherited many of the "excessive" traits of their parents, such as intemperance or violence. Men who exhibited such characteristics, they warned, should be avoided. Some even advocated legal restrictions on "unhygienic" marriages.[113] Pillsbury emphasized the importance of both environment and heredity. "It is the whole atmosphere of society which impregnates and nourishes and influences the mothers of the generations," he asserted. "It is not half enough that the natural father and mother of the child are healthy, in body, virtuous in soul and spirit" ; society itself must also be healthy and virtuous.[114]

Pillsbury and other feminists also employed the scientific concept of "symmetry" for feminist ends. Nature perfectly balanced men and women by providing them with symmetrical characteristics, according to this theory. If one sex or the other dominated at any level of society, therefore, irregularity and instability would result. Pillsbury applied this idea to all aspects of nature: "In vegetation as well as throughout the animal kingdom, the law of sex is universal and irrepealable," he claimed. "It is even held that . . . all the planets and orbs that swing in illimitable space are as really male and female as are men and women."[115] This symmetry was necessary in religion and even government, according to women's rights activists. In fact, without the balancing effect of women in politics, Pillsbury argued, an unnatural and unhealthy political system resulted. By offering women an equal role in government this imbalance could be eliminated, and societal ills would be corrected. "All wise and reflecting men say the women alone are now the country's only salvation; and until they have the ballot, there is no hope, no help for us as a people and a nation."[116] Moreover, only the balance ensured by women's presence in government would result in other much-needed social reform: "Colored male suffrage will not be safe, nor will labor reform ever make much progress, until woman comes to possess of her right of ballot."[117]

Pillsbury became increasingly disappointed with the women's rights movement, however. He noticed that more and more women's groups were abandoning their perfectionist roots and making compromises for the sake of success. By the 1880s, women activists began to focus exclusively on the vote, ignoring such confrontational topics as women's problems within the institution of marriage and control over their sexuality. Racism and nativism became more common as themes of women's suffrage advocacy. Pillsbury deplored these trends. He longed to see the radical tactics of the Garrisonian abolitionists adopted by women suffragists. At a reunion of abolitionists in 1893, Pillsbury announced that the suffrage movement had failed to make headway because it did not employ radical tactics. "There is nobody demanding woman's suffrage on the principle of Garrisonianism," he declared. "I am trying to act on that principle myself. I will not vote for any government that taxes my wife without representation, any more than I will vote for any government that made slavery and returned fugitive slaves."[118] Even at the age of eighty-four, Pillsbury remained committed to the perfectionist principles he adopted at the time of the antislavery movement, reproaching his feminist colleagues for their leanings toward expediency.

Pillsbury's dissatisfaction with the women's rights movement prompted him to devote more time to other social movements, and labor reform certainly proved to be one of the most important for him in the postwar period. Although he had long been interested in the difficulties working people confronted, especially following his two-year stay in England in the mid-1850s where he witnessed the devastating effects of factory work, it was not until the 1870s that Pillsbury began lecturing on this issue. "COME ONE AND ALL!" an 1878 handbill sang out, "Parker Pillsbury on the Portents and Perils of the Hour! A Lecture for Working Men, Working Women and Growing Children."[119] Pillsbury's lectures addressed diverse aspects of the labor question; some were directed toward the working class, while others spoke to a more general audience. The placard advertising Pillsbury's lecture on "Capital and Labor" exclaimed: "The RICH whose children may become poor, and the POOR who may desire to become rich, in short all classes of people who feel any interest in human progress and human happiness should hear this lecture."[120]

As with many of the other reforms Pillsbury endorsed in the postwar period, his support for the labor movement reflected his antislavery experiences and his perfectionist philosophy. Although a variety of different labor reform groups emerged in the late nineteenth century—ranging from liberals who advocated laissez-faire to anarchists who demanded a complete overthrow of the capitalist system—Pillsbury never joined any particular labor group.[121] Unable to find an organization that satisfied his perfectionist, activist, and moral standards, Pillsbury simply admonished labor groups, focusing especially on their failure to develop a strong moral foundation. Even the Knights of Labor, an organization that excluded those working in such "immoral" occupations as barkeeping, did not emphasize virtue to the satisfaction of Pillsbury. "Mr. Powderly talks wisely on some particulars but not on all," he concluded about the leader of the Knights.[122] Once again reflecting the perfectionist strains of the antebellum period, Pillsbury expected all reform organizations to value individual morality above all else. Perhaps most closely aligned with the Christian labor reformers led by men like Walter Rauschenbach and William Bliss, Pillsbury encouraged both workers and capitalists to embrace the virtues of Christian self-sacrifice and cooperation.[123] Sensitive to the oppression laborers often endured, Pillsbury nonetheless criticized any labor organization that did not emphasize moral issues. In discussing the massive march on Washington to protest unemployment known as Coxey's Army, Pillsbury pronounced this verdict: "Had

Coxey in good, solemn, holy Faith inscribed *Christ* on his banner, and under it, walked worthily to Washington, followed by one hundred, or one hundred thousand devout, peace-loving, peace-pursuing men and women, they would have been invincible."[124] Pillsbury was unable to understand the new social context of labor activism that led it to focus less on morality and more on the practical issues of working conditions and wages. In evaluating a mass meeting of workers in 1868, for example, he praised the speakers' "constant exhortation to moderation and wisdom in making demands" as well as their emphasis on "temperance and sobriety" and "honest industry."[125] Assuming these working people to be in need of such advice, Pillsbury's editorial certainly mirrored the concerns of most middle-class white reformers who expected everyone to adhere to their moral standards.

Pillsbury's concern with moral issues led him to support a few specific labor reforms, including Henry George's popular "single tax." Pillsbury concurred with George's assertion that land monopoly was at the root of inequality in the nation, earnestly supporting his idea of a special elevated tax which singled out large landholders. "I have no respect for any system of Human Economy, which does not begin with absolute *Freedom of the Soil* as source of human subsistence," Pillsbury informed his old friend Stephen Foster.[126] He was firmly convinced that working on the land inculcated in men and women a unique morality impossible to sustain in large urban areas. Land monopoly, of course, prevented this moral development. And yet Pillsbury did not completely romanticize life on the farm, as did many other land reformers. "The poorest of the poor are often kindly counselled to hasten to the West, and settle on the public lands," he explained. "But how is the man who just keeps from starvation here, to get a thousand, or two thousand miles with his family? . . . This editor has seen too much of Western emigrant life to hastily recommend it, especially to the very poor."[127] Land monopoly also represented the corruption of the political system. Almost all land monopolists, Pillsbury averred, had gained their acres through bribes, manipulation, and swindling. "Do you know how the Northern Pacific Railroad Company came by so much of the best land in all the West?" he asked. "Congress gave that stupendous monopoly 47,000,000 acres of the public lands, . . . of your land and mine!"[128] Pillsbury encouraged workers to oust the politicians who had stolen their land and replace them with honest, reliable working people.

Pillsbury hoped that labor's problems would be solved through peaceful political organization, yet he predicted bloodshed if such political solutions failed. Indeed, he often compared the oppression of workers to the servitude of slaves, and so naturally envisioned another civil war to end this oppression. "The North enslaved the negro until the rebellion released him," Pillsbury reminded his readers. "Now labor everywhere is in chains, and we are fast ripening for Revolution."[129] He often wrote and spoke about the degraded position of laborers, emphasizing the poor working conditions and low wages experienced by most working men, women, and children. He blamed greedy and heartless capitalists for this situation, comparing them to slave masters. "Factory owners in all great establishments grow rich, live in palaces, ride in chariots, travel abroad."[130] These greedy capitalists, like slaveholders, lived in luxury that was earned not by themselves, but by the sweat of their low-paid workers. "Capital massed, monopolized, rules the nation, ruling, grinding labor of both men and women to death," he concluded in 1872.[131] Such inequality and injustice, Pillsbury predicted, would eventually lead to violent revolution, unless workers united and used the ballot to unseat their oppressors. "Is there no hope for the nation but through violence?" he asked. "Shall the starving striker now become our savior, as did the slave before?" He provided the answer, "*Outvote* your opponent for the right, and if he resort to violence for the wrong, on him alone be the responsibility, on him the guilt."[132] Even as socialist reformers offered the nation a radical alternative to the capitalist system, Pillsbury's labor reform recommendations proved a bit obsolete and naive. His advocacy of George's single tax on land monopolists and the political organization of working people reflected both the moral and the individualist elements of perfectionism, which permeated all his reform activities. Unable to envision an alternative economic system that eschewed individualism, Pillsbury favored the more familiar morally based solutions.

Although Pillsbury devoted most of his time following the Civil War to lecturing on behalf of the causes he espoused, he employed other methods of reform activism as well, including publishing. Fully aware of the value of the written word, he continued to pen letters, articles, and pamphlets for public consumption, employing the skillful writing style he had developed during his antislavery years. Throughout the 1870s, his musings on Free Religion and other reform topics could be found in his column, "Notes from the Field," in *The Index*. He also wrote occasional editorials for such radical papers as *The Truth Seeker, The World's Advance Thought, New Northwest,* and others. City newspapers such as the New York *Tribune* periodically printed his political and economic commentaries. He also published several pamphlets, focused on his favorite reform topics. His most cherished publishing endeavor, however, had little to do with the reform topics of the period. In the mid-1880s, Pillsbury not only reissued several abolitionist tracts, he also wrote and published his own history of the antislavery movement, the *Acts of the Anti Slavery Apostles.*

Pillsbury was motivated to offer his version of the abolitionist movement above all by the desire to combat what he considered to be growing ignorance of the history of the antislavery campaign.[133] In 1880, Pillsbury complained to his old radical friend Stephen Foster about this general lack of knowledge: "If you were able to come with me abroad, you would be astounded to find how little is thought, felt, or known of the Anti Slavery enterprise beyond the war."[134] While Pillsbury acknowledged the importance of the war, he insisted that the decades of protest preceding it should be recognized as equally significant. The Garrisonian abolitionists, after all, had warned the nation of the inevitable consequences of engaging in the sin of slavery. To emphasize this prophetic element in abolition, Pillsbury used stationery that had on the side of every sheet an excerpt from an article he had written in 1847 warning of the inevitability of bloodshed: "This nation is hastening to its baptism," it began, "it is a baptism of blood."[135] Concerned that the history of the abolitionist movement would be lost with the death of the last abolitionist, Pillsbury wrote anxiously to a colleague: "The present generation knows little of the . . . 'thirty years war' before one shot was fired on Fort Sumter, with its trials and persecutions, its sacrifices and sufferings, its mobs and martyrdoms, who shall ever sing of them?"[136]

What little information the public did have about antislavery, moreover, was misleading and sometimes grossly inaccurate, according to Pillsbury. He could not endure, for example, the popular tendency to lump all abolitionists together. "Greeley is as well known, *as an abolitionist*, as Phillips," he fumed, "and Sumner, quite as well as Garrison."[137] One of the most uncompromising Garrisonians, Pillsbury was maddened at the thought that history would fail to differentiate between the no-voting, come-outer radicals and the compromising "halfway" conservatives like Horace Greeley.[138] Even more frustrating for Pillsbury, however, was the popular association of the antislavery movement with the church. A passionate critic of the clergy, Pillsbury was horrified that the institution that he considered abolition's most persistent enemy was receiving acclaim for its role in freeing the slaves. "I was compelled into a longer chapter of the Acts of the *Pro* Slavery apostles," explained Pillsbury to Frederick Douglass, "in consequence of the insolence of some of the Clergy and their discipleship who now claim . . . that they or their fathers abolished slavery!"[139]

The deaths of so many of the movement's "earliest comrades" also motivated Pillsbury to write a history of abolition. "The execution seems to have fallen on me as by divine appointment," he explained to his old colleague, James Miller McKim.[140] As one of the few remaining Garrisonians, he felt an obligation to record the group's achievements. The loss of his old friends motivated him in other ways, as well. By reconstructing a history of the

Fig. 10. Parker Pillsbury Late in Life. Courtesy of the New Hampshire Historical Society, F3571.

movement, he legitimized his past against the onslaught of inaccuracies and ignorance, but he also brought his friends back to life and reminisced about a time when he felt purposeful and important. Before he wrote the *Acts*, Pillsbury began recording the deaths of his old friends. "Few and far between are the survivors of those who first greeted and welcomed you to the stern encounters of Antislavery," Pillsbury ruefully informed Frederick Douglass. "I keep a little Registry in my Diary of the deaths of our old worthies as they come to my knowledge; and already this year numbers over thirty."[141] By

recording the loss of abolitionists in a most private space, his personal journal, Pillsbury hoped to keep sacred and safe the memories of his life as an
abolitionist, which seemed to slip away with the death of every old friend.
Even on the road, he was constantly reminded of these losses; no longer did
he find himself warmly welcomed in comfortable homes in the dozens of
cities he visited, for his hosts had long since passed away. But Pillsbury refused to abandon their memory, and with each death he wrote long missives
to friends and relatives remembering his abolitionist encounters with those
who now were deceased. Most difficult for Pillsbury of all the losses was the
death of his oldest friend, Stephen S. Foster, with whom he shared his earliest and most perilous antislavery experiences. "On reaching Lowell yesterday the tidings met me that my earliest, best, truest Anti Slavery and fellow-
worker, Stephen Foster, was on Earth no more!" Pillsbury despairingly
wrote his wife. "I was never so alone as now."[142] Two years later Pillsbury
wrote *Acts of the Anti Slavery Apostles*, devoting several chapters to his early
adventures with Foster.

Several former abolitionists, and sometimes their children, published historical reminiscences of the antislavery movement in the postwar period.[143]
Pillsbury's monograph, however, stands out for predictable reasons—his intimate portrait of life in the field and his emphasis on the opposition of the
church. His five-hundred-page book begins with the usual homage to
William Lloyd Garrison and continues with a brief biographical sketch of
his old mentor, Nathaniel P. Rogers. The remaining fourteen chapters are
devoted to describing the glorious efforts of "antislavery apostles," especially
field-workers. Pillsbury offers his readers a painstaking and intimate por-
trayal of the lives of antislavery lecturing agents, describing the typical
cramped, bleak accommodations, the weary hours of difficult travel, and the
failed meetings when not a single person attended. Mostly, however, Pillsbury recounts the efforts of the church to obstruct antislavery meetings and
undermine field-workers. In almost every chapter of his history, Pillsbury
describes the often violent encounters between Garrisonian field-workers
and the religious establishment which sought to stifle their lectures.

Although Pillsbury received favorable reviews of his book from old colleagues and radical newspapers, he failed to sell many copies and lost money
on the endeavor.[144] Financial reward did not interest him, however. "I
printed, as well as wrote the Acts of the Anti Slavery Apostles for History,
for Humanity, and for Posterity, regardless of money cost and loss," he explained.[145] In fact, the publication of the *Acts* as well as the reissuing of other
antislavery tracts became for Pillsbury a part of his reform activism. After
publishing the *Acts* in 1883, Pillsbury reprinted three other anticlerical pamphlets which were originally written in the antebellum period: his own *The*

Church as It Is; or, The Forlorn Hope of Slavery, Stephen Foster's *Brotherhood of Thieves, or, A True Picture of the American Church and Clergy*, and finally, James G. Birney's *The American Churches: The Bulwarks of American Slavery*. The reissuing of these pamphlets allowed Pillsbury to remind the public of how the church had obstructed efforts toward abolition. In order to ensure that future generations were also well informed, Pillsbury donated copies of the pamphlets to libraries across the country.[146] "I have sent a copy to every University, College and Theological Seminary Library in all the Northern and Western States," Pillsbury informed a friend, "and to many lesser libraries, and by hundreds, to individuals, where there was prospect of appreciation and usefulness."[147] Even if the public seemed uninterested in Pillsbury's antislavery memories, he determined to guarantee their place in history. By placing these publications in libraries across the country, Pillsbury attempted to legitimize his vision of the abolition movement, and rescue his self-identity.

During the final two decades of his life Pillsbury devoted himself to radical agitation, friendship, and family. Although often during the height of the antislavery movement these three important aspects of his life had come into conflict, as he grew old he established a comfortable harmony among them. Sarah and Helen continued to provide Parker with a stable and comfortable home, though they managed to maintain their own independent lives. Helen often traveled during the postwar years and became active in the Unitarian church. She and Parker sustained a lively and voluminous correspondence during this period, sharing their experiences, hopes, and disappointments. Helen married in 1888, at the age of forty-five, but she did not leave home. By this time her husband, P. Brainard Cogswell, had been a boarder in the Pillsbury home for four decades and they remained settled with Sarah on School Street for the rest of their lives. Friends and relatives expressed surprise at the wedding announcement, not because the relationship was hidden, but because it took so long to reach the point of marriage. "We were a little surprised at the announcement," explained Parker's brother Gilbert, "the subject had for a long time been alluded to, and talked over, and even looked upon as at least a probable event to occur in the family. The only wonderment to us was, that after withstanding the great temptation so long, you should at length . . . yield to the inevitable."[148] In homage to Parker, Helen and Brainard married on the old radical's eightieth birthday. Both Parker and Sarah were heartened to see their only child happily married but still close to home. "You are a favored mother," a friend wrote Sarah, "to marry your daughter and keep her too. That is charming."[149]

There are few extant letters between Sarah and Parker from the last few

Fig. 11. Sarah Pillsbury. Courtesy of the New Hampshire Historical Society, F4406.

decades of the nineteenth century, but Pillsbury often expressed his affection for his wife in his letters to Helen. The passion of their early love had long since diminished, but they remained close in their final years together. After Parker experienced debilitating physical problems in the mid-1890s, he remained at home with Sarah, though still writing and publishing as much as possible. Both died within a few months of one another, in 1898.

Long before his death, however, Pillsbury successfully renewed several important friendships with remaining Garrisonian comrades. The highly esteemed elder statesman, William Lloyd Garrison, cheerfully responded to Pillsbury's friendly correspondence in 1878, even including a picture of himself. Pillsbury understood that this simple offering symbolized Garrison's consent to forgive past conflicts and remember the closeness and genuine affection of times past. "It is a truly wonderful and lifelike picture you have sent me!" Pillsbury exclaimed. "I am complimented, I am honored by such a gift. No suitable return on my part, is possible. Accept unspoken, unwritten, unwritable thanks."[150] Garrison died within a year of this correspondence and Pillsbury was grateful to have renewed their relationship before it was too late.

Pillsbury also resurrected his friendships with Stephen and Abby Kelley Foster and Frederick Douglass. Douglass, who served in prestigious positions with the Republican Party in the postwar years, including marshal of the District of Columbia, welcomed his old friend's letters. "No man ever wrote and spoke mightier words, in those earlier days than yourself," Douglass gushed. "Your name is engraved upon the hearts of all who honestly labored to bring about the destruction of the horrible and hell black system."[151]

In reestablishing these friendships, Pillsbury hoped to remind himself of days long past. His attempt to find a fulfilling replacement for the antislavery movement had failed, so he tried to turn back the clock by writing his reminiscences and reviving past relationships. These efforts could only offer him short-lived satisfaction, however. He persevered in his radical agitation even though he felt out of place and old-fashioned. But how could he give it up? When he died in 1898, Pillsbury was not hopeful that the nation had made progress toward the millennium. He remained confident, however, that he had done everything humanly possible to "agitate the people" and help prepare for a better world.

Notes

Introduction

1. Letter from Peleg Clark, "The Phrenological Character of Parker Pillsbury," *Herald of Freedom*, 11 November 1842. For more on phrenology see John Davies, *Phrenology: Fad and Science: A Nineteenth-Century American Crusade* (New Haven, Conn.: Yale University Press, 1955).

2. Carlos Martyn, *Wendell Phillips: The Agitator* (New York: Funk and Wagnalls, 1890), 261.

3. Merton L. Dillon, *The Abolitionists: The Growth of a Dissenting Minority* (DeKalb: Northern Illinois University Press, 1974), 114.

4. Aileen Kraditor, perhaps the radical Garrisonians' most sympathetic historian, referred to Pillsbury solely in relation to his "notorious" "Come-Outer" activity, for which he was often "ejected forcibly" from churches. Aileen S. Kraditor, *Means and Ends in American Abolitionism: Garrison and His Critics on Strategy and Tactics, 1834–1850* (New York: Pantheon, 1967), 104, 105, 114. John L. Thomas in his biography of William Lloyd Garrison characterized Pillsbury as only slightly "more intelligent" than his "aggressive and humorless" "partner in disorder" Stephen S. Foster. These "fanatics," according to Thomas, threatened cohesion among Garrisonians by "chasing the illusion of purity." John L. Thomas, *The Liberator: William Lloyd Garrison* (Boston: Little, Brown and Company, 1963), 321–23. James B. Stewart depicted Pillsbury and Foster as "extremely disruptive practitioners of moral suasion." James B. Stewart, *Holy Warriors: The Abolitionists and American Slavery* (New York: Hill and Wang, 1967), 90.

5. The only scholarly publications focused on Pillsbury are Louis Filler, "Parker Pillsbury: An Antislavery Apostle," *New England Quarterly* 19 (September 1946): 315–37; and my own two articles: Stacey M. Robertson, " 'Aunt Nancy Men': Parker Pillsbury, Masculinity, and Women's Rights Activism in the Nineteenth-Century United States," *American Studies* 37 (Fall 1996): 33–60; and " 'A Hard, Cold, Stern Life': Parker Pillsbury and Grassroots Abolitionism, 1840–1865," *New England Quarterly* 70 (June 1997): 179–210.

6. Most important among these collections of correspondence is the previously unknown cache of letters in the John Greenleaf Whittier Papers at the Wardman Library, Whittier College.

7. See Thomas, *William Lloyd Garrison*, 323.

8. Scholarship on women in the antislavery movement has developed significantly over the past few decades. See, for example, Ellen Carol DuBois, *Feminism and Suffrage: The Emergence of an Independent Women's Movement in America, 1848–1869* (Ithaca: Cornell University Press, 1978); Debra Gold Hansen, *Strained Sisterhood: Gender and Class in the Boston Female Anti-*

Slavery Society (Amherst: University of Massachusetts Press, 1993); Blanche Glassman Hersh, *The Slavery of Sex: Feminist-Abolitionists in America* (Urbana: University of Illinois Press, 1978); Julie Roy Jeffrey, *The Great Silent Army of Abolitionism: Ordinary Women in the Antislavery Movement* (Chapel Hill: University of North Carolina Press, 1998); Deborah Van Broekhoven, " 'Better than a Clay Club': The Organization of Anti-Slavery Fairs, 1835–1860," *Slavery and Abolition* 19 (April 1998): 24–45; Judith Wellman, "Women and Radical Reform in Antebellum Upstate New York: A Profile of Grassroots Female Abolitionists," in *Clio Was a Woman: Studies in the History of American Women*, ed. Mabel Deutrich and Virginia Purdy (Washington, D.C.: Howard University Press, 1980), 113–27; Shirley J. Yee, *Black Women Abolitionists: A Study in Activism, 1828–1860* (Knoxville: University of Tennessee Press, 1992); and Jean Fagan Yellin and John C. Van Horne, eds., *The Abolitionist Sisterhood: Women's Political Culture in Antebellum America* (Ithaca: Cornell University Press, 1994).

9. See Kristin Hoganson, "Garrisonian Abolitionists and the Rhetoric of Gender, 1850–1860," *American Quarterly* 45 (December 1993): 558–95; and Margaret M. R. Kellow, " 'For the Sake of Suffering Kansas': Lydia Maria Child, Gender and the Politics of the 1850s," *Journal of Women's History* 5 (Fall 1993): 32–49.

10. See, for example, Anne C. Loveland, "Evangelicalism and 'Immediate Emancipation' in American Antislavery Thought," *Journal of Southern History* 32 (May 1966): 172–88; and John R. McKivigan, *The War against Proslavery Religion: Abolitionism and the Northern Churches, 1830–1865* (Ithaca: Cornell University Press, 1984).

Chapter One. The Roots of Radicalism

1. According to one account, Pillsbury was so dark in complexion that he was sometimes mistaken for an African American. See John White Chadwick, ed., *A Life for Liberty: Anti-Slavery and Other Letters of Sallie Holley* (1899; New York: Negro Universities Press, 1969), 62. Elizabeth Buffum Chace characterized Pillsbury as "a swarthy man of portentous appearance." See Lillie Buffum Chace Wyman and Arthur Crawford Wyman, eds., *Elizabeth Buffum Chace, 1806–1899: Her Life and Its Environment*, vol. 1 (Boston: W. B. Clarke, 1914), 192. Even Pillsbury referred to the dark color of his skin. See, for example, "From the Liberty Bell for 1848—Incidents in the Life of an Anti-Slavery Agent," *National Anti-Slavery Standard* (New York), 16 May 1848; and "Anti-Slavery Festival in Commemoration of the Twenty-Fifth Anniversary of the Formation of the Massachusetts Anti-Slavery Society," *National Anti-Slavery Standard*, 17 January 1857. Elizabeth Cady Stanton described Pillsbury as a "great burly fellow," in "What the Press Says of Us," *The Revolution* (New York), 29 January 1868.

2. "Great Meeting at Andover, Massachusetts," *Herald of Freedom* (Concord, N.H.), 28 January 1841.

3. Parker Pillsbury, *Acts of the Anti-Slavery Apostles* (Concord, N.H., 1883), 370.

4. Ibid., 377. Pillsbury was not the first abolitionist to excommunicate an entire church. Henry Clarke Wright, a Garrisonian and ex-Congregationalist minister, excommunicated the Essex North Association in 1839, two years before Pillsbury. See Lewis Perry, *Childhood, Marriage, and Reform: Henry Clarke Wright, 1797–1870* (Chicago: University of Chicago Press, 1980), 134.

5. See Pillsbury, *Anti-Slavery Apostles*, 377; Pillsbury, "Suffolk North Association," *Herald of Freedom*, 12 March 1841; and Frank Ramsdell to "Mr. Carpenter," 19 May 1899, FTL.

6. William Lloyd Garrison, Jr., used this phrase to describe Pillsbury after his death. See "Discourse Delivered at Parker Pillsbury's Funeral," *Free Thought Magazine* 16 (October 1898): 411.

7. Nathaniel P. Rogers, "The Hancock Convention," *Herald of Freedom*, 21 October 1842.

8. David B. Pillsbury and Emily A. Getchall, comps., *The Pillsbury Family* (Everett, Mass.: Massachusetts Publishing Co., 1898), 1–7.

9. See *Biographical Review: Containing Sketches of Leading Citizens of Merrimack and Sullivan*

Counties, New Hampshire, vol. 22 (1892), 40–48. On the economic difficulties caused by the Embargo Act of 1807 and the War of 1812 see Douglass C. North, *The Economic Growth of the United States, 1790–1860* (New York: Norton, 1966), 26. It is not clear, however, exactly how the War of 1812 would have affected Pillsbury's blacksmithing occupation.

10. See Nancy Coffey Heffernan and Ann Page Stecker, *New Hampshire: Crosscurrents in Its Development* (Grantham, N.H.: Thompson and Rutter, 1986), 80; and Elizabeth Forbes Morison and Elting E. Morison, *New Hampshire: A Bicentennial History* (New York: Norton, 1976), 92.

11. See Heffernan, *New Hampshire,* 89; and John Hayward, *The New England Gazetteer; Containing Descriptions of all the States, Counties and Towns in New England* (Concord, N.H.: Israel S. Boyd and William White, 1839).

12. Several private academies opened their doors by the Civil War. See David F. Allmendinger, Jr., *Paupers and Scholars: The Transformation of Student Life in Nineteenth-Century New England* (New York: St. Martin's Press, 1974), 11.

13. See Heffernan, *New Hampshire,* 151–67.

14. Pillsbury to Helen Pillsbury, 11 February 1853, JGW.

15. Parker Pillsbury's Personal History Form for the *Boston Journal,* NHHS. Capitalization of "Dirtiest" is Pillsbury's.

16. Pillsbury to Stephen S. and Abby Kelley Foster, 5 April 1846, Abby Kelley Foster Papers, AAS.

17. Pillsbury to Wendell Phillips, 4 December 1853, Crawford Blagden Papers, bMS Am 1953 (1001), HouL.

18. James Russell Lowell used this phrase to describe Pillsbury in an antislavery poem. See *The Complete Poetical Works of James Russell Lowell* (Boston: Houghton Mifflin, 1899), 151.

19. Pillsbury, "Editorial Correspondence," *The Revolution,* 27 May 1869.

20. Pillsbury to Helen Pillsbury, 30 October 1854, JGW.

21. *Biographical Review,* 45. Unfortunately, very little information is available on Pillsbury's mother.

22. Leander W. Cogswell, *History of the Town of Henniker, Merrimack County, New Hampshire, 1735 to 1880* (Concord, N.H.: Republican Press Association, 1880), 684.

23. Ibid.

24. On similar trends in neighboring Vermont see Randolph A. Roth, *The Democratic Dilemma: Religion, Reform, and the Social Order in the Connecticut River Valley of Vermont, 1791–1850* (Cambridge: Cambridge University Press, 1987), 80–141.

25. Cogswell, *Town of Henniker,* 684–85. New Hampshire experienced increased interest in a variety of reform movements in this period, even at the statewide level. See Lynn Warren Turner, *The Ninth State: New Hampshire's Formative Years* (Chapel Hill: University of North Carolina Press, 1983), 344–57.

26. Cogswell, *Town of Henniker,* 687. See also Pillsbury and Getchall, *Pillsbury Family,* 131–38. Oliver Pillsbury adopted the values of the emerging middle class, especially in regard to temperance and other moral reforms. See Stuart Blumin, *The Emergence of the Middle Class: Social Experience in the American City, 1760–1900* (Cambridge: Cambridge University Press, 1989); Paul E. Johnson, *A Shopkeeper's Millennium: Society and Revivals in Rochester, New York, 1815–1837* (New York: Hill and Wang, 1978); and Mary P. Ryan, *Cradle of the Middle Class: The Family in Oneida County, New York, 1790–1865* (Cambridge: Cambridge University Press, 1981).

27. See Donald M. Scott, *From Office to Profession: The New England Ministry, 1750–1850* (Philadelphia: University of Pennsylvania Press, 1978), 18–51. Some historians have argued that community leaders used religious benevolence as a tool to maintain their dominance in society. See Clyde S. Griffen, "Religious Benevolence as Social Control, 1815–1860," *Mississippi Valley Historical Review* 44 (December 1957): 423–44. For a different interpretation see Lois Banner, "Religious Benevolence as Social Control: A Critique of Interpretation," *Journal of American History* 60 (June 1973): 23–41.

28. This is how Sarah Pillsbury, Parker's spouse, described her father-in-law's vision of appropriate religious activity. See Sarah Pillsbury to Pillsbury, 11 March 1855, JGW.

29. Pillsbury, "A Sunday School Anniversary," *The Revolution*, 1 April 1869.

30. Pillsbury to Stephen and Abby Kelley Foster, 5 April 1846, A. K. Foster Papers, AAS. The phrase "organ of self esteem" is a phrenological reference. See John Davies, *Phrenology: Fad and Science: A Nineteenth-Century American Crusade* (New Haven, Conn.: Yale University Press, 1955).

31. Nathaniel P. Rogers, "Journey to Northampton," *Herald of Freedom*, 5 July 1844 (emphasis added).

32. Sarah Pillsbury to Pillsbury, 11 March 1855, JGW.

33. James M. McPherson documents the improved status of abolitionists during the Civil War in *The Struggle for Equality: Abolitionists and the Negro in the Civil War and Reconstruction* (Princeton, N.J.: Princeton University Press, 1964).

34. Pillsbury to William Lloyd Garrison, Jr., and Ellen Wright Garrison, 14 January 1875, SSC.

35. On express wagon driving see Personal History Form, NHHS; and Pillsbury to Helen Pillsbury, 25 September 1881, JGW. On soap boiling, see Pillsbury's speech in "Anti-Slavery Festival in Commemoration of the Twenty-Fifth Anniversary of the Formation of the Massachusetts Anti-Slavery Society," *National Anti-Slavery Standard*, 17 January 1857.

36. See W. J. Rorabaugh, *The Alcoholic Republic: An American Tradition* (New York: Oxford University Press, 1979), 140–41.

37. See Johnson, *Shopkeeper's Millennium*, 79–94.

38. Charles Buffum, "Parker Pillsbury and His Work," *Free Thought Magazine* 16 (October 1898): 416.

39. Advocates of temperance in Lynn during this period were primarily manufacturers. Workingmen in Lynn opposed the temperance movement because it focused on eliminating rum, their favorite drink. They perceived it to be an attack on working people. See Paul G. Faler, *Mechanics and Manufacturers in the Early Industrial Revolution: Lynn, Massachusetts, 1800–1860* (Albany: State University of New York Press, 1981), 206–7.

40. "New England Anti-Slavery Convention," *North Star* (Rochester, N.Y.), June 1848. Pillsbury would continue to encourage temperance among the working class, however. See Pillsbury, "Work and the Workers," *The Revolution*, 20 August 1868.

41. "Biographical: Parker Pillsbury, The Reformer," n.d., NHHS.

42. Personal History Form, NHHS. Parker's brothers Webster and Gilbert eventually graduated from Dartmouth College, although neither chose to enter the clerical profession. See Pillsbury and Getchall, *Pillsbury Family*, 132, 135.

43. Pillsbury, "An Irish 'Model Farm,' " *Liberator* (Boston, Mass.), 25 April 1856.

44. See William G. McLoughlin, *Revivals, Awakenings, and Reform: An Essay on Religion and Social Change in America, 1607–1977* (Chicago: University of Chicago Press, 1978), 98–140; and Sydney E. Ahlstrom, *A Religious History of the American People*, vol. 1 (1972; New York: Image Books, 1975), 574–79.

45. See Ronald G. Walters, *American Reformers, 1815–1860* (New York: Hill and Wang, 1978), 21–37.

46. Ibid.; and Roth, *Democratic Dilemma*, 187–219.

47. Personal History Form, NHHS. Temperance supporters in other locations also attempted to convince local militias to abstain from alcohol. See Roth, *Democratic Dilemma*, 169. On the growing intensity of the temperance movement see Robert H. Abzug, *Cosmos Crumbling: American Reform and the Religious Imagination* (New York: Oxford University Press, 1994), 81–104.

48. See Pillsbury and Getchall, *Pillsbury Family*, 132. Parker's brother Gilbert signed the constitution of the New Hampshire Anti-Slavery Society in November 1834. See the Records of the New Hampshire Anti-Slavery Society, NHHS.

49. Pillsbury, "To Washington Berry, A Leading Member of the Congregational Church in Henniker," *Herald of Freedom*, 3 May 1844.

50. Little information is available on Foster. See Joel Bernard, "Authority, Autonomy and

Radical Commitment: Stephen and Abby Kelley Foster," *Proceedings of the American Antiquarian Society* 90 (October 1980): 347–86; Parker Pillsbury, "Stephen Symonds Foster," *Granite Monthly* (August 1882): 1–7; and Dorothy Sterling, *Ahead of Her Time: Abby Kelley and the Politics of Antislavery* (New York: Norton, 1991).

51. Lillie Buffum Chace Wyman, "Parker Pillsbury and the Fosters," in *American Chivalry* (Boston: W. B. Clarke, 1913), 73.

52. Pillsbury, "Stephen Symonds Foster."

53. Personal History Form, NHHS.

54. Benjamin F. Underwood, "Broad-Shouldered Pillsbury," *Free Thought Magazine* 16 (October 1898): 424.

55. Elizabeth Cady Stanton described Pillsbury as "burly," in "What the Press Says of Us." Lucy Stone saw Pillsbury as a "thinker," quoted in Belle McArthur, *Lucinda Hinsdale Stone: Her Life Story and Reminiscences* (Detroit, Mich.: Elinn Publishing, 1902), 317.

56. Rogers, "The Hancock Convention," *Herald of Freedom*, 21 October 1842.

57. John R. McKivigan, *The War against Proslavery Religion: Abolitionism and the Northern Churches, 1830–1865* (Ithaca: Cornell University Press, 1984), 20. See also Gilbert Barnes, *The Antislavery Impulse, 1830–1844* (1933; New York: Harcourt, Brace and World, 1964).

58. McKivigan, *Proslavery Religion*, 29. For a different perspective see Victor B. Howard, *Conscience and Slavery: The Evangelicalistic Calvinist Domestic Missions, 1837–1861* (Kent, Ohio: Kent State University Press, 1990).

59. McKivigan, *Proslavery Religion*.

60. See Leonard L. Richards, *"Gentlemen of Property and Standing": Anti-Abolition Mobs in Jacksonian America* (London: Oxford University Press, 1970).

61. On Thompson see John L. Myers, "The Beginning of Antislavery Agencies in New Hampshire, 1832–1835," *Historical New Hampshire* 25 (Fall 1970): 21–22. On Storrs see John L. Myers, "The Major Effort of Antislavery Agents in New Hampshire, 1835–1837," ibid., vol. 26 (Fall 1971): 3–27.

62. Extract of letter from Pillsbury to Samuel May, Jr., *Liberator*, 14 December 1855.

63. Pillsbury, "New England Correspondence," *Anti-Slavery Bugle* (Salem, Ohio), 12 March 1853.

64. See Daniel Lancaster, *The History of Gilmanton* (Gilmanton, N.H.: Alfred Prescott, 1845), 169–79.

65. Ahlstrom, *Religious History*, 478.

66. J. Earl Thompson, Jr., "Abolitionism and Theological Education at Andover," *New England Quarterly* 47 (1974): 239.

67. Thompson, "Education at Andover," 246–47.

68. Pillsbury, *Herald of Freedom*, 5 November 1841.

69. Pillsbury to William Page, 26 November 1838, MS Am. 1993 (2), BPL.

70. Ibid. On Moses Stuart see McKivigan, *Proslavery Religion*, 30.

71. Pillsbury to unknown, 6 July 1882, FTL.

72. Pillsbury to William Lloyd Garrison, 15 December 1874, MS A.1.2 vol. 37, p. 131, BPL.

73. On the development of reform activism as a career see Walters, *American Reformers*, 13.

74. Pillsbury, "Andover Theological Seminary," *Anti-Slavery Bugle*, 29 August 1845.

75. Scott, *Office to Profession*, 87.

76. Ibid., 52–75.

77. Anne C. Loveland, "Evangelicalism and 'Immediate Emancipation' in American Antislavery Thought," *Journal of Southern History* 32 (May 1966): 179. See also Donald M. Scott, "Abolition as a Sacred Vocation," in *Antislavery Reconsidered: New Perspectives on the Abolitionists*, ed. Lewis Perry and Michael Fellman (Baton Rouge: Louisiana State University Press, 1979), 51–74.

78. Loveland, "Evangelicalism," 180.

79. Pillsbury, *Anti-Slavery Apostles*, 10–11.

80. See Perry, *Henry Clarke Wright*, 96–170; Bernard, "Stephen and Abby Kelley Foster";

and Pillsbury, "Stephen Symonds Foster." It is important to note, however, that antislavery did not replace religion for Pillsbury. As Anna M. Speicher points out in her thoughtful dissertation, many abolitionists were passionate about their reform convictions, but they still had specific theological ideas underpinning their activism (especially the belief in a merciful God and the innate goodness of human nature). The rejection of institutional religion did not necessitate the absence of all religion. Anna M. Speicher, " 'Faith Which Worketh By Love': The Religious World of Female Antislavery Lecturers" (Ph.D. diss., George Washington University, 1996).

81. For a description of Pillsbury's orthodox religious position see Pillsbury, *Anti-Slavery Apostles*, 86–87.

82. Pillsbury to unknown, 6 July 1882, FTL.

83. Scott, *Office to Profession*, 52–75.

84. Pillsbury to John A. Collins, November 1839, MS A 9.2 vol. 12, no. 91, BPL.

85. Ibid.

86. Most antislavery societies employed a few men and women as full-time lecturing agents. These "field workers" traveled from town to town delivering antislavery lectures, collecting donations, selling subscriptions to antislavery newspapers, and gathering signatures on antislavery petitions. Field work is described more fully in chapter 5, below. See also John L. Myers, "The Agency System of the Anti-Slavery Movement, 1832–1837, and Its Antecedents in Other Benevolent and Reform Societies" (Ph.D. diss., University of Michigan, 1961).

87. Pillsbury to Collins, November 1839, BPL.

88. On the Grimké sisters see Gerda Lerner, *The Grimké Sisters from South Carolina: Pioneers for Woman's Rights and Abolition* (New York: Schocken Books, 1971); and Katharine Du Pre Lumpkin, *The Emancipation of Angelina Grimké* (Chapel Hill: University of North Carolina Press, 1974).

89. For more on the relationship between ministers and women in the nineteenth century, see Anne Douglass, *The Feminization of American Culture* (New York: Knopf, 1977); and Carolyn Williams, "Religion, Race, and Gender in Antebellum American Radicalism: The Philadelphia Female Anti-Slavery Society, 1833–1870" (Ph.D. diss., University of California, Los Angeles, 1991).

90. See Richard H. Sewell, *Ballots for Freedom: Antislavery Politics in the United States, 1837–1860* (1976; New York: Norton, 1980); and Vernon L. Volpe, *Forlorn Hope for Freedom: The Liberty Party in the Old Northwest, 1838–1848* (Kent, Ohio: Kent State University Press, 1990).

91. See John Demos, "The Antislavery Movement and the Problem of Violent 'Means,' " *New England Quarterly* 37 (December 1964): 501–26; Lewis Perry, *Radical Abolitionism: Anarchy and the Government of God in Antislavery Thought* (Knoxville: University of Tennessee Press, 1995); and Valarie Ziegler, *The Advocates of Peace in Antebellum America* (Bloomington: Indiana University Press, 1992).

92. For insightful discussions of the antislavery divide see Aileen S. Kraditor, *Means and Ends in American Abolitionism: Garrison and His Critics on Strategy and Tactics, 1834–1850* (New York: Pantheon, 1969); and Lawrence Friedman, *Gregarious Saints: Self and Community in American Abolitionism, 1830–1870* (Cambridge: Cambridge University Press, 1982).

93. Wendell Phillips to Pillsbury, 4 January 1884, CSC.

94. Pillsbury to Collins, November 1839, BPL.

95. Rev. R. A. Putnam to "Brother Phelps and also Brother St. Clair," 28 September 1839, MS A.21.10, p. 94, BPL.

96. Pillsbury to Emily and Marius Robinson, 15 September 1865, ALutz.

97. Scott, "Sacred Vocation," 70.

98. Pillsbury, *Anti-Slavery Apostles*, 10.

99. Pillsbury to Collins, November 1839, BPL.

100. Friedman, *Gregarious Saints*, 43–67.

101. Pillsbury to Collins, November 1839, BPL.

102. Very little biographical information is available on Collins, who remained in the aboli-

tionist movement until he converted to Fourierism after a lecturing tour in England in 1840. See "Collins, John Anderson," *Dictionary of American Biography*, S. V.; and John A. Collins, *A Bird's Eye View of Society As It Is, and As It Should Be* (Boston: J. P. Mendum, 1844).

103. Pillsbury to Collins, November 1839, BPL.

104. Pillsbury to Samuel May, Jr., 25 June 1859, MS B.1.6 vol. 7, no. 52, BPL.

105. This was true at least until Rogers broke ranks with Garrison in 1845 by advocating a "no-organization" policy in New Hampshire antislavery. See Perry, *Radical Abolitionism*, 117–28; Friedman, *Gregarious Saints*, 59–61; and Nathaniel P. Rogers, *A Collection From the Newspaper Writings of Nathaniel Peabody Rogers* (Concord, N.H.: John R. French, 1847). See also my discussion of this topic in chapter 4, below.

106. Nathaniel P. Rogers, "Lecturing Agents," *Herald of Freedom*, 31 August 1839.

107. Ibid.

108. Nathaniel P. Rogers, ibid., 9 May 1840.

109. For Pillsbury's reaction to Kelley's election, see "The Annual Meeting at New York," ibid., 23 May 1840; for general comments on the role of women in antislavery societies, see the following editorials in the *Herald*: 6 June 1840; "Massachusetts Abolitionist," 10 July 1840; and "State Convention," 7 August 1840.

110. In his autobiographical account of the abolition movement Pillsbury devoted the second chapter to Rogers (Garrison was the subject of his first chapter). See Pillsbury, *Anti-Slavery Apostles*.

111. Nathaniel P. Rogers to Pillsbury, January 1844, CSC.

112. Nathaniel P. Rogers, "Hancock Convention," *Herald of Freedom*, 21 October 1842.

113. Nathaniel P. Rogers, "Parker Pillsbury," ibid., 30 August and 6 September 1844.

114. Pillsbury, " 'The' Herald of Freedom," *Liberator*, 4 April 1845.

115. See Pillsbury to Samuel May, Jr., 25 June 1859, B.1.6 vol. 7, no. 52, BPL.

116. Pillsbury, *Anti-Slavery Apostles*, 152–53.

117. Ibid.

118. Letter from Pillsbury, *Herald of Freedom*, 22 July 1842.

119. Pillsbury, *Anti-Slavery Apostles*, 152.

120. McKivigan, *Proslavery Religion*, 36–55.

121. Letter "To the Suffolk Co. North Association" from Pillsbury, *Herald of Freedom*, 22 January 1841.

122. See Ahlstrom, *Religious History;* Griffen, "Religious Benevolence"; and McKivigan, *Proslavery Religion*, 112.

123. James G. Birney, *American Churches, the Bulwarks of American Slavery* (Newburyport, Mass., 1834).

124. Betty L. Fladeland, *James Gillespie Birney: Slaveholder to Abolitionist* (Ithaca: Cornell University Press, 1955); and Ahlstrom, *Religious History*, 97.

125. Louis Filler, "Parker Pillsbury: An Anti-Slavery Apostle," *New England Quarterly* 19 (September 1946): 315–37.

126. Pillsbury, "S. S. Foster," *Herald of Freedom*, 20 August 1841.

127. See Donald Yacovone, *Samuel Joseph May and the Dilemmas of the Liberal Persuasion, 1797–1871* (Philadelphia: Temple University Press, 1991).

128. See Hugh Davis, *Joshua Leavitt, Evangelical Abolitionist* (Baton Rouge: Louisiana State University Press, 1990); and Bertram Wyatt-Brown, *Lewis Tappan and the Evangelical War against Slavery* (Cleveland: Press of Case Western University, 1969).

129. See Kraditor, *Means and Ends*.

130. For examples of Garrisonians' critiques of Pillsbury's religious radicalism, see Jane Wigham to Anne Warren Weston, 18 November 1852, MS A.9.2 vol. 26, p. 71, BPL; Mary Estlin to Anne Warren Weston, 20 March 1853, MS A.9.2 vol. 27, p. 15, BPL; and Maria Weston Chapman to Charlotte P. Remond, 4 September 1859, Mary Estlin Papers, Yale.

131. See John McKivigan, "The Antislavery 'Comeouter' Sects: A Neglected Dimension of the Abolitionist Movement," *Civil War History* 26 (1980): 142–60.

132. Pillbury, "S. S. Foster," *Herald of Freedom*, 20 August 1841.

133. See Pillsbury, *Anti-Slavery Apostles*; and McKivigan, *Proslavery Religion*, 56–73.

134. Pillsbury, *Anti-Slavery Apostles*, 201.

135. Antisabbatarianism called into question the validity of the "divine appointment" of the Sabbath by arguing that *all* days of the week should be considered spiritual. See Perry, *Henry Clarke Wright*, 147–54. Pillsbury's involvement with the Free Religion movement is discussed more extensively in chapter 9, below.

136. Friedman, *Gregarious Saints*, 56.

137. Pillsbury to Sarah Pillsbury, [January 1850], JGW.

138. Valarie Ziegler used these phrases to describe the theology that guided early participants in the peace movement. But these same theological ideas influenced the Garrisonians. In fact, many radicals became strong supporters of nonresistance. See Ziegler, *Advocates of Peace*, 28.

Chapter Two. Marriage, Family, and the Business of Reform

1. *Biographical Review: Containing Sketches of Leading Citizens of Merrimack and Sullivan Counties, N.H.* 22 (1892): 40–48.

2. Ibid.

3. In February 1836, Sarah Sargent wrote an essay entitled "On the Death of a Sister," which describes the unexpected death of a young sister who simply did not wake one morning. See "Remembrance Book of Sarah Sargent," NHHS. This handwritten journal contains Sarah Sargent's thoughts on a variety of specific topics, ranging from "Early Piety" to "On the Choice of Friends."

4. See Carroll Smith-Rosenberg's ground-breaking article: "The Female World of Love and Ritual: Relations between Women in Nineteenth-Century America," in *Disorderly Conduct: Visions of Gender in Victorian America* (New York: Oxford University Press, 1985), 53–76.

5. There are dozens of works on women's changing role in the nineteenth century. Useful introductions to the field include: Nancy Cott, *The Bonds of Womanhood: "Woman's Sphere" in New England, 1780–1835* (New Haven, Conn.: Yale University Press, 1977); Nancy Hewitt, *Women's Activism and Social Change: Rochester, New York, 1822–1872* (Ithaca: Cornell University Press, 1984); Smith-Rosenberg, "The Female World of Love and Ritual"; and Barbara Welter, "The Cult of True Womanhood: 1820–1860," *American Quarterly* 18 (Summer 1966): 151–74.

6. On women's education see Eleanor Flexner, *Century of Struggle: The Woman's Rights Movement in the United States* (1958; New York: Atheneum, 1974), 23–40; and Kathryn Kish Sklar, *Catharine Beecher: A Study in American Domesticity* (1973; New York: Norton, 1976).

7. "Music," "Remembrance Book," 19 September 1835, NHHS.

8. "Why Is Conversation in the Social Parties Generally So Trifling?" "Remembrance Book," 18 November 1835, NHHS.

9. On urban working women in this period see Christine Stansell, *City of Women: Sex and Class in New York, 1789–1860* (1982; Urbana: University of Illinois Press, 1987).

10. Nancy Hewitt discusses the differences between 1820s benevolent groups, 1830s evangelical reformers, and 1840s women's rights activists in her *Women's Activism*. See also Carroll Smith-Rosenberg, "Beauty, the Beast, and the Militant Woman in Jacksonian America," *American Quarterly* 23 (October 1971): 562–84.

11. On Chandler see Merton L. Dillon, "Elizabeth Chandler and the Spread of Antislavery Sentiment to Michigan," *Michigan History* 39 (1955): 481–94; Bonnie Arlene Geers, "Elizabeth Margaret Chandler: A Third Sphere" (M.A. thesis, Michigan State University, 1988); and Blanche Glassman Hersh, *The Slavery of Sex: Feminist-Abolitionists in America* (Urbana: University of Illinois Press, 1978), 7–10. On women's roles in antislavery see Gerda Lerner, "The Political Activities of Antislavery Women," in *The Majority Finds Its Past: Placing Women in History* (New York: Oxford University Press, 1979), 112–28.

12. *Freedom's Alarm, or Lovejoy's Voice from the Grave*, words by Miss S. H. Sargent (Concord, N.H.: William White, Printer, 1838), NHHS.

13. Sarah and three other women excommunicated the South Congregational church in Concord, N.H. See Sarah Pillsbury, "First and Second Steps," *Herald of Freedom* (Concord, N.H.), 26 March 1841; Parker Pillsbury, *Acts of the Anti-Slavery Apostles* (Concord, N.H., 1883), 157–58; and letter to Sarah Pillsbury from Daniel Noyes, minister of the South Congregational Church, excommunicating her, 17 February 1841, NHHS. Parker also excommunicated his church in Henniker, N.H. See Pillsbury, "Communications," *Herald of Freedom*, 19 March 1841.

14. Sarah Pillsbury, "First and Second Steps."

15. Sarah Pillsbury to Pillsbury, 11 March [1855], JGW.

16. Pillsbury to Sarah Pillsbury, 25 May 1855, JGW.

17. Nancy Hewitt argues that among women's rights activists in western New York, the abandonment of orthodox religion was a precondition for their feminism. See Hewitt, "Feminist Friends: Agrarian Quakers and the Emergence of Woman's Rights in America," *Feminist Studies* 12 (Spring 1986): 27–49. Blanche Glassman Hersh found that both feminist-abolitionists and their husbands abandoned traditional and orthodox religion for more liberal denominations, including Universalism and Unitarianism. See Hersh, *Slavery of Sex*, 136–50, 221–22.

18. Elizabeth Cady Stanton, Susan B. Anthony, and Matilda Joslyn Gage, eds., *History of Woman Suffrage*, vol. 1 (New York: Fowler and Wells, 1881), 284; quoted in Hersh, *Slavery of Sex*, 141.

19. For references to Sarah traveling with Parker see the following letters to the editor in the *Herald of Freedom*: Parker Pillsbury, 9 July 1841; Persis Seavey, 14 October 1842; and Peter G. Mason, 28 October 1842.

20. Hersh profiled thirty-seven feminist-abolitionist couples and found that most of the men supported the public careers of their wives and also supported women's rights; *Slavery of Sex*, 218–51.

21. On Sarah's interaction with other women's antislavery groups see Sarah Pillsbury to Maria Weston Chapman, 25 December 1844, MS A.9.2 vol. 20, p. 135, BPL; and "Notices," *Herald of Freedom*, 5 February 1841.

22. Hersh uses this phrase to describe other feminist-abolitionist couples; *Slavery of Sex*, 218.

23. Hersh discusses the attitude of several feminist-abolitionists toward child-rearing, *Slavery of Sex*, 218–51.

24. Kelley returned part time to the lecturing field, however, during her daughter's second year. See Dorothy Sterling, *Ahead of Her Time: Abby Kelley and The Politics of Antislavery* (New York: Norton, 1991), 234–62.

25. See the following by Debra Gold Hansen: *Strained Sisterhood: Gender and Class in the Boston Female Anti-Slavery Society* (Amherst: University of Massachusetts Press, 1993); and "The Boston Female Anti-Slavery Society and the Limits of Gender Politics," in *The Abolitionist Sisterhood: Women's Political Culture in Antebellum America*, ed. Jean Fagan Yellin and John C. Van Horne (Ithaca: Cornell University Press, 1994), 45–66.

26. See, for example, Hansen, *Strained Sisterhood*; Jean R. Soderlund, "Priorities and Power: The Philadelphia Female Anti-Slavery Society," in *Abolitionist Sisterhood*, 67–88; Amy Swerdlow, "Abolition's Conservative Sisters: The Ladies' New York City Anti-Slavery Societies, 1834–1840," ibid., 31–44; and Carolyn L. Williams, "Religion, Race, and Gender in Antebellum American Radicalism: The Philadelphia Female Antislavery Society, 1833–1870" (Ph.D. diss., University of California, Los Angeles, 1991).

27. On antislavery fairs see Lee Chambers-Schiller, " 'A Good Work among the People': The Political Culture of the Boston Antislavery Fair," in *Abolitionist Sisterhood*, 249–74; Hansen, *Strained Sisterhood*, 124–39; and Williams, "Religion, Race and Gender." On petitioning see Lerner, "Political Activities of Antislavery Women"; and Deborah Bingham Van Broekhoven, " 'Let Your Names Be Enrolled': Method and Ideology in Women's Antislavery Petitioning," in *Abolitionist Sisterhood*, 179–200.

28. Parker received less than $300 annually his first few years as a lecturer. See Pillsbury,

"Salaries of the Agents," *Herald of Freedom*, 10 June 1842; and New Hampshire Anti-Slavery Society Minutes of the Board of Managers Meeting, Records of the New Hampshire Anti-Slavery Society, NHHS. Lillie Buffum Chace Wyman mentions that Parker Pillsbury and Stephen Foster returned from one of their early lecturing tours to find Sarah Pillsbury "without money" and "destitute of food." See Wyman's *American Chivalry* (Boston: W. B. Clarke Co., 1913), 77.

29. Sarah Pillsbury, "To the Anti-Slavery Women of New Hampshire," *Herald of Freedom*, 30 September 1842.

30. Indeed, this points to the flexibility of the separate sphere ideology and the extent to which women managed to subvert their confining role and affect male-dominated areas. Dozens of female antislavery societies held fairs and raised money to support the movement and, to some extent, the men who controlled the movement. The twenty-four Boston Female Anti-Slavery Society fairs, for example, raised over $65,000 for New England abolitionists; see Hansen, *Strained Sisterhood*, 138.

31. On the importance of hosting antislavery lecturers see Janice Sumler-Lewis, "The Forten-Purvis Women of Philadelphia and the American Anti-Slavery Crusade," *Journal of Negro History* 66 (Winter 1981–1982): 281–88. For references to Sarah boarding abolitionists see: Sarah Pillsbury to Pillsbury, 24 December 1854, JGW; Sarah Pillsbury to Charles Sargent, 25 June 1855, JGW; Sarah Pillsbury to Pillsbury, 16 December 1855, JGW; and Pillsbury to William Lloyd Garrison, 28 December 1859, MS A.1.2 vol. 29, p. 146, BPL.

32. Sarah Pillsbury to Pillsbury, 16 December 1855, JGW.

33. "Letter to Parker Pillsbury," *Liberator* (Boston, Mass.), 4 January 1856.

34. Sarah Pillsbury to Pillsbury, 24 December 1854, JGW.

35. Ibid. Lucy Stone finally married Henry Blackwell in 1855, after he had bombarded her for months with entreaties to become his wife. See Andrea Moore Kerr, *Lucy Stone: Speaking Out for Equality* (New Brunswick, N.J.: Rutgers University Press, 1992), 71–81.

36. Sarah Pillsbury to Pillsbury, 22 October 1854, JGW.

37. Pillsbury to Helen and Sarah Pillsbury, 16 May 1852, JGW.

38. Ibid.

39. Sarah Pillsbury to Pillsbury, 2 July 1854, JGW.

40. Sarah Pillsbury to Pillsbury, 6 April 1856, JGW.

41. Pillsbury to Sarah Pillsbury, 26 August 1854, JGW.

42. Pillsbury to Sarah Pillsbury, 14 February 1856, JGW.

43. Sarah Pillsbury to Pillsbury, 24 December 1854, JGW.

44. Ibid.

45. For more on the significance of friendships among Garrisonians see Donald Yacovone, "Abolitionists and the 'Language of Fraternal Love,'" in *Meanings for Manhood: Constructions of Masculinity in Victorian America*, ed. Mark C. Carnes and Clyde Griffen (Chicago: University of Chicago Press, 1990), 85–95.

46. See, for example, Pillsbury to Wendell Phillips, 17 May 1859, Crawford Blagden Papers, bMS Am 1953 (1001), HouL; William Lloyd Garrison to Pillsbury, 3 June 1859, MS A.1.1 vol. 5, p. 93, BPL; Pillsbury to Samuel May, Jr., 9 August 1850, MS B.1.6 vol. 7, no. 59, BPL; and Samuel May, Jr., to Richard Webb, 30 June 1862, MS B.1.6 vol. 9, no. 37, BPL.

47. Pillsbury to Marius R. Robinson, 15 September 1865, ALutz.

48. Sarah Pillsbury to Pillsbury, 2 July 1854, JGW.

49. Sarah Pillsbury to Helen Pillsbury, 8 November 1854, JGW.

50. Sarah Pillsbury to Pillsbury, 16 December 1855, JGW.

51. Sarah Pillsbury to Pillsbury, 24 February 1856, JGW.

52. On the importance of "visiting" among New Englanders see Karen Hansen, *A Very Social Time: Crafting Community in Antebellum New England* (Berkeley: University of California Press, 1994), 79–113.

53. Sarah Pillsbury to Pillsbury, 24 December 1854, JGW.

54. Sarah Pillsbury to Pillsbury, 11 March 1855, JGW.

55. Sarah Pillsbury to Pillsbury, 13 January 1856, JGW.

56. Stuart Blumin, *The Emergence of the Middle Class: Social Experience in the American City, 1760–1900* (Cambridge: Cambridge University Press, 1989), 185.

57. Sarah Pillsbury to Pillsbury, 13 January 1856, JGW.

58. Ibid.

59. Pillsbury to Charles Sargent, 16 June 1843, JGW.

60. Pillsbury to Stephen Foster, 27 October 1847, Abby Kelley Foster Papers, AAS.

61. Pillsbury to Sarah and Helen Pillsbury, 1 September 1857, JGW.

62. Pillsbury to Abby Kelly Foster, 9 January 1846, A. K. Foster Papers, AAS.

63. On the Grimké sisters see Gerda Lerner, *The Grimké Sisters from South Carolina: Pioneers for Woman's Rights and Abolition* (New York: Schocken Books, 1970); and Katherine Du Pre Lumpkin, *The Emancipation of Angelina Grimké* (Chapel Hill: University of North Carolina Press, 1974).

64. Pillsbury to William Lloyd Garrison, 22 March 1845, MS A.9.2 vol. 21, p. 17, BPL.

65. On changing visions of masculinity in the nineteenth century see E. Anthony Rotundo, "Body and Soul: Changing Ideals of American Middle-Class Manhood, 1770–1920," *Journal of Social History* 16 (Summer 1983): 23–38. The literature on the history of masculinity has grown extensively in the past several years. A diverse introduction to the field includes: Ava Baron, "The Masculinization of Production: The Gendering of Work and Skill in U.S. Newspaper Printing, 1850–1920," in *Gendered Domains: Rethinking Public and Private in Women's History*, ed. Dorothy O. Helly and Susan M. Reverby (Ithaca: Cornell University Press, 1992), 277–88; Gail Bederman, " 'Civilization,' the Decline of Middle-Class Manliness and Ida B. Wells's Lynching Campaign (1892–94)," *American Quarterly* 45 (December 1993): 558–95; Carnes and Griffen, eds., *Meanings for Manhood*; and E. Anthony Rotundo, *American Manhood: Transformations in Masculinity from the Revolution to the Modern Era* (New York: Basic Books, 1993).

66. Sarah Pillsbury to Pillsbury, 16 December 1855, JGW.

67. Ibid.

68. The Free Soil Party emerged as an abolitionist third party in the late 1840s. Many members of the Liberty Party eventually joined the Free Soilers. See Richard H. Sewell, *Ballots for Freedom: Antislavery Politics in the United States, 1837–1860* (1976; New York: Norton, 1980).

69. For more on Cogswell see *Biographical Review* 22 (1892): 40–48; James O. Lyford, ed., *History of Concord, New Hampshire from the Original Grant in Seventeen Hundred and Twenty-Five to the Opening of the Twentieth Century*, vol. 11 (Concord, N.H.: Rumford Press, 1903), 1041–42; "Necrology: Hon. P. B. Cogswell," *Granite Monthly* 19 (December 1895): 483; Pillsbury to Lucia Rogers, 17 February 1882, HAV; and Parker Pillsbury to B. F. Underwood, 23 December 1896, NHHS.

70. Sarah Pillsbury to Pillsbury, 27 August 1854, JGW.

71. Pillsbury to William Lloyd Garrison, Jr., 6 January 1896, SSC.

72. Sarah Pillsbury to Pillsbury, 13 February 1854, JGW; and Frederick Douglass to P. Brainard Cogswell, 18 March 1854, CSC.

73. See CSC for correspondence between potential lyceum speakers and Cogswell.

74. Sarah Pillsbury to Pillsbury, 13 January 1856, JGW. The orator was "Mrs. Webb," probably M. E. Webb who at this time performed readings of Harriet Beecher Stowe's novel, *Uncle Tom's Cabin*. See Louis Ruchames, ed., *The Letters of William Lloyd Garrison*, vol. 4, *From Disunionism to the Brink of War, 1850–1860* (Cambridge, Mass: Belknap Press, 1975), 366.

75. "Necrology: Hon. P. B. Cogswell."

76. As Mary P. Ryan has documented in her study of nineteenth-century Utica, New York, the emerging culture of the middle class depended very much on a particular domestic ideal. See Mary P. Ryan, *Cradle of the Middle Class: The Family in Oneida County, New York, 1790–1860* (Cambridge: Cambridge University Press, 1981).

77. For an excellent discussion of declining birth rates see John D'Emilio and Estelle B. Freedman, *Intimate Matters: A History of Sexuality in America* (New York: Harper and Row, 1988), 55–84.

78. Nancy Cott, "Passionlessness: An Interpretation of Victorian Sexual Ideology, 1790–1850," *Signs* 4 (Winter 1978): 219–36.

79. Sarah Pillsbury to Pillsbury, 22 October 1854, JGW.

80. D'Emilio and Freedman, *Intimate Matters*, 59–63.

81. Ronald Walters argues that major changes occurring in the nineteenth century, from the economy to politics, catalyzed antebellum reform. See Ronald G. Walters, *American Reformers, 1815–1860* (New York: Hill and Wang, 1978), 3–20.

82. Two excellent introductory texts on these reform trends are: Stephen Nissenbaum, *Sex, Diet, and Debility in Jacksonian America: Sylvester Graham and Health Reform* (Westport, Conn.: Greenwood Press, 1980); and James C. Whorton, *Crusaders for Fitness: The History of American Health Reformers* (Princeton N.J.: Princeton University Press, 1982).

83. Pillsbury to Helen Pillsbury, 7 March 1850, JGW.

84. Pillsbury to Sarah Pillsbury, 14 February 1856, JGW.

85. See William Leach, *True Love and Perfect Union: The Feminist Reform of Sex and Society* (New York: Basic Books, 1980), 19–37.

86. Pillsbury to Helen Pillsbury, January 1854, JGW.

87. Pillsbury to Helen Pillsbury, 30 October 1854, JGW.

88. Pillsbury to Helen Pillsbury, 24 December 1851, NHHS.

89. Pillsbury to Helen Pillsbury, 17 April 1852, JGW.

90. Pillsbury to Helen Pillsbury, 3 March 1852, JGW.

91. Pillsbury to Helen Pillsbury, 25 September 1850, JGW.

92. Pillsbury to Helen Pillsbury, 26 October 1851, JGW.

93. After describing for Helen his excursion to the well-respected Troy Female Seminary, he asked, "At what age do you expect to be ready for such a distant boarding school? If you live, we shall have to send you to one, some time or other." Pillsbury to Helen Pillsbury, 3 March 1852, JGW.

94. Pillsbury to Helen Pillsbury, 6 June 1878, JGW.

95. See Sydney E. Ahlstrom, *A Religious History of the American People*, vol. 1 (1972; New York: Image Books, 1975), 481–88; and Hersh, *Slavery of Sex*, 136–50.

96. Helen Pillsbury to Pillsbury, 14 January 1855, JGW.

97. Pillsbury to Ellen Wright Garrison, 11 July 1860, SSC.

Chapter Three. Masculinity and Women's Rights

1. Quoted in *Against the Tide: Pro-Feminist Men in the United States, 1776–1990: A Documentary History*, ed. Michael S. Kimmel and Thomas E. Mosmiller (Boston: Beacon Press, 1992), 6.

2. For more on attacks against profeminist men see Michael S. Kimmel, "The Contemporary 'Crisis' of Masculinity in Historical Perspective," in *The Making of Masculinities: The New Men's Studies*, ed. Harry Brod (Boston: Allen and Unwin, 1987), 121–53; and Kimmel and Mosmiller, *Against the Tide*, 47.

3. Garrisonians embraced disunionism and anticlericalism in the early 1840s. Both were based on the religious call to "come out" from sinful institutions. Believing the Constitution and Union to be proslavery, Garrison called for the North to secede from the Union and thus escape the sinful influences of the South. Religious institutions proved equally proslavery, so Garrisonians encouraged abolitionists to abandon their church memberships as well. See John L. Thomas, *The Liberator: William Lloyd Garrison* (Boston: Little, Brown, 1963), 328–37.

4. See Phillip Foner, ed., *Frederick Douglass on Women's Rights* (1976; New York: Da Capo Press, 1992); Nathaniel P. Rogers, *A Collection from the Newspaper Writings of Nathaniel Peabody Rogers* (Concord, N. H.: John R. French, 1847); and Thomas, *William Lloyd Garrison*.

5. For more on feminist-abolitionist couples see Blanche Glassman Hersh, *The Slavery of Sex: Feminist Abolitionists in America* (Urbana: University of Illinois Press, 1978), 218–51.

6. And yet, as the historian Kristin Hoganson has shown, despite their women's rights activism many profeminist men (including Pillsbury) employed traditional gender ideals in their antislavery rhetoric, emphasizing slave men's inability to protect their female dependents and slave women's inability to fulfill their domestic roles as mothers and wives. Kristin Hoganson, "Garrisonian Abolitionists and the Rhetoric of Gender, 1850–1860," *American Quarterly* 45 (December 1993): 558–95.

7. The analysis here relies on Joan Scott's two-part definition of gender in which she argues that gender is "a constitutive element of social relationships based on perceived differences between the sexes," but also a "primary way of signifying relationships of power." See Joan Scott, "Gender: A Useful Category of Historical Analysis," in *Gender and the Politics of History* (New York: Columbia University Press, 1988), 42.

8. For more on the variety of masculinities in the nineteenth century see Mark C. Carnes and Clyde Griffen, eds., *Meanings for Manhood: Constructions of Masculinity in Victorian America* (Chicago: University of Chicago Press, 1990); and E. Anthony Rotundo, *American Manhood: Transformations in Masculinity from the Revolution to the Modern Era* (New York: Basic Books, 1993). On working-class masculinity see Ava Baron, "The Masculinization of Production: The Gendering of Work and Skill in U.S. Newspaper Printing, 1850–1920," in *Gendered Domains: Rethinking Public and Private in Women's History*, ed. Dorothy O. Helly and Susan M. Reverby (Ithaca: Cornell University Press, 1992), 277–88; and Mary H. Blewett, "Manhood and the Market: The Politics of Gender and Class among the Textile Workers of Fall River, Massachusetts, 1870–1880," in *Work Engendered: Toward a New History of American Labor*, ed. Ava Baron (Ithaca: Cornell University Press, 1991), 92–113. On race and masculinity see Gail Bederman, " 'Civilization,' the Decline of Middle-Class Manliness, and Ida B. Wells's Antilynching Campaign (1892–94)," *Radical History Review* 52 (Winter 1992): 5–30. On masculinity and antislavery see Hoganson, "Garrisonian Abolitionists"; Margaret M. R. Kellow, " 'For the Sake of Suffering Kansas': Lydia Maria Child, Gender and the Politics of the 1850s," *Journal of Women's History* 5 (Fall 1993): 32–49; Ronald G. Walters, "The Erotic South: Civilization and Sexuality in American Abolitionism," *American Quarterly* 25 (May 1973): 177–201; and Donald Yacovone, "Abolitionists and the 'Language of Fraternal Love,' " in *Meanings for Manhood*, 85–95.

9. See E. Anthony Rotundo, "Body and Soul: Changing Ideals of American Middle-Class Manhood, 1770–1920," *Journal of Social History* 16 (Summer 1983): 23–38.

10. Although E. Anthony Rotundo has convincingly argued in *American Manhood* that the term "manhood" often meant "adulthood" in the nineteenth century, Pillsbury understood manliness as a gendered concept. True men achieved manhood through very particular activities and duties, according to Pillsbury.

11. Parker Pillsbury's Personal History Form for the *Boston Journal*, NHHS.

12. Pillsbury, "New England Correspondence," *Anti-Slavery Bugle* (Salem, Ohio), 12 March 1853.

13. *Journals of Ralph Waldo Emerson*, ed. Edward Waldo Emerson and Waldo Emerson Forbes, vol. 7 (Cambridge, Mass.: Riverside Press, 1912), 202.

14. Pillsbury, "New England Correspondence," *Anti-Slavery Bugle*, 30 August 1853.

15. Pillsbury to Helen Pillsbury, 8 May 1878, JGW. Pillsbury's concern with the decline in popularity and status of yeoman farmers represented a common concern among many Northern reformers. See, for example, William Ellery Channing, *Lectures on the Elevation of the Labouring Portion of the Community* (Boston, 1840).

16. Pillsbury, "The Mob and the Ministers on the Cape," *Liberator* (Boston, Mass.), 24 November 1848.

17. Nathaniel P. Rogers, "Lecturing Agents," *Herald of Freedom* (Concord, N.H.), 31 August 1839; Pillsbury, "Convention at Livonia," *Liberator*, 15 February 1861.

18. On male athleticism see Rotundo, *American Manhood*, 222–46; and Rotundo, "Body and Soul." See also Susan Curtis's description of the emergence of a masculinized Jesus, "The Son of Man and God the Father: The Social Gospel and Victorian Masculinity," in *Meanings for Manhood*. On muscular Christianity in Britain see J. A. Mangan, "Social Darwinism and Upper-

Class Education in Late Victorian and Edwardian England," in *Manliness and Morality: Middle-Class Masculinity in Britain and America*, ed. J. A. Mangan and James Walvin (New York: St. Martin's Press, 1987).

19. Carroll Smith-Rosenberg, "Davy Crockett as Trickster: Pornography, Liminality and Symbolic Inversions in Victorian America," in *Disorderly Conduct: Visions of Gender in Victorian America* (New York: Oxford University Press, 1985), 108.

20. Pillsbury, "Woman's Work and Wages," *The Revolution* (New York), 22 April 1869.

21. Ibid.

22. "Letter from Mr. Pillsbury," *Liberator*, 16 November 1860.

23. Pillsbury to Helen Pillsbury, 3 October 1853, JGW.

24. For more on the importance of self-discipline among abolitionists see Ronald G. Walters, *American Reformers, 1815–1860* (New York: Hill and Wang, 1978), 77–100.

25. Letter from Pillsbury, *Anti-Slavery Bugle*, 4 August 1848.

26. See W. J. Rorabaugh, *The Alcoholic Republic: An American Tradition* (Oxford: Oxford University Press, 1979).

27. "Letter from Parker Pillsbury," *National Anti-Slavery Standard* (New York), 18 March 1852.

28. Pillsbury, "Teetotal Convention," *Herald of Freedom*, 4 September 1840.

29. See Paul E. Johnson, *A Shopkeeper's Millennium: Society and Revivals in Rochester, New York, 1815–1837* (New York: Hill and Wang, 1978); and Clyde S. Griffen, "Religious Benevolence as Social Control, 1815–1860," *Mississippi Valley Historical Review* 44 (December 1957): 423–44.

30. Foner, *Frederick Douglass*, 60. On the antebellum temperance movement see Robert H. Abzug, *Cosmos Crumbling: American Reform and the Religious Imagination* (New York: Oxford University Press, 1994), 81–104.

31. His resolution stated: "Resolved, That the Temperance Societies in this State have proved recreant to their trust, and have suffered the great cause of Humanity to decline under their unfaithful management and want of zeal in its behalf." See "State Tee-Total Convention," *Herald of Freedom*, 18 September 1840.

32. By the middle of the century women, primarily concerned with protecting womanhood and punishing besotted manhood, dominated most temperance organizations. See Barbara L. Epstein, *The Politics of Domesticity: Women, Evangelism and Temperance in Nineteenth-Century America* (Middletown, Conn.: Wesleyan University Press, 1981).

33. Statement of Parker Pillsbury, May 1845, Papers of the Western Anti-Slavery Society, LOC.

34. Pillsbury to Helen Pillsbury, 8 May 1878, JGW.

35. See Lee Benson, *The Concept of Jacksonian Democracy: New York as a Test Case* (Princeton, N.J.: Princeton University Press, 1961); Ronald Formisano, "Deferential-Participant Politics: The Early Republic's Political Culture, 1789–1840," *American Political Science Review* 68 (1974): 473–87; and Richard Hofstader, *The Idea of a Party System* (Berkeley: University of California Press, 1969).

36. See Paula Baker, "The Domestication of American Politics: Women and American Political Society, 1780–1920," *American Historical Review* 89 (June 1984): 620–47.

37. Pillsbury to Gerrit Smith, 23 September 1868, SYR.

38. See William Leach, *True Love and Perfect Union: The Feminist Reform of Sex and Society* (New York: Basic Books, 1980).

39. Pillsbury to William Lloyd Garrison, Jr., 12 February 1892, SSC.

40. For a discussion of republicanism and the political economy see Drew McCoy, *The Elusive Republic: Political Economy in Jeffersonian America* (Chapel Hill: University of North Carolina Press, 1980).

41. "Ninth Annual Meeting of the Essex County Anti-Slavery Society," *Herald of Freedom*, 21 July 1843.

42. "Editorial Correspondence," *The Revolution*, 11 March 1868.

43. Pillsbury, "Noisy Women and Gentle Women," *The Revolution*, 12 August 1869.

44. Kimmel and Mosmiller, *Against the Tide*, 216–17. Foner, *Frederick Douglass*, 96.

45. Pillsbury, "The Mortality of Nations, an Address Delivered Before the American Equal Rights Association," 9 May 1867, NHHS.

46. "Free love" in nineteenth-century America was a term of opprobrium. It was used by its detractors as a denotation of sexual impropriety. Its proponents, on the other hand, argued that free love involved opposition to marriage laws that denigrated women and support for sexual intercourse based on love, not economic or legal ties. It was not, they contended, a call for frequent and uninhibited sexual relations. See Ann Braude, *Radical Spirits: Spiritualism and Women's Rights in Nineteenth-Century America* (Boston: Beacon Press, 1989), 127–36; Leach, *True Love*; Stephen Nissenbaum, *Sex, Diet, and Debility in Jacksonian America* (Westport, Conn.: Greenwood Press, 1980); and Hal D. Sears, *The Sex Radicals: Free Love in High Victorian America* (Lawrence: Regents Press of Kansas, 1977).

47. Charles Griffing to Samuel May, Jr., 1 March 1863, MS B.1.6 vol. 9, no. 87, BPL (emphasis in original). Griffing accurately quoted Pillsbury's article, which appeared in the *Anti-Slavery Bugle*, 30 April 1853.

48. Ibid.

49. Ibid. (emphasis in original).

50. Marius R. Robinson to Samuel May, Jr., 24 April 1863, MS B.1.6 vol. 9, no. 91, BPL.

51. On Pillsbury's concern with diet and good health see, for example, Pillsbury to Helen Pillsbury, 7 March 1850, JGW; and Pillsbury to Sarah Pillsbury, 14 February 1856, JGW. For information on similar trends in relation to the body and health in Victorian England see Bruce Haley, *The Healthy Body and Victorian Culture* (Cambridge, Mass.: Harvard University Press, 1978).

52. For example, Pillsbury told his wife in a letter from England that she should exhort her bachelor brother, Charles Sargent "to hold his head high and maintain his right to sleep alone as long as he pleases. A true man's history can be written in other characters *than baby hieroglyphics*." Pillsbury to Sarah Pillsbury, 14 February 1856, JGW.

53. See John D'Emilio and Estelle B. Freedman, *Intimate Matters: A History of Sexuality in America* (New York: Harper and Row, 1988), 66–73; and Leach, *True Love*, 19–37.

54. See Leach, *True Love*, 85–106.

55. Pillsbury, "New England Correspondence," *Anti-Slavery Bugle*, 30 April 1853.

56. During the colonial period women were considered dangerous as a result of their powerful and "uncontrolled" sexual nature. Although the nineteenth-century ideology of passionlessness disarmed women's sexual power they gained status as spiritual and moral beings. See Nancy Cott, "Passionlessness: An Interpretation of Victorian Sexual Ideology, 1790–1850," *Signs* 4 (Winter 1978): 219–36; D'Emilio and Freedman, *Intimate Matters*, 45–46, 70–71; and Ellen Rothman, *Hands and Hearts: A History of Courtship in America* (Cambridge, Mass.: Harvard University Press, 1987), 119–43.

57. See the following articles by Robert L. Griswold: "Divorce and the Legal Redefinition of Victorian Manhood," in *Meanings for Manhood*, 96–110; "The Evolution of the Doctrine of Mental Cruelty in Victorian American Divorce, 1790–1900," *Journal of Social History* 20 (Fall 1986): 127–48; "Law, Sex, Cruelty, and Divorce in Victorian America, 1840–1900," *American Quarterly* 38 (Winter 1986): 721–45; and "Sexual Cruelty and the Case for Divorce in Victorian America," *Signs* 2 (Spring 1986): 529–41. Even some physicians toward the end of the century expounded on the sexual exploitation of women and the need to regulate male promiscuity. See John S. Haller and Robin M. Haller, *The Physician and Sexuality in Victorian America* (Urbana: University of Illinois Press, 1974), 236–70.

58. In his egalitarian perspective on sexuality Pillsbury distinguished himself from other antebellum male moral reformers whose concerns with controlling male sexuality, according to Carroll Smith-Rosenberg, reflected anxiety about their declining status. Unlike female moral reformers who were concerned with the double standard and sexual exploitation (much like Pillsbury), male moral reformers were focused on maintaining their own power. See the following by Smith-Rosenberg, "Beauty, the Beast, and the Militant Woman in Jacksonian Amer-

ica," *American Quarterly* 23 (October 1971): 562–84; and "Sex as a Symbol in Victorian Purity: An Ethnohistorical Analysis of Jacksonian America," *American Journal of Sociology* 84 suppl. (1978): 212–47.

59. See Hoganson, "Garrisonian Abolitionists"; and Walters, "The Erotic South."

60. Pillsbury, "Swapping Wives," *The Revolution*, 24 June 1869.

61. Pillsbury attended women's rights conventions in 1850, 1858, and 1859. See Pillsbury to Wendell Phillips, 21 September 1859, Crawford Blagden Papers, bMS Am 1953 (1001), HouL; Alma Lutz, *Susan B. Anthony: Rebel, Crusader, Humanitarian* (Boston: Beacon Press, 1959), 25; and "The National Woman's Rights Convention," *National Anti-Slavery Standard*, 22 May 1858. Several other male abolitionists also regularly attended women's rights conventions, including Frederick Douglass, Thomas Wentworth Higginson, Samuel J. May, and Gerrit Smith.

62. Pillsbury, "Women's Rights Convention," *Anti-Slavery Bugle*, 9 November 1850.

63. Pillsbury, "New England Correspondence," ibid., 20 August 1853.

64. For the most recent discussion of dress reform see Sylvia D. Hoffert, *When Hens Crow: The Woman's Rights Movement in Antebellum America* (Bloomington: Indiana University Press, 1995), 23–31.

65. Pillsbury to Helen Pillsbury, 18 August 1853, JGW.

66. See Leach, *True Love*, 213–62.

67. Pillsbury to Wendell Phillips, 21 September 1859, Blagden Papers, bMS Am 1953 (1001), HouL.

Chapter Four. Abolitionism Organized or Unorganized?

1. Nathaniel P. Rogers, "Parker Pillsbury," *Herald of Freedom* (Concord, N.H.), 6 September 1844.

2. See Parker Pillsbury, *Acts of the Anti-Slavery Apostles* (Concord, N.H., 1883), 10–11; "The Warfare: Plan of Operations for September," *Herald of Freedom*, 4 September 1840; and Pillsbury, "The Warfare," ibid., 20 November 1840.

3. On Rogers's personal history see Robert Adams, "Nathaniel Peabody Rogers: 1794–1846," *New England Quarterly* (September 1947): 365–76; Steven Cox, "Nathaniel P. Rogers and the Rogers Collection," *Historical New Hampshire* 22 (Spring 1978): 52–61; and Pillsbury, *Anti-Slavery Apostles*, 28–46.

4. For Rogers's writings see *A Collection from the Newspaper Writings of Nathaniel Peabody Rogers* (Concord, N.H.: John R. French, 1847); and the *Herald of Freedom*, 1838–1845.

5. Anne C. Loveland, "Evangelicalism and 'Immediate Emancipation' in American Antislavery Thought," *Journal of Southern History* 32 (May 1966): 175.

6. Ronald G. Walters, *American Reformers, 1815–1860* (New York: Hill and Wang, 1978), 25.

7. John R. McKivigan, *The War against Proslavery Religion: Abolitionism and the Northern Churches, 1830–1865* (Ithaca: Cornell University Press, 1984), 20. See also Walters, *American Reformers*, 21–38.

8. *Newspaper Writings*, 220. Quoted in Adams, "Rogers," 368.

9. Ibid.

10. Nathaniel P. Rogers, "Pro-Slavery 'Excommunication,' " *Herald of Freedom*, 19 March 1841.

11. On Rogers's no-organization ideas see Lewis Perry, *Radical Abolitionism: Anarchy and the Government of God in Antislavery Thought* (1973; Knoxville: University of Tennessee Press, 1995), 117–23.

12. Perry, *Radical Abolitionism*, 114.

13. Nathaniel P. Rogers, "Free Meeting at Nashua," *Herald of Freedom*, 2 August 1844.

14. Nathaniel P. Rogers, "The Herald of Freedom," ibid., 14 June 1844.

15. Letter from Stephen S. Foster, "To the Subscribers and Friends of the Herald of Freedom," ibid., 9 August 1844.
16. Nathaniel P. Rogers, "Organization in New Hampshire," ibid., 23 August 1844.
17. Ibid.
18. Nathaniel P. Rogers, "Parker Pillsbury," ibid., 6 September 1844.
19. Rogers printed this letter, dated 13 September 1844, ibid., 18 July 1845.
20. Letter from Stephen Foster and Nathaniel P. Rogers's response, ibid., 13 September 1844; and letter from Stephen Foster and John French's response, ibid., 20 September 1844.
21. Nathaniel P. Rogers, "The Convention," ibid., 6 December 1844.
22. John R. French, "Reply to friend Foster's Charges," ibid., 20 September 1844. See also letter from Nathaniel P. Rogers, "The Herald of Freedom," *National Anti-Slavery Standard* (New York), 16 January 1845.
23. The report from the arbitration committee stated specifically that the conflict over no-organization had no influence on the issue of who owned the *Herald*. See "Proceedings of the Anti-Slavery Convention in Concord, N.H.," *National Anti-Slavery Standard*, 26 December 1844.
24. " 'The' Herald of Freedom," *Liberator* (Boston, Mass.), 4 April 1845.
25. For two contrasting descriptions of this meeting see Nathaniel P. Rogers, "The Convention," *Herald of Freedom*, 6 December 1844; and Edmund Quincy, "Special Meeting of the New Hampshire Anti-Slavery Society," *National Anti-Slavery Standard*, 12 December 1844.
26. See letter from Nathaniel P. Rogers, "The Herald of Freedom," *National Anti-Slavery Standard*, 16 January 1845; "Circular," by John French and Nathaniel P. Rogers, MS A.1.2 vol. 15, no. 12, BPL; William Lloyd Garrison, "Extraordinary Circular," *Liberator*, 14 February 1845; letter from Nathaniel P. Rogers, "To William Lloyd Garrison," ibid., 21 February 1845; and William Lloyd Garrison, " 'The Herald of Freedom,' " ibid., 18 April 1845.
27. Nathaniel P. Rogers, "A Word of Remark," *Herald of Freedom*, 18 July 1845.
28. John French, "Parker Pillsbury," ibid., 6 December 1844.
29. Lawrence Friedman, *Gregarious Saints: Self and Community in American Abolitionism, 1830–1870* (Cambridge: Cambridge University Press, 1982), 59–61.
30. Perry, *Radical Abolitionism*, 127.
31. James Brewer Stewart, *Wendell Phillips, Liberty's Hero* (Baton Rouge: Louisiana State University Press, 1986), 132.
32. See "Anti-Slavery Conventions, Lectures and Meetings for Discussions," *Herald of Freedom*, 11 October 1844; and Letter from Pillsbury, "Convention at Milford," ibid., 8 November 1844.
33. Nathaniel P. Rogers, "Parker Pillsbury," ibid., 27 September 1844.
34. Nathaniel P. Rogers, "Parker Pillsbury," ibid., 6 September 1844.
35. Pillsbury to David Boutelle, 22 January 1848, John Parker Hale Papers, Dartmouth College Library, Hanover, N.H.
36. Sarah Pillsbury to Maria Weston Chapman, 25 December 1844, MS A.9.2 vol. 20, p. 135, BPL.
37. Pillsbury to William Lloyd Garrison, 22 March 1845, MS A.9.2 vol. 21, p. 17, BPL.
38. The Rogers conflict also affected other New England antislavery communities. Nearly forty Rhode Island abolitionists met in Providence and wrote a series of resolutions supporting Rogers. See "The Herald of Freedom," *National Anti-Slavery Standard*, 26 December 1844.
39. Pillsbury to Wendell Phillips, 29 December 1844, Crawford Blagden Papers, bMS Am 1953 (1001), HouL.
40. Ibid.
41. For a variety of reports on the chaotic nature of the meeting see the following articles in the *Liberator*, 13 June 1845: "Annual Meeting of the New Hampshire Anti-Slavery Society"; "Letter from Wendell Phillips"; "Letter from James N. Buffum"; and "Letter from C. L. Remond."
42. *National Anti-Slavery Standard*, 12 June 1845.

43. Pillsbury to Wendell Phillips, 8 January 1845, Blagden Papers, bMS Am 1953 (1001), HouL.

44. Ibid.

45. Garrison printed a letter containing this quote and expressed his disagreement with it. See William Lloyd Garrison, " 'The Herald of Freedom,' " *Liberator*, 18 April 1845.

46. Rogers's paper first appeared in February 1845 and was published irregularly for several months before it ceased with Rogers's illness. See "Circular," BPL.

47. Pillsbury to William Lloyd Garrison, 22 March 1845, MS A.9.2 vol. 21, p. 17, BPL.

48. Pillsbury to Stephen S. Foster, 30 September 1845, Abby Kelley Foster Papers, AAS.

49. Pillsbury to William Lloyd Garrison, 11 June 1845, MS A.1.2 vol. 15, p. 40, BPL.

50. Pillsbury to David Wood and David Boutelle, 3 January 1845, J. P. Hale Papers, Dartmouth.

51. Pillsbury to William Lloyd Garrison, 13 February 1845, MS A.1.2 vol. 15, p. 16, BPL.

52. Ibid.

53. "Letter from the Editor," *Herald of Freedom*, 28 March 1845.

54. " 'The' Herald of Freedom," *Liberator*, 4 April 1845.

55. "Rhode Island Anti-Slavery Society," *National Anti-Slavery Standard*, 10 December 1846.

56. See Pillsbury, *Anti-Slavery Apostles*, 28–46.

57. Pillsbury, "Woman's Right of Petition," *The Revolution*, 24 June 1869.

58. Pillsbury to Lucia Rogers, 22 December 1881, HAV.

59. Pillsbury, *Anti-Slavery Apostles*, 28.

60. See, for example, "The 'Garrisonians' Sketched by an Opponent," *Anti-Slavery Bugle*, 6 September 1851.

Chapter Five. Grassroots Abolition

1. The Western Anti-Slavery Society grew out of the Ohio American Anti-Slavery Society in 1845. It attracted mostly radical Garrisonians who rejected the extensive antislavery third party movement in the West. Although initially limited to Ohio, it eventually expanded to include abolition groups in Michigan, Indiana, Illinois, Iowa, and Wisconsin. See Douglas Gamble, "Moral Suasion in the West: Garrisonian Abolitionism, 1831–1861" (Ph.D. diss., Ohio State University, 1973), 18–48.

2. "You don't know how importunate the Ohio folks have been," he explained to Samuel May, Jr., the General Agent of the American Anti-Slavery Society. "I have received five letters from them written the last three days." See Pillsbury to Samuel May, Jr., 30 July 1850, MS A.1.2 vol. 19, p. 62, BPL.

3. Pillsbury's speech is fully reported in "Remarks of Mr. Pillsbury," *Anti-Slavery Bugle* (Salem, Ohio), 3 September 1853.

4. Pillsbury to Samuel May, Jr., 1 September 1853, MS A.1.2 vol. 23, p. 50, BPL.

5. For a description of the resolutions see "Proceedings of the Eleventh Anniversary," *Anti-Slavery Bugle*, 3 September 1853.

6. See the following by John L. Myers: "The Agency System of the Anti-Slavery Movement, 1832–1837, and Its Antecedents in Other Benevolent and Reform Societies" (Ph.D. diss., University of Michigan, 1961); "The Beginning of Antislavery Agencies in New Hampshire, 1832–1835," *Historical New Hampshire* 25 (Fall 1970): 3–25; and "The Early Antislavery Agency System in Pennsylvania, 1833–1837," *Pennsylvania History* 46 (January 1964): 62–86.

7. These quotes describing the effects of field lecturing are from Pillsbury, "Government, Education, and Religion in Indiana," *Liberator*, 28 October 1853. As John L. Thomas asserted, "the best way of spreading the gospel now appeared to be the spontaneous local meeting, where itinerant antislavery lecturers like Stephen S. Foster and Parker Pillsbury performed in their best Old Testament manner." John L. Thomas, *The Liberator: William Lloyd Garrison* (Boston: Little, Brown, 1963), 324.

8. See the papers of the Western Anti-Slavery Society, LOC; and the regular "Notices" of meetings in the *Anti-Slavery Bugle* between 1845 and 1860.

9. On the purpose of Pillsbury's trip to England see the following letters in the BPL: Pillsbury to Maria Weston Chapman, 17 and 28 January 1854, MS A.9.2, vol. 28, pp. 2, 5; Pillsbury to Samuel May, Jr., 11 April 1855, MS B.1.6, vol. 5, no. 63. For more on Pillsbury's antislavery activities abroad see his European Journal, NHHS.

10. Letter from Henry Wright, "Will the North Submit?" *Liberator* (Boston), 27 March 1857.

11. Pillsbury, "Travelling Accommodations," ibid., 17 October 1851.

12. John White Chadwick, ed., *A Life for Liberty: Anti-Slavery and Other Letters of Sallie Holley* (1899; New York: Negro Universities Press, 1969), 140.

13. Pillsbury, "Foreign Correspondence," *Anti-Slavery Bugle*, 1 July 1854.

14. Charles Lenox Remond to Pillsbury, 12 January 1844, CSC; Judson, John, Asa, and Abby Hutchinson to Pillsbury, 23 November 1843, CSC; Pillsbury to Wendell Phillips, 14 February 1844, Crawford Blagden Papers, bMS Am 1953 (1001), HouL; "Parker Pillsbury," *Herald of Freedom*, 3 and 10 November 1843.

15. For more on the demographic background of abolitionists see Edward Magdol, *The Antislavery Rank and File: A Social Profile of the Abolitionists' Constituency* (New York: Greenwood Press, 1986).

16. Pillsbury to Helen Pillsbury, 22 February 1848, JGW.

17. Pillsbury to Helen Pillsbury, 12 April 1892, JGW.

18. Pillsbury to Helen Pillsbury, 22 February 1848, JGW.

19. "Mr. Pillsbury at Plymouth," *Liberator*, 4 April 1851.

20. Martha Barrett Diary, 2 February 1852, PEM.

21. Pillsbury, "The Campaign in Ohio," *Liberator*, 10 October 1851.

22. Ibid.

23. Pillsbury, "Pertinent Question," *Anti-Slavery Bugle*, 22 June 1850. For other examples of churches closing their doors to Pillsbury see his letters in the *Herald of Freedom* (Concord, N.H.): 11 and 18 December 1840; 24 September and 12 February 1841; 4 March 1842. See also the following in the *Liberator*: "Ministry of Cape Ann," 23 April 1847; "Convention at Hyannis," 15 September 1848; "Anti-Slavery in Connecticut," 12 March 1852; and the following in the *Anti-Slavery Bugle*: "Meetings at Sullivan and Westfield," 31 August 1850; "Meetings at Andover and Dorset," 8 November 1851; and "Letter from Indiana," 15 October 1853.

24. Pillsbury, "One Week's Experience of a 'Field Hand,' " *Liberator*, 16 April 1852.

25. See the following in the *Liberator*: "Our Cause in Ohio," 3 July 1846; and "Anniversary of the Western Anti-Slavery Society," 5 September 1851. On Pillsbury's smaller meetings see letter from Pillsbury, *Herald of Freedom*, 23 December 1842 and 12 July 1844; "The Barnstable Convention," *Liberator*, 24 September 1842; and "Meetings in Herkimer County," *National Anti-Slavery Standard* (New York), 22 January 1852.

26. For example, Pillsbury's annual visits to the Western Society (often accompanied by Stephen S. Foster and Abby Kelley Foster) resulted in its reputation for extremely radical positions. Westerners insisted on condemning the Republican Party in the late 1850s even when Garrison became more conciliatory. See Gamble, "Moral Suasion in the West." See also the description of Pillsbury's effect on the New Hampshire Anti-Slavery Society in the letter from John W. Lewis, *Herald of Freedom*, 24 July 1840.

27. This includes every major Christian denomination: Methodist, Congregational, Presbyterian, Baptist, and Unitarian. Even those denominations or breakaway groups that forbade slaveholding (Quakers, Freewill Baptists, Wesleyan Methodists, and Free Presbyterians) still found themselves at odds with the Garrisonians. See the superb discussion of this topic by John R. McKivigan, *The War against Proslavery Religion: Abolitionism and the Northern Churches, 1830–1865* (Ithaca: Cornell University Press, 1984).

28. For more on the relationship between antislavery and religion see Anne C. Loveland, "Evangelicalism and 'Immediate Emancipation' in American Antislavery Thought," *Journal of*

Southern History 32 (May 1966): 172–88; McKivigan, *Proslavery Religion*; and Donald M. Scott, "Abolition as a Sacred Vocation," in *Antislavery Reconsidered: New Perspectives on the Abolitionists*, ed. Lewis Perry and Michael Fellman (Baton Rouge: Louisiana State University Press, 1979), 51–74.

29. McKivigan, *Proslavery Religion*, 56–73; and J. Earl Thompson, Jr., "Abolitionism and Theological Education at Andover," *New England Quarterly* 47 (1974): 238–61.

30. No major denomination endorsed immediate emancipation prior to the Civil War. See McKivigan, *Proslavery Religion*, 56–73.

31. Letter from Pillsbury, *Herald of Freedom*, 5 November 1841.

32. Letter from Pillsbury, ibid., 19 November 1841.

33. See Parker Pillsbury, *Acts of the Anti-Slavery Apostles* (Concord, N.H., 1983); and McKivigan, *Proslavery Religion*, 56–73. For more on come-outerism see John R. McKivigan, "The Antislavery 'Comeouter' Sects: A Neglected Dimension of the Abolitionist Movement," *Civil War History* 26 (June 1980): 142–60.

34. Letter from Pillsbury, *Herald of Freedom*, 5 November 1841.

35. "Annual Meeting of the Essex Co. A.S. Society," *Liberator*, 12 July 1850.

36. Letter from Pillsbury, *Herald of Freedom*, 4 March 1842.

37. "Convention at Abington," *Liberator*, 25 April 1851.

38. See the following letters in the BPL: Jane Wigham to Anne Warren Weston, 18 November 1852, MS A.9.2 vol. 26, p. 71; and Richard Webb to Maria Weston Chapman, 1 July 1857, MS A.9.2 vol. 29, p. 11.

39. Mary Estlin to Anne Warren Weston, 4 March 1853, MS A.9.2 vol. 27, p. 15, BPL.

40. "Speech of Mr. Pillsbury," *National Anti-Slavery Standard*, 16 May 1857.

41. Quoted in the *North Star* (Rochester, N.Y.), 31 July 1851.

42. Ibid.

43. Quoted in "Satanic Misrepresentation," *Liberator*, 3 October 1851.

44. See ibid. and "Mr. Pillsbury—Misrepresentation," *Anti-Slavery Bugle*, 20 September 1851.

45. "Barnstable County Convention," *Liberator*, 5 September 1851.

46. See "Meetings at New Market, Massillon and Akron," *Anti-Slavery Bugle*, 4 October 1851; "The Campaign in Ohio," *Liberator*, 10 October 1851; "Miss Holley and Parker Pillsbury," *Anti-Slavery Bugle*, 11 October 1851; "Wesleyanism at the West" and "Travelling Accommodations," *Liberator*, 17 October 1851; and "Meetings at Westfield," *Anti-Slavery Bugle*, 18 October 1851.

47. "From the Oberlin *Evangelist*: Letter from Parker Pillsbury," *Anti-Slavery Bugle*, 25 October 1851.

48. Ibid.

49. Pillsbury, "Meetings at Andover and Dorset," ibid., 8 November 1851.

50. Letter from Lewis Ford, "The Lecturing Field," *Liberator*, 9 January 1852.

51. Ibid.

52. Pillsbury to Samuel May, Jr., 14 February 1856, MS B.1.6 vol. 6, no. 11, BPL.

53. The column is reproduced in the *Liberator*; see "An Exploded Slander Revived," 14 August 1857.

54. "Sigma and His Dogs," ibid., 21 August 1857.

55. Ibid.

56. "New England Anti-Slavery Convention," *National Anti-Slavery Standard*, 3 June 1847.

57. For a brief summary of Pillsbury's speech see "Sketches of the Sayings and Doings at the N.E. Anti-Slavery Convention," *Liberator*, 4 June 1847.

58. Ibid.

59. This description of Pillsbury's speaking abilities is found in Leander Cogswell's *History of the Town of Henniker, Merrimack County, New Hampshire, 1735 to 1880* (Concord, N.H.: Republican Press Association, 1880), 686. Some of the other antislavery organizations that passed antichurch resolutions in 1847 were the Old Colony Anti-Slavery Society of Plymouth, Mass-

achusetts ("Annual Meeting," *Liberator*, 16 July 1847), the Worcester County South Anti-Slavery Society ("Worcester County South Anti-Slavery Society," ibid., 3 December 1847), and the New Hampshire Anti-Slavery Society ("Annual Meeting of the N.H. Anti-Slavery Society," ibid., 11 June 1847).

60. Although the *Syracuse Daily Star* used this phrase in reference to an anticlerical speech Pillsbury presented a few years later, the press reacted similarly in 1847. Quoted in "Pro-Slavery and Anti-Slavery Advocates," *National Anti-Slavery Standard*, 31 May 1849.

61. From the *Savannah Georgian*. Quoted in "The Abolitionists," *Liberator*, 25 June 1847.

62. "Annual Meeting of the N.H. Anti-Slavery Society," ibid., 11 June 1847.

63. Pillsbury, "Liberty Party," *Anti-Slavery Bugle*, 10 July 1846.

64. See Thomas, *William Lloyd Garrison*, 388–408.

65. See, for example, Pillsbury's resolutions in the following articles in the *Liberator*: "Annual Meeting of the Essex County Anti-Slavery Society," 7 July 1848; "East Lexington," 16 February 1849; "Anniversary of the Western A.S. Society," 5 September 1851; "First of August in Salem," 6 August 1852; and "New England Anti-Slavery Convention," 5 June 1857.

66. See Richard H. Sewell, *Ballots for Freedom: Antislavery Politics in the United States, 1837–1860* (1976; New York: Norton, 1980), 80–106.

67. See Eric Foner, *Free Soil, Free Labor, Free Men: The Ideology of the Republican Party before the Civil War* (New York: Oxford University Press, 1970); William E. Gienapp, *The Origins of the Republican Party, 1852–1856* (New York: Oxford University Press, 1987); and Sewell, *Ballots for Freedom*.

68. James B. Stewart established the practicality and effectiveness of the Garrisonian moral suasion tactic in "The Aims and Impact of Garrisonian Abolitionism, 1840–1860," *Civil War History* 16 (September 1969): 197–209.

69. "Twenty-Sixth Annual Meeting of the American Anti-Slavery Society," *National Anti-Slavery Standard*, 21 May 1859.

70. Pillsbury, "The Third Party," *Herald of Freedom*, 4 February 1841; and Pillsbury, "Liberty Party," *Anti-Slavery Bugle*, 10 July 1846.

71. Pillsbury, "Meetings in Herkimer County," *National Anti-Slavery Standard*, 22 January 1852.

72. On the Free Soil Party see Douglas Gamble, "Joshua Giddings and the Ohio Abolitionists: A Study in Radical Politics," *Ohio History* 88 (Winter 1979): 37–56; and Sewell, *Ballots for Freedom*, 152–201.

73. "Letter from Parker Pillsbury," *Anti-Slavery Bugle*, 20 November 1852.

74. "Speech of Parker Pillsbury at the Annual Meeting of the Massachusetts A.S. Society," *National Anti-Slavery Standard*, 10 March 1853.

75. "Twenty-First Annual Meeting of the Massachusetts Anti-Slavery Society," ibid., 3 February 1853.

76. For more on the intense opposition to the antislavery movement in the 1830s see Lorman Ratner, *Powder Keg: Northern Opposition to the Antislavery Movement, 1831–1840* (New York: Basic Books, 1968); and Leonard L. Richards, *"Gentlemen of Property and Standing": Anti-Abolition Mobs in Jacksonian America* (London: Oxford University Press, 1970).

77. See Loveland, "Evangelicalism"; and Scott, "Sacred Vocation." Pillsbury even entitled his account of the abolition movement *Acts of the Anti-Slavery Apostles*.

78. The Garrisonians embraced the policies of disunionism and no-voting in the early 1840s. They contended that without Northern support, the Southern slave system would collapse. See Aileen S. Kraditor, *Means and Ends in American Abolitionism: Garrison and His Critics on Strategy and Tactics, 1834–1850* (New York: Pantheon, 1967), 178–234.

79. Pillsbury, "Meetings at Andover and Dorset," *Anti-Slavery Bugle*, 8 November 1851.

80. Letter from Sabina Small, "Anti-Slavery Convention at Harwich," ibid., 15 September 1848. Sabina Small was the president of the Harwich Anti-Slavery Society and an eyewitness of the mob. Two other observers also wrote to newspapers and provided similar descriptions of the event: letter from R. Y., "Disgraceful Mob at Harwich," ibid., 8 September 1848 (reprinted

from the Boston *Daily Republican*); and letter from Harriet A. Jones, "The Harwich Mob," ibid., 15 September 1848.

81. Pillsbury, "Mob in Harwich, Massachusetts," *National Anti-Slavery Standard*, 7 September 1848. Both the *Liberator* (15 September 1848) and the *Anti-Slavery Bugle* (22 September 1848) reprinted this letter from Pillsbury.

82. Pillsbury to "Editor," 27 August 1848, MS A.1.2 vol. 18, p. 30, BPL. Pillsbury does not specify which newspaper he is writing to in this letter.

83. Pillsbury, "Meetings at the Bridgewaters," *Liberator*, 14 July 1848.

84. Ibid.

85. Abby Kelley, one of the first female antislavery lecturers to travel alone, began her public speaking career in 1839, and endured years of vituperative and personal attacks. See Dorothy Sterling, *Ahead of Her Time: Abby Kelley and The Politics of Antislavery* (New York: Norton, 1991), 107–28. Lucy Stone's women's rights activities also made her a favorite target for mobs. See Andrea Moore Kerr, *Lucy Stone: Speaking Out for Equality* (New Brunswick, N.J.: Rutgers University Press, 1992). The clerical leadership in Massachusetts attacked the Grimké sisters for violating the boundaries of the "woman's sphere" through their antislavery lecturing. See Gerda Lerner, *The Grimké Sisters from South Carolina: Pioneers for Woman's Rights and Abolition* (New York: Schocken Books, 1971), 165–204; and Katharine Du Pre Lumpkin, *The Emancipation of Angelina Grimké* (Chapel Hill: University of North Carolina Press, 1974), 78–154. Pillsbury often traveled and lectured with women abolitionists, including Sojourner Truth, Abby Kelley Foster, Lucy Stone, and Sallie Holley, and he treated them as equals even in the midst of mob assaults. Because the Garrisonians practiced nonresistance, both male and female field workers responded similarly to violence—shielding their bodies and refusing to be provoked into physical retaliation.

86. "Miss Holley and Parker Pillsbury," *Anti-Slavery Bugle*, 11 October 1851.

Chapter Six. An American Abolitionist Abroad

1. Letter from Parker Pillsbury, "New England Correspondence," *Anti-Slavery Bugle* (Salem, Ohio), 10 December 1853. I have been unable to determine who issued this invitation.

2. Pillsbury to Wendell Phillips, 4 December 1853, Crawford Blagden Papers, bMS Am 1953 (1001), HouL.

3. See Pillsbury's letter to Elizabeth Buffum Chace requesting financial aid, in Lillie Buffum Chace Wyman and Arthur Crawford Wyman, eds., *Elizabeth Buffum Chace, 1806–1899; Her Life and Its Environment*, vol. 1 (Boston: W. B. Clarke, 1914), 154.

4. "Visit to Europe," *Liberator* (Boston), 23 December 1853.

5. Pillsbury, "New England Correspondence," *Anti-Slavery Bugle*, 10 December 1853.

6. Pillsbury to Wendell Phillips, 4 December 1853, Blagden Papers, bMS Am 1953 (1001), HouL.

7. "Safe Arrival of Mr. Pillsbury," *Liberator*, 10 February 1854.

8. See Pillsbury's European Journal, 18 January 1854, NHHS.

9. Richard Webb to Maria Weston Chapman, 22 January 1854, MS A.9.2 vol. 28, p. 4., BPL.

10. European Journal, 22 February 1854. Pillsbury's illness was later referred to as hydrothorax. See "Letter from Mr. Pillsbury," *Liberator*, 28 April 1854.

11. European Journal, 19 March 1854, NHHS.

12. Ibid., 26 March 1854.

13. Ibid., 24 April 1854.

14. Mary Estlin to Maria Weston Chapman, 25 March 1854, MS A.9.2 vol. 28, p. 7, BPL. After describing her dancing lessons with Pillsbury, Estlin parenthetically warned Chapman, "don't blazon us abroad, or teacher and pupil will be alike pronounced demented."

15. Eliza Lee Follen to Mary Estlin, n.d., Yale.

16. Sarah Pillsbury to Pillsbury, 12 February 1855, JGW.
17. Sarah Pillsbury to Pillsbury, 11 March 1855, JGW.
18. Helen Pillsbury to Pillsbury, 11 March 1855, JGW.
19. European Journal, 4 April 1854.
20. Henry Clarke Wright to Pillsbury, 21 March 1854, CSC.
21. William Lloyd Garrison to Pillsbury, 21 March 1854, CSC.
22. Mary Estlin to Wendell Phillips, 7 April 1854, Blagden Collection, bMS Am 1953 (1001), HouL.
23. European Journal, 19 May 1854.
24. Ibid., 24 May 1854.
25. On British and American antislavery relations see Betty L. Fladeland, *Men and Brothers: Anglo-American Antislavery Cooperation* (Urbana: University of Illinois Press, 1972); and Clare Taylor, *British and American Abolitionists: An Episode in Transatlantic Understanding* (Edinburgh: Edinburgh University Press, 1974).
26. The Kansas-Nebraska Act nullified the 1820 Missouri Compromise and made slavery legal north of 36°30'. It led to armed battles between pro- and antislavery forces on the borders of Kansas. See David M. Potter, *The Impending Crisis, 1848–1861* (New York: Harper and Row, 1976), 199–224.
27. S. Alfred Steinthal to Samuel May, Jr., 4 May 1854, MS B.1.6 vol. 5, no. 22, BPL.
28. Pillsbury to John and Mary Estlin, 24 May 1854, MS A.7.2, p. 36, BPL.
29. For Pillsbury's interpretation of the event, see ibid. For a secondhand description of Chamerovzow's opinion see Richard Webb to Samuel May, Jr., 16 August 1854, quoted in Taylor, *British and American Abolitionists*, 407–8.
30. Pillsbury to Samuel May, Jr., 2 June 1854, MS B.1.6 vol. 5, no. 24, BPL. Excerpts from this letter regarding the anniversary were published in the *Liberator*, see "Letter From Mr. Pillsbury," 23 June 1854.
31. Ibid.
32. On Pillsbury's doubts about attending the meeting (as expressed afterward) see Pillsbury to Samuel May, Jr., 21 December 1854, MS B.1.6 vol. 5, no. 33, BPL; and Pillsbury to Maria Weston Chapman, 7 January 1854, MS A.9.2 vol. 28, p. 1, BPL.
33. Pillsbury to Samuel May, Jr., 5 October 1854, MS B.1.6 vol. 5, no. 31, BPL.
34. Samuel May, Jr., to Richard Webb, 25 October 1854, MS B.1.6 vol. 5, no. 32, BPL.
35. See Minutes of the Bristol and Clifton Ladies Auxiliary Antislavery Society, 4 December 1854, Yale; and Fladeland, *Men and Brothers*, 363–64.
36. Pillsbury to Samuel May, Jr., 21 December 1854, MS B.1.6 vol. 5, no. 33, BPL.
37. Louis Chamerovzow to John Estlin, 6 February 1855, MS A.9.2 vol. 28, p. 39, BPL.
38. Louis Chamerovzow to Pillsbury, 15 February 1855, MS B.1.6 vol. 5, nos. 43–47, BPL. This is a copy of the correspondence made by Mary Estlin.
39. Pillsbury to John and Mary Estlin, 18 February 1855, MS B.1.6 vol. 5, no. 52, BPL.
40. Mary Estlin's copy of the Pillsbury-Chamerovzow correspondence, MS B.1.6 vol. 5, nos. 43–47, BPL.
41. Ibid.
42. See Pillsbury's European Journal for more on his stay with the Estlins and his trip with Hovey.
43. On Chamerovzow's apology to Wells Brown see Richard Webb to Samuel May, Jr., 16 August 1854, MS B.1.6 vol. 15, BPL.
44. Sarah Pugh to Mary Estlin, 28 August 1854, Yale.
45. Chamerovzow-Pillsbury correspondence (see above, note 40).
46. Mary Estlin to Louis Chamerovzow, 25 February 1855, MS B.1.6 vol. 5, nos. 43–47, BPL.
47. Richard Webb to "Mrs. Mitchell," 5 March 1855, MS B.1.6 vol. 5, no. 48, BPL.
48. Francis Bishop to Mary Estlin, 5 May 1855, MS B.1.5 vol. 5, no. 50, BPL. Copied by Mary Estlin.

49. Francis Bishop to Mary Estlin, 30 May 1855, MS B.1.6 vol. 5, no. 51, BPL.
50. Francis Bishop to Mary Estlin, 5 May 1855, MS B.1.5 vol. 5, no. 50, BPL.
51. Pillsbury to Mary Estlin, 2 March 1855, MS B.1.6 vol. 5, no. 54, BPL.
52. Sarah Pugh to Mary Estlin, n.d., Yale.
53. Richard Webb to Maria Weston Chapman, 22 January 1854, MS A.9.2 vol. 28, p. 4, BPL.
54. Pillsbury to Samuel May, Jr., 2 June 1854, MS B.1.6 vol. 5, no. 24, BPL.
55. Pillsbury to Samuel May, Jr., 4 May 1855, MS B.1.6 vol. 5, no. 67, BPL.
56. Historians disagree about the wisdom of Pillsbury's position. R. J. M. Blackett determined that Pillsbury was "right" in his insistence that the British and Foreign Society "recognize the contribution of a society it had long vilified," while Betty Fladeland argued that Pillsbury caused much "damage" by refusing to "let the matter drop" and insisting on speaking about the "old injustices." See R. J. M. Blackett, *Building an Antislavery Wall: Black Americans in the Atlantic Abolitionist Movement, 1830–1860,* 2d ed. (Ithaca: Cornell University Press, 1989), 138; and Fladeland, *Men and Brothers,* 364.
57. *European Journal,* 21 October 1854.
58. Ibid., 22 March 1854.
59. See Clare Midgley, *Women against Slavery: The British Campaigns, 1780–1870* (London: Routledge, 1992).
60. *Anti-Slavery Reporter,* vol. 1, no. 16 (January 1854), 126–27. Quoted in Midgley, *Women against Slavery,* 125.
61. Pillsbury to Sarah Pillsbury, 25 October 1855, JGW.
62. On Stowe's British tour see Midgley, *Women against Slavery,* 126–27. See also Fladeland's more critical account which suggests that Stowe pocketed the money, Fladeland, *Men and Brothers,* 350–58.
63. Midgley, *Women against Slavery,* 129.
64. *European Journal,* 5 January 1855.
65. Pillsbury to Sarah Pillsbury, 26 August 1854, JGW.
66. Minutes of the Edinburgh Ladies Emancipation Committee, 4 October 1855, NHHS.
67. Louisa Leonard to Parker Pillsbury, 12 May 1854, NHHS.
68. Pillsbury to Samuel May, Jr., 1 February 1856, MS B.1.6 vol. 6, no. 13, BPL.
69. "Mr. Pillsbury in Liverpool," *Liberator,* 22 June 1855; and Pillsbury to Samuel May, Jr., 22 November 1855, MS B.1.6 vol. 5, no. 88, BPL.
70. Wendell Phillips to Pillsbury, 25 April 1854, CSC.
71. See Pillsbury's European Journal, 1854–1855.
72. Mary Estlin to Anne Warren Weston, 30 November 1854, MS A.9.2 vol. 28, p. 33, BPL.
73. Wendell Phillips to Pillsbury, 25 April 1854, CSC.
74. *European Journal,* 19 June 1854.
75. "Agent for Great Britain and Ireland," *National Anti-Slavery Standard* (New York), 24 March 1855.
76. "Speech of Parker Pillsbury," *Liberator,* 1 September 1854. On the tendency of black abolitionists in Britain to emphasize their alienation from the United States see Jane H. Pease and William H. Pease, *They Who Would Be Free: Blacks' Search for Freedom, 1830–1861* (1974; Urbana: University of Illinois Press, 1990), 48–67.
77. "Letter from Rev. S. A. Steinthal," *Liberator,* 9 February 1855.
78. Richard Webb to Samuel May, Jr., 15 February 1856, MS B.1.6 vol. 6, no. 15, BPL.
79. Francis Bishop to Mary Estlin, 1 August 1854, MS A.9.2 vol. 28, p. 19, BPL.
80. "The Anti-Slavery Conference," *National Anti-Slavery Standard,* 6 January 1855. This description of the London conference was culled from the London *Empire.*
81. As quoted in the *Liberator,* 23 February 1855.
82. On the Garrisonians and the American Board of Commissioners of Foreign Missions, see John R. McKivigan, *The War against Proslavery Religion: Abolitionism and the Northern Churches, 1830–1865* (Ithaca: Cornell University Press, 1984), 112–19.

83. "The American Board of Foreign Missions," *Liberator*, 6 April 1855; and "Parker Pillsbury and 'The Independent,'" *National Anti-Slavery Standard*, 7 April 1855.

84. "Act and Testimony," *National Anti-Slavery Standard*, 26 May 1855.

85. "Parker Pillsbury in Liverpool," *Liberator*, 9 March 1855.

86. "Letter from Pillsbury," ibid., 29 September 1854.

87. See Donald M. Jacobs, "David Walker and William Lloyd Garrison: Racial Cooperation and the Shaping of Boston Abolition," in *Courage and Conscience: Black and White Abolitionists in Boston* (Bloomington: Indiana University Press, 1993), 1–20; and Leon Litwack, "The Emancipation of the Negro Abolitionist," in *The Antislavery Vanguard: New Essays on the Abolitionists*, ed. Martin Duberman (Princeton, N.J.: Princeton University Press, 1965), 137–55.

88. See James Oliver Horton and Lois E. Horton, "The Affirmation of Manhood: Black Garrisonians in Antebellum Boston," in *Courage and Conscience*, 127–54; Pease and Pease, *They Who Would Be Free*; Benjamin Quarles, *Black Abolitionists* (London: Oxford University Press, 1969); and Adam D. Simmons, "Ideologies and Programs of the Negro Antislavery Movement, 1830–1861" (Ph.D. diss., Northwestern University, 1983). It is important to note that blacks developed many different visions of antislavery, disagreeing on key issues. However, most black abolitionists did focus more on prejudice and building the black community than white abolitionists.

89. On blacks in Britain see Blackett, *Building an Antislavery Wall*. On Frederick Douglass see William McFeely, *Frederick Douglass* (New York: Touchstone, 1991).

90. See Fladeland, *Men and Brothers*, 345–46.

91. Blackett, *Building an Antislavery Wall*, 118–61.

92. Pillsbury to Sarah Pillsbury, 25 October 1855, JGW.

93. Letter from Pillsbury to the Bristol *Gazette*, as copied in the *Liberator*. See "Boston Anti-Slavery Bazaar," 11 August 1855.

94. Ibid.

95. Wendell Phillips to Pillsbury, 25 April 1854, CSC.

96. European Journal, 29 August 1854.

97. See Blackett, *Antislavery Wall*, 131–33. Blackett argues that Pennington probably did pocket some funds intended for his purchase.

98. Pillsbury's letter is copied in the *Liberator*, see "Letter from Parker Pillsbury," 29 September 1854.

99. Ibid.

100. Lois E. Horton, "Community Organization and Social Activism: Black Boston and the Antislavery Movement," *Sociological Inquiry* 55, no. 2 (1985): 182–99.

101. On the breakdown of relations between Garrison and Douglass see Blackett, *Antislavery Wall*, 79–117; Lawrence Friedman, *Gregarious Saints: Self and Community in American Abolitionism, 1830–1870* (Cambridge: Cambridge University Press, 1982), 187–92; Litwack, "Negro Abolitionist"; and Pease and Pease, *They Who Would Be Free*, 88–93.

102. Pillsbury to Maria Weston Chapman, 17 January 1854, MS A.9.2 vol. 28, p. 2, BPL.

103. For Douglass's editorials on Pillsbury see "New England Anti-Slavery Convention," *North Star* (Rochester, N.Y.), June 1848; and "From Frederick Douglass's *North Star*," *Liberator*, 25 May 1849. Cogswell took too long considering Douglass's offer, and by the time he accepted Douglass had already found another printer. See Sarah Pillsbury to Pillsbury, 13 February 1854, JGW; and Frederick Douglass to P. Brainard Cogswell, 18 February 1854, CSC.

104. On Griffiths and Douglass see Blackett, *Antislavery Wall*, 115–17; McFeely, *Frederick Douglass*, 163–82; and Midgley, *Women against Slavery*, 140–42.

105. Blackett, *Antislavery Wall*, 115.

106. Pillsbury to Maria Weston Chapman, 3 September 1855, MS A.9.2 vol. 28, p. 57, BPL.

107. Pillsbury to Samuel May, Jr., 22 February 1856, MS B.1.6 vol. 6, no. 17, BPL.

108. Pillsbury to Samuel May, Jr., 7 December 1855, MS B.1.6 vol. 5, no. 91, BPL. For examples of Pillsbury's comments on Griffiths, see the following letters from Pillsbury to Samuel

May, Jr., in the BPL: 26 September 1855, MS B.1.6 vol. 5, no. 82; 5 November 1855, MS B.1.6 vol. 5, no. 85; 21 December 1855, MS B.1.6 vol. 5, no. 93; 4 January 1856, MS B.1.6 vol. 6, no. 2; 29 January 1856, MS B.1.6 vol. 6, no. 7; 14 February 1856, MS B.1.6 vol. 6, no. 11; 22 February 1856, MS B.1.6 vol. 6, no. 17; and 27 March 1856, MS B.1.6 vol. 6, no. 27.

109. On the Jezebel stereotype see Debra Gray White, *Ar'n't I a Woman? Female Slaves in the Plantation South* (New York: Norton, 1985), 27–46. For an excellent general account of female sexuality in the nineteenth century see John D'Emilio and Estelle B. Freedman, *Intimate Matters: A History of Sexuality in America* (New York: Harper and Row, 1988), 55–167.

110. Letter from Pillsbury, "Anti-Slavery in Rhode Island—A Free-will Baptist Mob!!!— The cause of Humanity driven from the Meeting-House to a Tavern!" *Herald of Freedom* (Concord, N.H.), 31 December 1841.

111. Letter from Pillsbury, ibid., 4 March 1842.

112. See, for example, the following letters from Pillsbury: "More Outrages—Howard Street Church in Salem Defended by Mobs," ibid., 18 March 1842; "Things to be Considered," ibid., 21 April 1843; "Slaughter of Washington Goode," *Liberator*, 11 May 1849; "From the Pittsburgh Saturday *Visitor*, Women's Rights Convention and the People of Color," *National Anti-Slavery Standard*, 5 December 1850; *Anti-Slavery Bugle*, 29 August 1857.

113. Quoted in James Brewer Stewart, *Holy Warriors: The Abolitionists and American Slavery* (New York: Hill and Wang, 1976), 138.

114. See, for example, "Letter from Parker Pillsbury," *Liberator*, 29 September 1854.

115. Pillsbury, "New England Correspondence," *Anti-Slavery Bugle*, 29 August 1857.

116. For examples of Pillsbury's concern with racial inequality see the following letters in the *National Anti-Slavery Standard*: "Western Operations: Letters from Parker Pillsbury," 9 February 1861; "Letter from Mrs. Griffing: A Word from Parker Pillsbury," 1 June 1861; "The Danger of Compromise: Letter from Parker Pillsbury," 22 June 1861; "Letter from Parker Pillsbury," 8 February 1862; and "Letter from Parker Pillsbury," 8 March 1862.

117. *European Journal*, 9 May 1854.

118. Ibid., 12 May 1854.

119. Ibid., 23 May 1854.

120. S. Alfred Steinthal to Samuel May, Jr., 4 May 1854, MS B.1.6 vol. 5, no. 22, BPL.

121. *European Journal*, 30 January 1854.

122. "Letter from Mr. Pillsbury," *Anti-Slavery Bugle*, 11 March 1854.

123. *European Journal*, 18 May 1854.

124. Pillsbury to Sarah and Helen Pillsbury, 26 August 1854, JGW.

125. Letter from George Putnam, "British Crime and Oppression," *Liberator*, 24 November 1854.

126. This is how Charlotte Forten Grimké described Pillsbury's address. See Brenda Stevenson, ed., *The Journals of Charlotte Forten Grimké* (New York: Oxford University Press, 1988), 156.

127. "Anti-Slavery Festival at Faneuil Hall," *National Anti-Slavery Standard*, 14 June 1856.

Chapter Seven. Perfectionism and the Civil War

1. "Report of Discussions at the Anniversary," *Anti-Slavery Bugle* (Salem, Ohio), 20 September 1856.

2. Pillsbury claimed to have five other job offers when he left the ministry to become a full-time lecturing agent. See Pillsbury to Samuel May, Jr., 25 June 1859, MS B.1.6 vol. 7, no. 52, BPL.

3. "Letter from Parker Pillsbury," *National Anti-Slavery Standard* (New York), 10 October 1857.

4. "Letter from Pillsbury," *Liberator* (Boston, Mass.), 6 November 1857.

5. The July 1857 call for a Disunion Convention attracted much support among abolition-

ists; field lecturers garnered six thousand signatures of endorsement by October 1857. The meeting was canceled on 17 October 1857, due to the nationwide depression which organizers feared would prevent strong attendance. See Louis Ruchames, ed., *The Letters of William Lloyd Garrison, vol. 4: From Disunion to the Brink of War, 1850–1860* (Cambridge: Belknap Press, 1975), 489–97; and "The Northern Convention," *Liberator*, 16 October 1857.

6. Pillsbury, "Northern Disunion Convention," *Liberator*, 13 November 1857.

7. "Report of Speeches and Discussions at the Cleveland Disunion Convention," *Anti-Slavery Bugle*, 7 November 1857.

8. Letter from Pillsbury, ibid., 28 November 1857.

9. John R. McKivigan, *The War against Proslavery Religion: Abolitionism and the Northern Churches, 1830–1865* (Ithaca: Cornell University Press, 1984), 128–42, 161–82.

10. See Pillsbury's resolutions at the following conventions: "Annual Meeting of the Massachusetts Anti-Slavery Society," *Liberator*, 4 February 1859; and "Twenty-Sixth Annual Meeting of the American Anti-Slavery Society," *National Anti-Slavery Standard*, 21 May 1859. See also the following letters and articles: Pillsbury to Samuel May, Jr., 9 August 1859, MS B.1.6 vol. 7, no. 59, BPL; Pillsbury to Wendell Phillips, 17 May 1859, Crawford Blagden Papers, bMS Am 1953 (1001), HouL; Letter from Pillsbury, *Anti-Slavery Bugle*, 13 August 1859; and "Remarks of Parker Pillsbury" at the Anti-Slavery Celebration of Independence Day, Framingham Grove, *Liberator*, 16 July 1858.

11. "Remarks of Parker Pillsbury," *Liberator*, 16 July 1858.

12. "Annual Meeting of the Massachusetts Anti-Slavery Society," ibid., 5 February 1858.

13. Ibid.

14. "Twenty-Sixth Annual Meeting of the American Anti-Slavery Society," *National Anti-Slavery Standard*, 21 May 1859.

15. For a thorough discussion of the complicated rise of the Republican Party see William E. Gienapp, *The Origins of the Republican Party, 1852–1856* (New York: Oxford University Press, 1987). On the ideology of the Republicans see Eric Foner, *Free Soil, Free Labor, Free Men: The Ideology of the Republican Party before the Civil War* (New York: Oxford University Press, 1970).

16. See David M. Potter, *The Impending Crisis, 1848–1861* (New York: Harper and Row, 1976), 130–39; and Richard H. Sewell, *Ballots for Freedom: Antislavery Politics in the United States, 1837–1860* (1976; New York: Norton, 1980), 236–39.

17. The novel was even made into a popular play in the mid-1850s. See Potter, *Impending Crisis*, 140; and Sewell, *Ballots for Freedom*, 234–35.

18. On the Kansas-Nebraska Bill see Potter, *Impending Crisis*, 145–76.

19. See Gienapp, *Republican Party*, 297–307; and Potter, *Impending Crisis*, 199–224.

20. For a detailed description of the attack see David Herbert Donald, *Charles Sumner and the Coming of the Civil War* (Chicago: University of Chicago Press, 1960), 293–311.

21. On the "slave power" see Gienapp, *Republican Party*, 353–65; and Foner, *Free Soil*, 73–102.

22. Sewell, *Ballots for Freedom*, 304–10.

23. Ibid., 324–26.

24. See Phyllis Field, "Party Politics and Antislavery Idealism: The Republican Approach to Racial Change in New York, 1855–1860," in *Crusaders and Compromisers: Essays on the Relationship of the Antislavery Struggle to the Antebellum Party System*, ed. Alan M. Kraut (Westport, Conn.: Greenwood Press, 1983), 125–39; Foner, *Free Soil*, 261–300; and Sewell, *Ballots for Freedom*, 321–42.

25. See Benjamin Quarles, *Black Abolitionists* (London: Oxford University Press, 1969), 187–90; and Sewell, *Ballots for Freedom*, 321–42.

26. On the relationship between Garrisonians and Republicans in the West see Douglas Gamble, "Joshua Giddings and the Ohio Abolitionists: A Study in Radical Politics," *Ohio History* 88 (Winter 1979): 37–56. See also Donald, *Charles Sumner*.

27. "Letters from Harriet Martineau . . . No. VIII," *National Anti-Slavery Standard*, 9 July 1859.

28. John L. Thomas, *The Liberator: William Lloyd Garrison* (Boston: Little, Brown, 1963), 368.

29. Pillsbury to Charles Sumner, 8 May 1864, Charles Sumner Papers, microfilm A 665, Reel 31, Frame 41, HouL.

30. Pillsbury to Charles Sumner, 24 May 1864, Sumner Papers, Reel 31, Frame 137, HouL.

31. "The New England Anti-Slavery Convention," *National Anti-Slavery Standard*, 18 June 1864.

32. "Annual Meeting of the Massachusetts Anti-Slavery Society," *Liberator*, 4 February 1859. For earlier examples of Pillsbury introducing this resolution see ibid., 29 May 1857; and "New England Anti-Slavery Convention," ibid., 5 June 1857.

33. "Annual Meeting of the Massachusetts Anti-Slavery Society," ibid., 4 February 1859.

34. Some moderate Garrisonians campaigned for Lincoln, including Theodore Tilton, Sydney Howard Gay, and David Lee Child. Most, however, agreed with Edmund Quincy that Lincoln's election would neither help nor hurt the antislavery movement. See James M. McPherson, *The Struggle for Equality: Abolitionists and the Negro in the Civil War and Reconstruction* (Princeton, N.J.: Princeton University Press, 1964), 9–28.

35. "Report of Discussions at the Anniversary," *Anti-Slavery Bugle*, 20 September 1856.

36. "Independence Day: Antislavery Celebration at Framingham," *Liberator*, 20 July 1860.

37. Pillsbury to William Lloyd Garrison, 29 October 1860, MS A.1.2 vol. 30, p. 139, BPL.

38. Douglas Gamble, "Moral Suasion in the West: Garrisonian Abolitionism, 1831–61" (Ph.D. diss., Ohio State University, 1973). See also Gamble, "Garrisonian Abolitionists in the West: Some Suggestions for Study," *Civil War History* 23 (March 1977): 52–68.

39. See *Liberator*, 6 May 1859; and Ruchames, *The Letters of William Lloyd Garrison*, 4:636.

40. Pillsbury to Wendell Phillips, 15 August 1860, Blagden Papers, bMS AM 1953 (1001), HouL.

41. For a discussion of mob opposition to abolitionists during this period see McPherson, *Struggle for Equality*, 45. For examples of mobs obstructing Pillsbury's meetings see the following letters from Pillsbury: "Western Operations," *National Anti-Slavery Standard*, 17 November 1860; "Pro-Slavery Mob at Ann Arbor," *Liberator*, 8 February 1861; and "Letter from Parker Pillsbury," *National Anti-Slavery Standard*, 2 March 1861.

42. "Anti-Slavery Celebration at Rochester, N.Y.," *National Anti-Slavery Standard*, 13 July 1861.

43. See Nancy A. Hewitt, *Women's Activism and Social Change: Rochester, New York, 1822–1872* (Ithaca: Cornell University Press, 1984), 192.

44. This term is used in a letter to Oliver Johnson from William Lloyd Garrison, 27 June 1861, BPL. Quoted in McPherson, *Struggle for Equality*, 55.

45. Ibid.

46. Minutes of the Executive Committee of the American Anti-Slavery Society, 3 May 1861, BPL.

47. "A Word from Parker Pillsbury," *National Anti-Slavery Standard*, 1 June 1861.

48. "The New York State Anti-Slavery Convention," ibid., 15 February 1862.

49. "The Justice of God in Our National Calamities: Remarks of Parker Pillsbury," ibid., 22 February 1862.

50. "The Danger of Compromise: Letter from Parker Pillsbury," ibid., 22 June 1861.

51. "Western Anniversary Postponed," ibid., 17 August 1861.

52. Pillsbury to Theodore Tilton, 22 May 1864, Miscellaneous Manuscripts, Pillsbury, Parker, New York Historical Society.

53. See McPherson, *Struggle for Equality*, 90–93.

54. "A Word from Parker Pillsbury," *National Anti-Slavery Standard*, 23 November 1861.

55. William Lloyd Garrison describes his understanding of the conflict in a letter to Pillsbury, 3 June 1859, MS A.1.1 vol. 5, p. 93, BPL. This unfinished letter was probably never mailed.

56. Ibid.

57. Pillsbury to Samuel May, Jr., 24 March 1859, MS A.1.2 vol. 29, p. 37, BPL.

58. "Letters from Harriet Martineau . . . No. VIII," *National Anti-Slavery Standard*, 9 July 1859.

59. Ibid. See also Oliver Johnson to Harriet Martineau, 7 May 1859, MS A.9.2. vol. 29, p. 68, BPL; Oliver Johnson to Maria Weston Chapman, 31 August 1859, MS A.9.2 vol. 29, p. 70, BPL; and Maria Weston Chapman to Sarah Parker Remond, 4 September 1859, Yale.

60. Pillsbury to Wendell Phillips, 20 July 1859, Blagden Papers, bMS Am 1953 (1001), HouL. Pillsbury's use of the initials "HM" may also be a subtle reference to the term "Her Majesty," which the British often use. Thanks to Hal Morris for this suggestion.

61. Pillsbury to Wendell Phillips, 21 September 1859, Blagden Papers, bMS Am 1953 (1001), HouL.

62. Samuel May, Jr., to Richard Webb, 30 June 1862, MS B.1.6 vol. 9, no. 37, BPL.

63. Samuel May, Jr., to Elizabeth Buffum Chace [1862], quoted in Lillie Buffum Chace Wyman and Arthur Crawford Wyman, eds., *Elizabeth Buffum Chace, 1806–1899: Her Life and Its Environment*, vol. 1 (Boston: W. B. Clarke, 1914), 236.

64. Pillsbury to Theodore Tilton, 16 September 1862, New York Historical Society.

65. James Brewer Stewart, *Wendell Phillips, Liberty's Hero* (Baton Rouge: Louisiana State University Press, 1986), 209–42.

66. McPherson, *Struggle for Equality*, 99–133.

67. Pillsbury to Charles Sumner, Sumner Papers, Reel 32, Frame 18, HouL.

68. Samuel May, Jr., to Richard Webb, 29 May 1865, MS B.1.6 vol. 10, no. 26, BPL.

69. Pillsbury and Gerrit Smith exchanged friendly letters in the 1860s. See, for example, Pillsbury to Gerrit Smith, 14 March 1863, Gerrit Smith Papers, LOC; and Gerrit Smith to Pillsbury, 18 March 1863, CSC.

70. On abolitionists and the Fremont campaign see McPherson, *Struggle for Equality*, 264–86.

71. Pillsbury to Wendell Phillips, 3 May 1864, Blagden Papers, bMS Am 1953 (1001), HouL.

72. Pillsbury to Charles Sumner, 18 June 1864, Sumner Papers, Reel 31, Frame 245, HouL. See also McPherson, *Struggle for Equality*, 260–86.

73. Johnson Editorial, *National Anti-Slavery Standard*, 18 June 1864.

74. Pillsbury to Wendell Phillips, 27 August 1864, Blagden Papers, bMS Am 1953 (1001), HouL.

75. Ibid.

76. McPherson describes Pillsbury and Foster as "temperamentally incapable of supporting any government. They had been oppositionists and 'come-outers' so long that their hostility to authority was ingrained, no matter what the authority stood for." *Struggle for Equality*, 103–4.

77. "The New England Anti-Slavery Convention," *National Anti-Slavery Standard*, 7 June 1862.

78. On Garrison's strategic positioning see James B. Stewart, "The Aims and Impact of Garrisonian Abolitionism, 1840–1860," *Civil War History* 16 (September 1969): 197–209.

79. Pillsbury to Charles Sumner, 12 June 1860, Sumner Papers, Reel 19, Frame 606, HouL.

80. Pillsbury to Charles Sumner, 8 May 1864, Sumner Papers, Reel 31, Frame 41, HouL.

81. Pillsbury to Charles Sumner, 3 July 1864, Sumner Papers, Reel 31, Frame 358, HouL.

82. Many Garrisonians used traditional ideas about gender to promote their radical agenda, according to Kristin Hoganson, "Garrisonian Abolitionists and the Rhetoric of Gender, 1850–1860," *American Quarterly* 45 (December 1993): 558–95.

83. Pillsbury, "The Hour Without the Man," *National Anti-Slavery Standard*, 6 July 1861.

84. "Parker Pillsbury on the Times," ibid., 26 July 1862.

85. Lawrence Friedman, *Gregarious Saints: Self and Community in American Abolitionism, 1830–1870* (Cambridge: Cambridge University Press, 1982), 205–6; and Jane H. Pease and William H. Pease, *They Who Would Be Free: Blacks' Search for Freedom, 1830–1861* (1974; Urbana: University of Illinois Press, 1990), 233–51.

86. James Oliver Horton and Lois E. Horton, "The Affirmation of Manhood: Black Garrisonians in Antebellum Boston," in *Courage and Conscience: Black and White Abolitionists in Boston*, ed. Donald Jacobs (Bloomington: Indiana University Press, 1993), 127–54; Pease and Pease, *They Who Would Be Free*, 233–51; and Adam D. Simmons, "Ideologies and Programs of the Negro Antislavery Movement, 1830–1861" (Ph.D. diss., Northwestern University, 1983).

87. John Demos, "The Antislavery Movement and the Problem of Violent 'Means,'" *New England Quarterly* 37 (December 1964): 501–26; and Friedman, *Gregarious Saints*, 196–222.

88. Friedman, *Gregarious Saints*, 214–17.

89. "Anti-Slavery Meetings at Weymouth," *Liberator*, 19 November 1847.

90. "Ninth Annual Meeting of the N.E. Non-Resistance Society," ibid., 5 January 1849.

91. Pillsbury's European Journal, 16 June 1854, NHHS.

92. "Annual Meeting of the Massachusetts Anti-Slavery Society," *Liberator*, 4 February 1859.

93. "Annual Meeting of the Massachusetts Anti-Slavery Society," ibid., 13 February 1857.

94. "Report of Speeches and Discussions at the Cleveland Disunion Convention," *Anti-Slavery Bugle*, 14 November 1857.

95. F. B. Sanborn, ed., *The Life and Letters of John Brown, Liberator of Kansas, and Martyr of Virginia* (Boston: Roberts Brothers, 1885), 435.

96. See "Convention at Adrian," *Anti-Slavery Bugle*, 12 November 1859; "Parker Pillsbury on John Brown," *Liberator*, 2 December 1859; Letter from Pillsbury, *Anti-Slavery Bugle*, 17 December 1859; and "Parker Pillsbury in Illinois," *Liberator*, 21 December 1859.

97. "Annual Meeting of the Massachusetts Anti-Slavery Society," *Liberator*, 13 February 1857.

98. "Anti-Slavery Festival in Commemoration of the Twenty-Fifth Anniversary of the Formation of the Massachusetts Anti-Slavery Society," *National Anti-Slavery Standard*, 17 January 1857.

99. McPherson, *Struggle for Equality*, 52–55.

100. *National Anti-Slavery Standard*, 3 May 1862. Quoted in McPherson, *Struggle for Equality*, 161.

101. "The New England Anti-Slavery Convention," *National Anti-Slavery Standard*, 18 June 1864.

102. For a discussion of the Garrisonian divisions over universal suffrage and the continuation of antislavery societies see McPherson, *Struggle for Equality*, 287–307.

103. *Liberator*, 22 July 1864. Quoted in McPherson, *Struggle for Equality*, 294.

104. "The Standard," *National Anti-Slavery Standard*, 10 June 1855.

105. Pillsbury to Wendell Phillips, 15 February 1865, Blagden Papers, bMS Am 1953 (1001), HouL.

106. "Thirty-Second Annual Meeting of the American Anti-Slavery Society," *National Anti-Slavery Standard*, 27 May 1865.

107. Oliver Johnson to Maria Weston Chapman, 4 May 1865, MS A.9.2 vol. 32, p. 37, BPL.

108. Samuel May, Jr., to Richard Webb, 29 May 1865, MS B.1.6 vol. 10, no. 26, BPL.

109. McPherson, *Struggle for Equality*, 307.

Chapter Eight. Imperfect Reconstruction

1. Pillsbury to Frances Anne Blanchard, 3 August 1869, ALutz.

2. See Oliver Johnson, "The Coming Man," *National Anti-Slavery Standard* (New York), 20 May 1865. For a concurring opinion see Samuel May, Jr., "A Protest," ibid., 20 May 1865.

3. Pillsbury to Charles Sumner, 2 June 1865, Charles Sumner Papers, Microfilm A 665, Reel 33, Frame 526, HouL.

4. On abolitionists and Reconstruction see James M. McPherson, *The Struggle for Equality: Abolitionists and the Negro in the Civil War and Reconstruction* (Princeton, N.J.: Princeton Univer-

sity Press, 1964), 308–416. For a general history of Reconstruction see Eric Foner, *Reconstruction: America's Unfinished Revolution, 1863–1877* (New York: Harper and Row, 1984).

5. "It Is Only an Experiment," *National Anti-Slavery Standard*, 9 September 1865; and "The Church, North and South," ibid., 12 August 1865.

6. Pillsbury, "The Present Danger," ibid., 19 August 1865.

7. Ellen Carol DuBois, *Feminism and Suffrage: The Emergence of an Independent Women's Movement in America, 1848–1869* (Ithaca: Cornell University Press, 1978), 75.

8. Pillsbury to Wendell Phillips, 28 September 1865, Crawford Blagden Papers, bMS Am 1953 (1001), HouL.

9. "Meeting at Milton on the Hudson," *National Anti-Slavery Standard*, 25 November 1865.

10. "Will the People Sustain Congress?" ibid., 5 May 1866.

11. "The Church as the Light of the World," ibid., 12 May 1866.

12. "Beecher's Backsliding," ibid., 28 October 1865.

13. Pillsbury to Samuel Johnson, 2 March 1866, Samuel Johnson Papers, MSS 248, PEM.

14. Pillsbury to Samuel Johnson, 3 August 1865, Johnson Papers, PEM.

15. Pillsbury to Marius and Emily Robinson, 15 September 1865, ALutz.

16. Pillsbury to Charles H. Whipple, secretary of the American Anti-Slavery Society, 28 December 1865, MS AM 123 (72), BPL.

17. Wendell and Anne Phillips never had any children, but they adopted Phoebe Garnaut, the daughter of one of Anne's nurses who had died of cholera. Phoebe married George Smalley in 1862. See James Brewer Stewart, *Wendell Phillips, Liberty's Hero* (Baton Rouge: Louisiana State University Press, 1986), 91.

18. Minutes of the Executive Committee of the American Anti-Slavery Society, 5 December 1865, BPL.

19. Pillsbury to Phillips, 8 December 1865, Blagden Papers, bMS Am 1953 (1001), HouL.

20. Pillsbury to Phillips, 12 December 1865, Blagden Papers, bMS Am 1953 (1001), HouL.

21. Minutes of the Executive Committee of the American Anti-Slavery Society, 26 December 1865, BPL.

22. Pillsbury to Phillips, 12 December 1865, Blagden Papers, bMS Am 1953 (1001), HouL.

23. Pillsbury to Whipple, 28 December 1865, MS AM 123 (72), BPL.

24. Minutes of the Executive Committee of the American Anti-Slavery Society, 4 January 1866, BPL.

25. Letter from Elizabeth Cady Stanton, " 'This is the Negro's Hour,' " *National Anti-Slavery Standard*, 30 December 1865.

26. " 'Woman's Rights,' " ibid., 30 December 1865.

27. Pillsbury to Elizabeth Buffum Chace, 27 January 1866, in Lillie Buffum Chace Wyman and Arthur Crawford Wyman, eds., *Elizabeth Buffum Chace, 1806–1899; Her Life and Its Environment*, vol. 1 (Boston: W. B. Clarke, 1914), 287.

28. Pillsbury, "The Conflict—For Power or For Principle?" *National Anti-Slavery Standard*, 21 April 1866. The Fourteenth Amendment was frustrating for Pillsbury and women's rights supporters because it repeatedly used the phrase "male citizens," thus for the first time specifically excluding women from the protections and rights guaranteed by the Constitution. Moreover, the amendment did not force states to enfranchise blacks, but merely promised to punish them if they prevented black men from voting. For more on feminists' reaction to the Fourteenth Amendment see DuBois, *Feminism and Suffrage*, 21–52.

29. Pillsbury to the Executive Committee of the American Anti-Slavery Society, 11 May 1866, Blagden Papers, bMS Am 1953 (1001), HouL.

30. "Equal Rights for Women," *National Anti-Slavery Standard*, 2 June 1866.

31. Susan B. Anthony to unknown, 1867, quoted in Ida Husted Harper, ed., *The Life and Work of Susan B. Anthony*, vol. 1 (Indianapolis: Hollenbeck Press, 1898), 269.

32. Pillsbury to Gerrit Smith, 23 July 1866, SYR.

33. Ibid.

34. Pillsbury to Wendell Phillips, 5 September 1866, Blagden Papers, bMS Am 1953 (1001),

HouL. See also Pillsbury to Wendell Phillips, 15 August 1866, Blagden Papers, bMS Am 1953 (1001), HouL.

35. For a thorough discussion of the American Equal Rights Association see DuBois, *Feminism and Suffrage*, 63–78.

36. Pillsbury, "The Anniversary," *The Revolution* (New York), 20 May 1869.

37. Pillsbury to Benjamin Cheever, 17 June 1867, ALutz.

38. Pillsbury to Elizabeth Buffum Chace, 20 June 1867, in *Elizabeth Buffum Chace*, 304–5.

39. See, for example, the following in the *National Anti-Slavery Standard*: "Equal Rights Convention for the State of New York," 10 November 1866; "Convention at Albany," 17 November 1866; "State Constitutional Convention," 8 December 1866; "The Equal Rights Enterprise," 26 January 1867; "The State Constitutional Convention," 16 February 1867; "The Equal Rights Enterprise," 2 March 1867; and "The Forthcoming Convention," 25 May 1867.

40. Abolitionists were busy debating the Fourteenth Amendment and pushing for the impeachment of President Johnson in 1867. See McPherson, *Struggle for Equality*, 341–86.

41. "Proceedings of the New England Anti-Slavery Convention," *National Anti-Slavery Standard*, 15 June 1867.

42. Ibid.

43. Ibid.

44. On Pillsbury's brother-in-law see Pillsbury to Marius and Emily Robinson, 14 June 1867, Ulrich B. Phillips Papers, Yale; and *National Anti-Slavery Standard*, 20 July 1867. On Pillsbury's position with the Equal Rights Association see "Personal," *National Anti-Slavery Standard*, 7 September 1867. On the campaign in Kansas see DuBois, *Feminism and Suffrage*, 79–104.

45. For an excellent discussion of the influence of Train on the movement see DuBois, *Feminism and Suffrage*, 93–104. See also the conflicting views of Kathleen Barry, *Susan B. Anthony: A Biography* (New York: New York University Press, 1988), 178–89; and Andrea Moore Kerr, *Lucy Stone: Speaking Out for Equality* (New Brunswick, N.J.: Rutgers University Press, 1992), 127–34. Barry argues that Henry Blackwell conspired to bring Train into the campaign to undermine Anthony and Stanton and thus leave his wife, Lucy Stone, in control; Kerr retorts that Barry misread the evidence.

46. DuBois argues that Train probably had little influence on the campaign. See DuBois, *Feminism and Suffrage*, 97–98.

47. Quoted in Kerr, *Lucy Stone*, 129.

48. See Pillsbury to Wendell Phillips, 7 September 1867, Blagden Papers, bMS Am 1953 (1001), HouL.

49. Pillsbury to Gerrit Smith, 27 November 1867, SYR.

50. Pillsbury to [Gerrit Smith], 2 November 1867, NHHS.

51. Pillsbury to Gerrit Smith, 15 November 1867, SYR.

52. Pillsbury to Gerrit Smith, 27 November 1867, SYR.

53. Pillsbury to Marius and Emily Robinson, 15 September 1865, ALutz.

54. Helen Pillsbury to Sarah Pillsbury, 23 April [1869], JGW.

55. On *The Revolution* see DuBois, *Feminism and Suffrage*, 104.

56. For example, see the following in *The Revolution*: "What the Press Says of Us," 28 May 1868; and "Editorial Correspondence," 11 March 1869.

57. Pillsbury, "The Plague of Politicians," ibid., 5 February 1868.

58. Pillsbury, "Congressional Dignity and Decency," ibid., 14 May 1868.

59. Pillsbury, "Woman as Witch," ibid., 25 June 1868.

60. Pillsbury, "Presbyterianism Reconstructed," ibid., 10 June 1869.

61. Although Lawrence Friedman asserts that Pillsbury participated in the 1869–70 debate over the dissolution of antislavery societies I have found no evidence of this. See Lawrence Friedman, *Gregarious Saints: Self and Community in American Abolitionism, 1830–1870* (Cambridge: Cambridge University Press, 1982), 272–77.

62. Samuel May, Jr., to Samuel May, 26 March 1868, MS B.1.6 vol. 10, no. 51, BPL.

63. Oliver Johnson to Mary Estlin, 14 February 1869, Mary Estlin Papers, Yale.

64. Pillsbury to [Ellen Wright Garrison], 1 May 1869, SSC.

65. On the change in status of the abolitionists see McPherson, *Struggle for Equality*, 367.

66. Letter from Aurora C. Phelps, "Ballot, Bench and Barricade," *The Revolution*, 21 May 1868.

67. Pillsbury had earlier rejected educational qualifications for suffrage. See Pillsbury editorial, "The Test of Citizenship," *National Anti-Slavery Standard*, 10 March 1866.

68. Pillsbury, "Educated Suffrage," *The Revolution*, 16 April 1868.

69. "What the Press Says of Us," ibid., 28 May 1868.

70. "Freedom vs. Pillsbury," New York *Tribune*, 24 November 1867. Quoted in Tilden G. Edelstein, *Strange Enthusiasm: A Life of Thomas Wentworth Higginson* (New York: Atheneum, 1970), 299.

71. For Pillsbury's denunciation of racism at an 1850 women's rights convention, see "From the Pittsburgh Saturday Visiter: Women's Rights Convention and the People of Color," *National Anti-Slavery Standard*, 5 December 1850; and "Mrs. Swisshelm and the Worcester Convention," *Anti-Slavery Bugle* (Salem, Ohio), 11 January 1851.

72. Letter from Pillsbury, "Miss Anthony and the Labor Congress," *The Revolution*, 2 September 1869.

73. "Proceedings of the New England Anti-Slavery Convention," *National Anti-Slavery Standard*, 15 June 1867.

74. "The Mortality of Nations, an Address delivered before the American Equal Rights Association by Parker Pillsbury," 9 May 1869, NHHS.

75. For a discussion of the class and race influences on Anthony and Stanton see DuBois, *Feminism and Suffrage*, 174–78.

76. Letter from Pillsbury, "South Carolina," *The Revolution*, 14 October 1869.

77. See letters from Thomas Wentworth Higginson in New York *Tribune*, 24 November 1869; and *Independent*, 30 June 1870. Quoted in James M. McPherson, *The Abolitionist Legacy: From Reconstruction to the NAACP* (Princeton, N.J.: Princeton University Press, 1975), 57–58.

78. Gilbert Pillsbury to John Alvord, 10 January 1870, in Alvord, *Letters from the South, Relating to the Condition of Freedmen* (Washington, 1870), 11–12. Quoted in McPherson, *Abolitionist Legacy*, 58.

79. Letter from Pillsbury, "The South As It Is," *The Revolution*, 11 November 1869.

80. Pillsbury, "Educated Suffrage," ibid., 16 April 1868.

81. Ibid.

82. See DuBois, *Feminism and Suffrage*, 164–72.

83. Wendell Phillips, "The Fifteenth Amendment," *National Anti-Slavery Standard*, 3 July 1869.

84. Stewart, *Wendell Phillips*, 282.

85. Ibid.

86. Garrisonians frequently employed traditional gender ideals in their abolitionist literature. For example, they argued that female slaves could not become "true" women due to their enslavement, focusing on motherhood and sexual purity as the defining elements of womanhood. See Kristin Hoganson, "Garrisonian Abolitionists and the Rhetoric of Gender, 1850–1860," *American Quarterly* 45 (December 1993): 558–95.

87. Quoted in McPherson, *Struggle for Equality*, 426.

88. "Woman's Rights," *National Anti-Slavery Standard*, 21 August 1869.

89. Quoted in Michael S. Kimmel and Thomas E. Mosmiller, eds., *Against the Tide: Pro-Feminist Men in the United States, 1776–1990: A Documentary History* (Boston: Beacon Press, 1992), 18.

90. Ibid.

91. Pillsbury, "Fifteenth Amendment—Its Ludicrous Side," *The Revolution*, 22 July 1869.

92. Pillsbury, "The Present Danger," ibid., 3 December 1868.

93. Ibid.

94. "Proceedings of the New England Anti-Slavery Society Convention," *National Anti-Slavery Standard*, 8 June 1867.

95. Pillsbury to Martha Coffin Wright, 1 May 1871, SSC.

96. In fact, Pillsbury would continue to advocate women's rights in his public lectures for the next twenty years. See, for example, Pillsbury to Rebecca Anne Smith Janney, 10 February 1873, Charles A. Jones Collection, MIC 137, Ohio Historical Society, Columbus, Ohio; E. F. Eddy to Pillsbury, 4 February 1881, NHHS; Pillsbury to Helen Pillsbury, 22 May 1881, JGW; Pillsbury to Lucia Rogers, 17 February 1882, HAV; and Pillsbury to Clara B. Colby, 8 March 1894, Huntington Library, San Marino, Calif.

97. Lawrence Friedman discusses Weston's early call for dissolution in *Gregarious Saints*, 260–61.

98. For example, Foster and Kelley opposed Wendell Phillips when he tried to dissolve antislavery societies after the passage of the Fifteenth Amendment, using the same argument Phillips himself had employed in the 1865 debate over dissolution. Ibid., 72–77.

Chapter Nine. The Postbellum Quest for the Millennium

1. Pillsbury to Sarah Pillsbury, 21 November 1874, JGW.

2. See James Brewer Stewart, *Wendell Phillips, Liberty's Hero* (Baton Rouge: Louisiana State University Press, 1986), 296–335; Tilden G. Edelstein, *Strange Enthusiasm: A Life of Thomas Wentworth Higginson* (New York: Atheneum, 1970), 296–401; and Lawrence Goodheart, *Abolitionist, Actuary, Atheist: Elizur Wright and the Reform Impulse* (Kent, Ohio: Kent State University Press, 1990), 179–210. Most of the abolitionists who had been active since the 1830s and 1840s were well into old age by the end of the Civil War.

3. Pillsbury to Sarah Pillsbury, 21 November 1874, JGW.

4. Ibid.

5. Ibid.

6. For more on postwar reform see Peter J. Frederick, *Knights of the Golden Rule: The Intellectual as Social Christian Reformer in the 1890s* (Lexington: University of Kentucky Press, 1976); William Leach, *True Love and Perfect Union: The Feminist Reform of Sex and Society* (New York: Basic Books, 1980); Arthur Mann, *Yankee Reformers in the Urban Age: Social Reform in Boston, 1880–1900* (New York: Harper and Row, 1954); and John G. Sproat, *"The Best Men": Liberal Reformers in the Gilded Age* (New York: Oxford University Press, 1968). For an excellent discussion of the transformation of women's reform activism over the nineteenth century see Lori D. Ginzberg, *Women and the Work of Benevolence: Morality, Politics, and Class in the Nineteenth-Century United States* (New Haven: Yale University Press, 1990).

7. Quoted in "An Abolitionist of Old Time," *Cincinnati Commercial*, 15 May 1875.

8. Pillsbury to James Monroe, 28 September 1897, James Monroe Papers, Oberlin College, Oberlin, Ohio.

9. For more on the role of abolitionists in racial reform movements in the postwar period see James McPherson, *The Abolitionist Legacy: From Reconstruction to the NAACP* (Princeton, N.J.: Princeton University Press, 1975). On the rise of racial segregation and disfranchisement see C. Vann Woodward, *The Strange Career of Jim Crow*, 3d ed. (New York: Oxford University Press, 1974).

10. See Warren Sager to Helen Pillsbury, 13 November 1906, JGW; Mrs. Booker T. Washington to Helen Pillsbury, 21 December 1906 and 10 January 1907, JGW.

11. William Lloyd Garrison to Stephen and Abby Kelley Foster, 12 November 1877, Abby Kelley Foster Papers, AAS.

12. Stow Persons, *Free Religion: An American Faith* (Boston: Beacon Press, 1963), 12. See also Sydney E. Ahlstrom and Robert Bruce Mullin, *The Scientific Theist: A Life of Francis Ellingwood Abbot* (Macon, Ga.: Mercer University Press, 1987); W. Creighton Peden, *The Philosopher of Free Religion: Francis Ellingwood Abbot, 1836–1903* (New York: Peter Lang, 1992); and Sidney Warren, *American Freethought, 1860–1914* (New York: Garden Press, 1966).

13. Persons, *Free Religion*, 23–24.

14. Ibid., 18–41.

15. Ibid., 42.

16. Warren, *American Freethought*, 96–116. Pillsbury became so fascinated with Thomas Paine that he wrote a lecture on him and delivered it regularly at lyceums in the early 1880s. See NHHS.

17. Peden, *Francis Ellingwood Abbot*, 72.

18. Ibid., 79.

19. Pillsbury, "Free Religious Convention in Boston," *The Revolution* (New York), 11 June 1868.

20. Ibid.

21. Persons, *Free Religion*, 42–54.

22. Pillsbury, "Free Religious Conventions," *The Revolution*, 18 June 1868.

23. Ibid.

24. Persons, *Free Religion*, 77.

25. Pillsbury, "Notes from the Field," *The Index* (Toledo, Ohio), 6 May 1871.

26. Persons, *Free Religion*, 55.

27. Pillsbury to Helen Pillsbury, 23 July 1889, JGW.

28. Pillsbury, "Notes from the Field," *The Index*, 22 July 1871.

29. Ibid.

30. Persons, *Free Religion*, 99–129; and Warren, *American Freethought*, 45–74.

31. Pillsbury, *The Popular Religions, and What Shall Be Instead* (Concord, N.H.: Republican Press Association, 1893).

32. Ibid.

33. See Pillsbury to Helen Pillsbury, 27 April 1882, JGW; and Pillsbury to Helen Pillsbury, 28 May 1882, NHHS. The Institute of Heredity focused on improving the health of humanity in general, unlike its heir, the eugenics movement, which sought to weed out the "unfit." See Robert C. Bannister, *Social Darwinism: Science and Myth in Anglo-American Thought* (Philadelphia: Temple University Press, 1979), 171–73; and Leach, *True Love*, 135.

34. A few scientists and theologians, however, did offer theories that reconciled Christianity and evolution, including Asa Gray, a botanist at Harvard University. See Sydney E. Ahlstrom, *A Religious History of the American People*, vol. 2 (New York: Image Books, 1975), 229–34.

35. Persons, *Free Religion*, 112.

36. Mann, *Yankee Reformers*, 81.

37. The Spiritualists hoped that science would help to legitimize their claims of contact with spirit life through the study of parapsychology. See R. Laurence Moore, *In Search of White Crows: Spiritualism, Parapsychology, and American Culture* (New York: Oxford University Press, 1977), 36, 221–44.

38. Robert D. Thomas, *"With Bleeding Footsteps": Mary Baker Eddy's Path to Religious Leadership* (New York: Alfred A. Knopf, 1994).

39. Pillsbury, *Things New and Old* (Concord, N.H.: Republican Press Association, 1893).

40. Ibid.

41. Warren, *American Freethought*, 45–74; and Orvin Larson, *American Infidel: Robert G. Ingersoll* (New York: Citadel Press, 1962).

42. Persons, *Free Religion*, 75–98.

43. Pillsbury, "Notes from the Field," *The Index*, 6 May 1871. See also the advertisement for Pillsbury's Free Religion lectures, ibid., 22 July 1871.

44. Pillsbury to Helen Pillsbury, 28 July 1879, JGW.

45. Pillsbury to Lucia Rogers, 17 February 1882, HAV.

46. Pillsbury to Helen Pillsbury, 28 July 1879, JGW.

47. Pillsbury to Helen Pillsbury, 20 April 1878, JGW. On Beecher see Altina L. Waller, *Reverend Beecher and Mrs. Tilton: Sex and Class in Victorian America* (Amherst: University of Massachusetts Press, 1982).

48. See Pillsbury to William Lloyd Garrison, Jr., 3 October 1877, SSC; and Pillsbury to Stephen S. Foster, 3 June 1881, A. K. Foster Papers, AAS.

49. Pillsbury to Garrison, Jr., 3 October 1877, SSC.

50. Pillsbury, "Notes from the Field," *The Index*, 3 June 1871.

51. Pillsbury, "Notes from the Field," ibid., 1 July 1871. For other references to abolitionists see Pillsbury's "Notes from the Field" in the following editions of *The Index*: 20 May 1871, 6 July 1872, 10 August 1872, and 12 October 1872.

52. Pillsbury's antislavery co-worker Charles C. Burleigh, for example, formed a Free Church in Florence, Massachusetts, and another in Bloomington, Illinois. See Pillsbury, "God in the Constitution," *The Index*, 1 January 1874.

53. Pillsbury to William Lloyd Garrison, 29 April 1872, Oswald G. Villard Papers, bMS Am 1906 (25), HouL.

54. Frederick Douglass to Pillsbury, 8 December 1882, NHHS.

55. Pillsbury to William Lloyd Garrison, Jr., 11 May 1878, SSC. For other examples of Pillsbury describing himself as the last abolitionist in the field see Pillsbury to Lucia Rogers, 17 February 1882, HAV; Pillsbury to Anne Warren Weston, 19 June 1888, MS Am. 1993 (13), BPL; and Pillsbury to William Lloyd Garrison, Jr., 15 February 1895, SSC.

56. Ann Braude, *Radical Spirits: Spiritualism and Women's Rights in Nineteenth-Century America* (Boston: Beacon Press, 1989), 162–91.

57. On Spiritualism see ibid.; Paul A. Carter, *The Spiritual Crisis of the Gilded Age* (DeKalb: Northern Illinois University Press, 1971); and Moore, *White Crows*.

58. See Braude, *Radical Spirits*, 1–9; and Leach, *True Love*, 293–97.

59. Leach, *True Love*, 293.

60. Pillsbury, "Notes from the Field," *The Index*, 5 August 1871.

61. Braude, *Radical Spirits*, 56.

62. Persons, *Free Religion*, 75.

63. Ibid., 75–98; and Warren, *American Freethought*, 96–116.

64. Pillsbury, "Notes from the Field," *The Index*, 15 July 1871.

65. Ibid.

66. Pillsbury, "Notes from the Field," ibid., 5 August 1871.

67. Pillsbury, "Notes from the Field," ibid., 13 July 1872.

68. Pillsbury, *Things New and Old*.

69. Pillsbury, "Notes from the Field," *The Index*, 29 July 1871.

70. Ibid.

71. "A Letter from Parker Pillsbury," ibid., 25 October 1877.

72. See Carter, *Spiritual Crisis*, for more on the concerns of the church in this period.

73. Ahlstrom, *Religious History*, 226.

74. Warren, *American Freethought*, 176–83.

75. "Parker Pillsbury in Worcester," *The Index*, 8 February 1877.

76. "Parker Pillsbury on the Sixteenth Amendment," ibid., 7 February 1878.

77. Ibid.

78. Pillsbury, *Ecclesiastical vs. Civil Authority: God in the Federal Constitution, Man and Woman Out* (Concord, N.H.: Republican Press Association, 1893).

79. Cited in Goodheart, *Elizur Wright*, 185. See also Persons, *Free Religion*, 118–29; and Hal D. Sears, *The Sex Radicals: Free Love in High Victorian America* (Lawrence: Regents Press of Kansas, 1977), 37–40.

80. Martin Blatt, ed., *The Collected Works of Ezra H. Heywood* (Weston, Mass.: M & S Press, 1985), 231–64.

81. See *The Index*, 31 October, 7 November, and 20 December 1878; and Ahlstrom and Mullin, *Scientific Theist*, 112–27.

82. Pillsbury to Helen Pillsbury, 2 July 1878, JGW.

83. Ibid.

84. Pillsbury, "Whose Turn Next?" *The Index*, 12 December 1878.

85. Pillsbury, *"Cupid's Yokes" and the Holy Scriptures Contrasted in a Letter from Parker Pillsbury to Ezra H. Heywood* (Boston, Mass.: Albert Kendrick, Publisher, 1878).

86. Pillsbury published a few of these all-encompassing lectures, including *Things New and Old*, and *The Popular Religions*.

87. Anita C. Fellman and Michael Fellman, *Making Sense of Self: Medical Advice Literature in Late Nineteenth-Century America* (Philadelphia: University of Pennsylvania Press, 1981), 1–22; and James C. Whorton, *Crusaders for Fitness: The History of American Health Reformers* (Princeton, N.J.: Princeton University Press, 1982), 132–33. On antebellum health reform see Robert H. Abzug, *Cosmos Crumbling: American Reform and the Religious Imagination* (New York: Oxford University Press, 1994), 163–82.

88. Pillsbury, "Turkish Baths," *The Revolution*, 11 February 1869.

89. Ibid.

90. On Graham and the water-cure see Stephen Nissenbaum, *Sex, Diet, and Debility in Jacksonian America* (Westport, Conn.: Greenwood Press, 1980), 149–54. See also Susan E. Cayleff, *Wash and Be Healed: The Water-Cure Movement and Women's Health* (Philadelphia: Temple University Press, 1987); and Jane B. Donegan, *"Hydropathic Highway to Health": Women and Water-Cure in Antebellum America* (New York: Greenwood Press, 1986).

91. For examples of Pillsbury's employment of hydropathy see Pillsbury, "New England Correspondence," *Anti-Slavery Bugle* (Salem, Ohio), 30 July 1853; "Parker Pillsbury," *Liberator* (Boston, Mass.), 26 May 1854; and Pillsbury to Helen Pillsbury, 1 and 6 September 1857, JGW.

92. Nathaniel Peabody Rogers to Pillsbury [January 1844], CSC.

93. Pillsbury, "The Turkish Bath," *The Revolution*, 25 February 1868.

94. Nissenbaum, *Sex, Diet, and Debility*, 39–52.

95. Pillsbury to unknown, 19 January 1890, bMS Am 1752 (632), HouL.

96. Pillsbury to William Lloyd Garrison, Jr., April 1891, SSC.

97. Pillsbury, *Things New and Old*.

98. Pillsbury, *The Popular Religions*.

99. The Fellmans discuss the importance of control in medical literature in the period 1870–1890, *Making Sense of Self*, 1–22.

100. Nissenbaum, *Sex, Diet, and Debility*.

101. On the rise of exercise in the Gilded Age see Whorton, *Crusaders for Fitness*, 270–303.

102. Ibid., 275–82.

103. Pillsbury, "The Healing Art," *The Revolution*, 15 April 1869.

104. Ibid.

105. Ibid.

106. Ibid.

107. Cayleff, *Wash and Be Healed*, 16. See also Donegan, *"Hydropathic Highway."*

108. On the variety of women's activism in this period see Eleanor Flexner, *Century of Struggle: The Woman's Rights Movement in the United States* (New York: Atheneum, 1972). See also Ruth Bordin, *Woman and Temperance: The Quest for Power and Liberty, 1873–1900* (New Burnswick, N.J.: Rutgers University Press, 1990).

109. For more on Francis Willard and the Woman's Christian Temperance Union see Bordin, *Woman and Temperance*; and Barbara L. Epstein, *The Politics of Domesticity: Women, Evangelism, and Temperance in Nineteenth-Century America* (Middletown, Conn.: Wesleyan University Press, 1981). On moral educationists see Carol Smith-Rosenberg, "Beauty, the Beast and the Militant Woman in Jacksonian America," *American Quarterly* 23 (October 1971): 526–84. On Scudder see Frederick, *Knights of the Golden Rule*, 113–40. On Jane Addams see her autobiography, *Twenty Years at Hull House* (1910; Urbana: University of Illinois Press, 1990); and Kathryn Kish Sklar, "Hull House in the 1890s: A Community of Women Reformers," *Signs* 10 (Summer 1985): 658–77.

110. Pillsbury to Rebecca Smith Anne Janney, 10 February 1873, Charles A. Jones Collection, Microfilm 137, Ohio Historical Society, Columbus, Ohio.

111. He wrote letters to various libraries soliciting their orders and even offered to pay for

the books if the library was unable to afford them. See Susan Anthony to Pillsbury, 31 December 1896, James Copley Library, La Jolla, Calif.; and Susan Anthony to Pillsbury, 8 January 1897, American Museum of Historical Documents, Las Vegas, Nev.

112. Leach, *True Love*.

113. Ibid., 19–37.

114. Pillsbury, *Self-made Men and Society-made Men: Or, Men with Conscience and Men without* (1872).

115. Pillsbury, "The Vote of the Sturgis Women," *The Revolution*, 21 May 1868.

116. Pillsbury, "Who Is Responsible?" ibid., 13 January 1870.

117. Pillsbury, "Notes from the Field," *The Index*, 17 June 1871.

118. *Old Anti-Slavery Days: Proceedings of the Commemorative Meeting* (Danvers, Mass.: Danvers Mirror Print, 1893).

119. Handbill, Earlville, Illinois, 2 April 1878, JGW.

120. Handbill, Springfield, Ohio, 17 September 1879, JGW.

121. On the variety of labor reformers in the late nineteenth century, see Frederick, *Knights of the Golden Rule*; Mann, *Yankee Reformers*; and Sproat, *"The Best Men."*

122. Pillsbury to James Eddy, 15 June 1887, Henry E. Huntington Library, San Marino, Calif.

123. On Christian labor reformers see Frederick, *Knights of the Golden Rule*, 79–112, 141–84.

124. Pillsbury to Charles Elmer Rice, 4 May 1894, NHHS. For a historical treatment of Coxey's Army see Carlos A. Schwantes, *Coxey's Army: An American Odyssey* (Lincoln: University of Nebraska Press, 1985).

125. Pillsbury, "Work and the Workers," *The Revolution*, 20 August 1868.

126. Pillsbury to Stephen Foster, 22 May 1881, A. K. Foster Papers, AAS.

127. Pillsbury, "The Truth at Last: Fogg and Chandler," *The Revolution*, 4 June 1868.

128. Pillsbury, *The Plague and Peril of Monopoly* (Concord, N. H.: Republican Press Association, 1887).

129. Pillsbury, "The Chicago Platform," *The Revolution*, 4 June 1868.

130. Pillsbury, "Work and the Workers," ibid., 20 August 1868.

131. Pillsbury, *Self-made Men and Society-made Men*.

132. Pillsbury, *Peril of Monopoly*.

133. Even before Pillsbury wrote his history of the abolition movement, he tried to combat this ignorance by teaching his reform colleagues the lessons of antislavery. Among his writings in Free Religion's *The Index*, for example, was a series of articles on slavery and antislavery, focusing on the insidious role of the church. See the following articles by Pillsbury in *The Index*: "Slave-Holding Christianity," 2 July 1874; "Chattel Slavery and the Church," 23 July 1874; "Did Churches Own Slaves?" 13 August 1874; "What was American Slavery?" 20 August 1874; and five articles entitled "What Was Slavery?" 27 August 1874, 17 September 1874, 8 October 1874; 5 November 1874, and 3 December 1874.

134. Pillsbury to Stephen Foster, 2 February 1880, A. K. Foster Papers, AAS.

135. Pillsbury, "The Destiny of the Nation," reprinted from the *Liberty Bell* of 1847. See, for example, Pillsbury to "friend," 21 May 1864, Crawford Blagden Collection, HouL.

136. Pillsbury to James Miller McKim, 17 January 1883, Department of Rare Books, Cornell University Library, Ithaca, N.Y.

137. Pillsbury to Foster, 2 February 1880, A. K. Foster Papers, AAS.

138. Pillsbury would have been aghast at the revisionist history of the 1930s and 1940s which suggested that the extremism of the abolitionists, not slavery, caused the Civil War. See Betty L. Fladeland, "Revisionists vs. Abolitionists: The Historiographical Cold War of the 1930s and 1940s," *Journal of the Early Republic* 6 (Spring 1986): 1–21.

139. Pillsbury to Frederick Douglass, 13 November 1883, Frederick Douglass Papers, Yale.

140. Pillsbury to James Miller McKim, 17 January 1883, Cornell University.

141. Pillsbury to Frederick Douglass, 7 December 1882, F. Douglass Papers, Yale.

142. Pillsbury to Sarah Pillsbury, 10 September 1881, JGW.

143. See, for example, Wendell Phillips Garrison and Francis Jackson Garrison, *William Lloyd Garrison, 1805–1879: The Story of His Life Told by His Children*, 4 vols. (New York: Century Company, 1885–89); Thomas Wentworth Higginson, *Cheerful Yesterdays* (Boston: Houghton Mifflin, 1898); Samuel J. May, *Some Recollections of Our Antislavery Conflict* (Boston: Fields, Osgood, and Co., 1869); and Lillie Buffum Chace Wyman and Arthur Crawford Wyman, eds., *Elizabeth Buffum Chace, 1806–1899; Her Life and Its Environment* (Boston: W. B. Clarke, 1914).

144. For an example of a review of the *Acts* in a radical paper, see "Parker Pillsbury—A Modern Apostle and His Book," *Free Thought Magazine* (March 1898). For reactions of Pillsbury's old abolitionist friends see John Brown, Jr., to Pillsbury, 1 February 1884, JGW; Abby Kelley Foster to Pillsbury, 20 January 1884, NHHS; Wendell Phillips to Pillsbury, 4 January 1884, CSC; George Putnam to Pillsbury, 24 January 1885, JGW; and Elizur Wright to Pillsbury, 19 February 1884, JGW.

145. Pillsbury to unknown, 14 June 1887, Special Collections, Vassar College Library, Poughkeepsie, N.Y.

146. See the NHHS for dozens of letters from libraries acknowledging Pillsbury's donations.

147. Pillsbury to James Monroe, 27 August 1885, Monroe Papers, Oberlin College.

148. Gilbert and Ann Frances Pillsbury to Helen Pillsbury, 19 June 1888, JGW.

149. Mr. and Mrs. Tilden to Sarah Pillsbury, 1 October 1888, JGW.

150. Pillsbury to William Lloyd Garrison, 15 November 1878, MS A.1.2 vol. 40, p. 52, BPL. See also Pillsbury to William Lloyd Garrison, 22 November 1878, MS A.1.2 vol. 40, p. 57, BPL.

151. Frederick Douglass to Pillsbury, 18 July 1882, NHHS. See also Pillsbury to Frederick Douglass, 7 December 1882, F. Douglass Papers, Yale; and Frederick Douglass to Pillsbury, 8 December 1882, NHHS.

Index